PRACTICE MAKES PERFECT™

Arabic Verb Tenses

Jane Wightwick and Mahmoud Gaafar

McGraw Hill

New York   Chicago   San Francisco   Lisbon   London   Madrid   Mexico City
Milan   New Delhi   San Juan   Seoul   Singapore   Sydney   Toronto

Contents

VI OTHER ASPECTS OF VERBS 223

Preface

The richness of Arabic is based on its system of word roots, and nowhere is this more evident than in the verb system. Arabic tenses can be characterized as narrow but very deep. For while Arabic has only two basic tenses (past and present/future), the verb system encompasses a huge variety of types and variations within these tenses.

Practice Makes Perfect: Arabic Verb Tenses is perfect for all beginning and intermediate students who have a solid grasp of the Arabic script or for more advanced students who are in need of a good review workbook. It promotes the confident use of Arabic verbs through clear explanations and examples followed by extensive practice exercises. It is an invaluable aid for all learners who want to advance more quickly and is particularly useful for independent study.

The book is divided into six main parts:

- ◆ **Part I: Roots, nonverbal sentences, and pronouns.** It may seem odd to start a book about verb tenses without any verbs or tenses! However, Part I provides a very important grounding in the basics of Arabic word roots and pronouns, together with nonverbal sentences that express the equivalent of the English verbs "to be" and "to have." You will find the subsequent parts of the book fall into place much more easily after completing this introductory part.
- ◆ **Part II: Past tense.** The second part covers the complete conjugation in the past (or *perfect*) tense of all verbs types, both regular and irregular, together with sections on word order and use of the dual.
- ◆ **Part III: Present/future tense.** The third part covers the complete conjugation of regular and irregular verbs types in the present (or *imperfect*) tense, together with a section on using this tense to talk about the future.
- ◆ **Part IV: Forms of the verb.** The fourth part deals with the eight significant derived forms of the verb—the very important and commonly-used variations to the verbal root that modify the meaning of verbs. Both the past and present tenses of the derived forms are covered.
- ◆ **Part V: Moods of the verb and verbal nouns.** The fifth part concentrates on the "moods" of the verb—the *subjunctive*, the *jussive* and the *imperative*. Also included in this part are the important verbal nouns that are formed from verbs and often used in place of a second verb.
- ◆ **Part VI: Other aspects of verbs.** The sixth part looks at unusual and very irregular verbs, compound tenses, and the conditional and passive verbs.

Each part provides concise but complete explanations and ample exercises. An answer key is also provided. This will be especially useful to learners who are studying independently.

Every effort has been made to limit the range of additional vocabulary, and to organize material in such a way that key words are naturally absorbed. In this way, your understanding of the learning points and exercises will not be hampered by the inclusion of large amounts of unfamiliar vocabulary. In Part I almost all of the vocabulary needed for the exercises is given in the book. For subsequent parts much of the vocabulary is recycled, but there may be instances when you will need to use a dictionary to look up words unfamiliar to you.

Practice Makes Perfect: Arabic Verb Tenses is an excellent tool for the self-learner or a companion for any classroom-based textbook, as well as a source of reference for both students and teachers of Arabic. We hope you find it a valuable resource in your learning.

Basic terminology

Here is a brief explanation of some of the more common grammatical terms found in this text.

Compound tense: A tense made by combining two different verbs.

Conjugation: Changing the verb to agree with the subject, for example, أَزور (*I visit*), يَزور (*he visits*).

Derived form: Variation of the Arabic verbal root that modifies meaning.

Doubled verb: A verb that has the same second and third root letter.

Dual: Used in Arabic when referring to *two* people or things.

Hamzated **verb:** A verb that has *hamza* (ء) as one of the root letters.

Imperative: A *mood*, or variation, of the present tense verb used for commands or instructions.

Irregular verb: A verb that varies from the normal patterns.

Jussive: A *mood*, or variation, of the present tense verb used in certain structures.

Noun: A word naming a person, object or idea, for example, بَيت (*house*), وَلَد (*boy*), حُرِّيّة (*freedom*).

Passive: A verb where the subject undergoes the action of the verb rather than carries out the action, for example, حُمِلَت (*she was carried*), يُستَخدَم (*it is used*).

Past tense: A verb form showing something has happened in the past.

Plural: Used in Arabic when referring to *three or more* people or things.

Present/future tense: A verb form showing something is happening now, routinely or in the future.

Pronoun: A word replacing a noun, for example, هِيَ (*she*), أَنا (*I*), أَنتَ (*you*).

Quadriliteral verb: A verb with a 4-letter root, for example, تَرجَم/يُتَرجِم (*to translate*)

Regular verb: A verb that consistently follows the normal patterns.

Root: The sequence of (usually three) Arabic letters that carry the underlying meaning of a word, for example, ش/ر/ب (*to drink*), ح/م/ل (*to carry*).

Subjunctive: A *mood*, or variation, of the present tense verb used after certain particles (short words).

Tense: The tense of a verb tells you when the action takes place.

Verb: A word describing an action or a state of being, for example, ذَهَبْنا (*we came*), يَزور (*he visits*), سَأَكون (*I will be*).

Verb endings: What you add to the *end* of the verb stem to get the proper conjugation, for example, ذَهَبْتُ (*I went*).

Verbal noun: A noun formed from a verb describing a state or action, for example, سِباحة (*swimming*), تَدريس (*teaching*), اِجتِماع (*meeting*).

Verb prefixes: What you add to the *beginning* of the verb stem to get the proper conjugation, for example, يَذهَب (*he goes*).

Verb stem: The part of the verb to which endings and prefixes are added, for example, شَرِب (*drank*), ذَهَب (*went*).

Weak verb: A verb that has و or ي as one of the root letters.

ROOTS, NONVERBAL SENTENCES, AND PRONOUNS

The Arabic language is based on "roots" that link words of related meanings. A knowledge of these roots, together with the role played by gender and plural, is essential to understanding Arabic verb tenses and patterns.

Part I provides a grounding in the basics of Arabic word roots and also introduces the Arabic pronouns, genders, and plurals, together with nonverbal sentences that express the equivalent of the English verbs "to be" and "to have." You will find the subsequent parts of the book fall into place much more easily after completing this introductory part.

Word roots

3-letter (triliteral) roots

A knowledge of Arabic in general, and its verb system in particular, requires an understanding of the root system integral to the language.

General meaning patterns are associated with a sequence of (usually three) root consonants, for example (reading the Arabic root from right to left):

to sit	ج/ل/س
to wash	غ/س/ل
to find	و/ج/د

Most Arabic words, and almost all Arabic verbs, have a root sequence at their heart. This sequence can appear in a variety of word patterns, all associated with the general meaning:

he sits	يَجلِس
washing machine	غَسّالة
finding/existence	وُجود

Associated words may have additional letters and vowels inserted between, before, or after the root letters but the sequence of the letters within the root does not change.

Regular roots

Regular Arabic roots consist of three distinct stable consonants. The majority of Arabic consonants are stable and produce regular root sequences when combined with two other stable consonants. Some of the most common are in the following list (read columns right to left):

to leave	ت/ر/ك	to follow	ت/ب/ع	to search	ب/ح/ث
to reserve	ح/ج/ز	to gather	ج/م/ع	to sit	ج/ل/س
to move	ح/ر/ك	to burn	ح/ر/ق	to happen	ح/د/ث
to carry	ح/م/ل	to save/memorize	ح/ف/ظ	to attend	ح/ض/ر
to study	د/ر/س	to come in	د/خ/ل	to go out	خ/ر/ج
to go	ذ/ه/ب	to mention	ذ/ك/ر	to push/pay	د/ف/ع

3

to dance	د/ق/ص	to draw	ر/س/م	to return	ر/ج/ع
to travel	س/ف/ر	to plant	ز/ر/ع	to ride	ر/ك/ب
to reside/ to live	س/ك/ن	to fall	س/ق/ط	to steal	س/ر/ق
to thank	ش/ك/ر	to drink	ش/ر/ب	to hear	س/م/ع
to hit	ض/ر/ب	to laugh	ض/ح/ك	to make	ص/ن/ع
to appear	ظ/ه/ر	to request	ط/ل/ب	to cook	ط/ب/خ
to work	ع/م/ل	to learn	ع/ل/م	to know	ع/ر/ف
to do	ف/ع/ل	to open	ف/ت/ح	to wash	غ/س/ل
to cut	ق/ط/ع	to kill	ق/ت/ل	to understand	ف/ه/م
to write	ك/ت/ب	to close	ق/ف/ل	to jump	ق/ف/ز
to wear	ل/ب/س	to break	ك/س/ر	to hate	ك/ر/ه
to own	م/ل/ك	to hold	م/س/ك	to play	ل/ع/ب
to land/descend	ه/ب/ط	to look	ن/ظ/ر	to stay/go down	ن/ز/ل
				to escape	ه/ر/ب

EXERCISE

1·1

Give the general meaning for the following common regular roots.

EXAMPLE   <u>*to sit*</u> ج/ل/س

١ د/ر/س _____

٢ ك/ت/ب _____

٣ ف/ت/ح _____

٤ ن/ظ/ر _____

٥ ل/ب/س _____

٦ ك/س/ر _____

٧ ح/م/ل _____

٨ ذ/ه/ب _____

٩ س/م/ع _____

١٠ ش/ر/ب _____

١١ ع/م/ل _____

١٢ ق/ت/ل _____

١٣ ف/ع/ل _____

١٤ غ/س/ل _____

١٥ ف/ه/م _____

Write the three Arabic letters that make up the root conveying these general meanings.

EXAMPLE   <u>د/ خ /ل</u> to come in

_____ to reside/live ١

_____ to cook ٢

_____ to close ٣

_____ to know ٤

_____ to return ٥

_____ to jump ٦

_____ to play ٧

_____ to go out ٨

_____ to draw ٩

_____ to fall ١٠

_____ to hit ١١

_____ to appear ١٢

_____ to laugh ١٣

_____ to request ١٤

_____ to make ١٥

All the following verbs express something "I did," using the verb ending ـتُ *(-tu). Decide the meaning of each, using the list of regular roots to help you.*

EXAMPLE   طَبَختُ *I cooked*

١ دَرَستُ _____

٢ جَلَستُ _____

٣ خَرَجتُ _____

٤ عَمِلتُ _____

٥ فَتَحتُ _____

٦ لَبِستُ _____

٧ شَرِبتُ _____

٨ قَفَلتُ _____

٩ ضَحِكتُ _____

١٠ كَسَرتُ _____

Identify the root of these words, using the English meanings and the list of verbs in the "Regular roots" section earlier in this chapter.

EXAMPLE   مِفتاح (key) ف/ت/ح *to open*

_____ مَدرَسة (school) ١

_____ كُتُب (books) ٢

_____ أُعَلِّم (I teach) ٣

_____ مَلابِس (clothes) ٤

_____ باحِث (researcher) ٥

_____ مَهبَط (runway/landing strip) ٦

_____ حَمّال (porter) ٧

_____ اِستَمَعنا (we listened) ٨

_____ رَسّام (illustrator) ٩

_____ جامِع (mosque) ١٠

_____ يَنتَظِر (he waits) ١١

_____ مَنزِل (house/home) ١٢

_____ زِراعة (agriculture) ١٣

_____ فَعَّال (effective) ١٤

_____ مُلوك (kings) ١٥

Irregular roots

Irregular roots do not consist of three distinct stable consonants; instead, they fall into three categories:

- *Doubled roots*: where the second and third root letters are the same
- *Weak roots*: where one of the three root letters is و or ي
- *Hamzated roots*: where one of the root letters is *hamza* (ء)

Doubled roots

Doubled roots have the same second and third root letters; for example:

to reply	ر/د/د
to think/believe	ظ/ن/ن

The second and third root letters are sometimes written as one with a *shadda* (ّ) and sometimes written separately:

he replied	رَدَّ
I replied	رَدَدْتُ
we think	نَظُنّ
you (masc.) thought	ظَنَنْتَ

The rules for how to write doubled roots are reasonably straightforward and are summarized in Chapters 5, 11, and 18.

Common doubled roots include:

to bathe	ح/م/م	to finish	ت/م/م	to broadcast/ spread	ب/ث/ث
to cause	س/ب/ب	to reply	ر/د/د	to show/prove	د/ل/ل
to join	ض/م/م	to smell	ش/م/م	to doubt	ش/ك/ك
to repeat	ك/ر/ر	to cut	ق/ص/ص	to count	ع/د/د
to pass by	م/ر/ر	to stretch/extend	م/د/د	to turn	ل/ف/ف

EXERCISE
1·5

Identify the doubled root of these words from the preceding list.

EXAMPLE   حَمّام (bathroom) ح/م/م *to bathe*

١ سَبَب (reason) _____

٢ رَدّ (reply/response) _____

٣ دليل (guide) _____

٤ تِكرار (repetition) _____

٥ لَفّة (rotation) _____

٦ مِقَصّ (scissors) _____

٧ اِنضِمام (annexation) _____

٨ عَدَد (number) _____

٩ مَمَرّ (corridor) _____

١٠ تَشَكُّك (skepticism) _____

Weak roots

Roots with و or ي as one of the root letters are by far the largest irregular category. The letters و and ي are unstable, or "weak." They can change from a consonant to a vowel sound, or even disappear entirely, depending on the word pattern into which the root is put.

The و or ي can be any of the three root letters, and are subdivided as follows:

- *Assimilated*: with و or ي as the first root letter
- *Hollow*: with و or ي as the second root letter
- *Defective*: with و or ي as the third root letter

Common weak roots include:

Assimilated		Hollow		Defective	
to arrive	و/ص/ل	to say	ق/و/ل	to complain	ش/ك/و
to describe	و/ص/ف	to visit	ز/و/ر	to request	ر/ج/و
to find	و/ج/د	to return	ع/و/د	to appear	ب/د/و
to put/place	و/ض/ع	to stand up	ق/و/م	to buy	ش/ر/ي
to fall	و/ق/ع	to go round	د/و/ر	to finish	ن/ه/ي
to stop/stand	و/ق/ف	to sell	ب/ي/ع	to give	ع/ط/ي
to give birth	و/ل/د	to shout/cry out	ص/ي/ح	to weep/cry	ب/ك/ي
to wake up	ي/ق/ظ	to fly	ط/ي/ر	to meet	ل/ق/ي
to be certain	ي/ق/ن	to increase	ز/ي/د	to run	ج/ر/ي
				to sing	غ/ن/ي
				to walk	م/ش/ي

EXERCISE
1·6

Decide which category of weak root the following fall into and then give their general meaning.

EXAMPLE   *assimilated; to find* و/ج/د

_____ ١ ز/و/ر

_____ ٢ و/ص/ل

_____ ٣ م/ش/ي

_____ ٤ ق/و/ل

_____ ٥ ي/ق/ظ

_____ ٦ ط/ي/ر

_____ ٧ ر/ج/و

_____ ٨ و/ض/ع

_____ ٩ ع/ط/ي

_____ ١٠ ص/ي/ح

_____ ١١ غ/ن/ي

_____ ١٢ و/ل/د

Write the weak root that conveys these general meanings.

EXAMPLE   <u>ط/ي/ر</u> to fly

_____ ١ to walk

_____ ٢ to arrive

_____ ٣ to sell

_____ ٤ to describe

_____ ٥ to return

_____ ٦ to run

_____ ٧ to finish

_____ ٨ to meet

_____ ٩ to request

_____ ١٠ to stand up

_____ ١١ to wake up

_____ ١٢ to increase

_____ ١٣ to buy

_____ ١٤ to complain

_____ ١٥ to fall

Identify the weak root of these words from the earlier list of common weak roots.

EXAMPLE   نِهاية (ending) <u>ن/ه/ي</u> _to finish_

_____ ١ شَكوى (complaint)

_____ ٢ اِشتَرَيتُ (I bought)

_____ ٣ وَضع (position)

_____ ٤ وُجود (existence)

_____ ٥ طائِرة (airplane)

_____ ٦ أُغنية (song)

_____ ٧ يَبدو (it seems)

٨ مَولود (born) _____

٩ دائِرة (circle) _____

١٠ قُمنا (we stood up) _____

١١ يَقين (certainty) _____

١٢ مَجرًى (channel) _____

Hamzated roots

Hamza (ء) is a "half" letter; it is pronounced as a glottal stop. *Hamzated* roots have *hamza* as one of the root letters; for example:

to begin	ء/د/ب
to eat	ء/ك/ل
to ask	س/ء/ل

The *hamza* can be written in a variety of ways: by itself on the line (ء); carried by an *alif* (أ); carried by *yāʾ* (ـئـ/ئ); or carried by *wāw* (ؤ). For example:

he ate	أَكَلَ
questions	أَسئِلة
beginning	بَدء
we feed	نُؤَكِّل

Common *hamzated* roots include:

to eat	ء/ك/ل	to begin	ء/د/ب
to read	ق/ر/ء	to ask	س/ء/ل
to command	ء/م/ر	to take	ء/خ/ذ
to be slow	ب/ط/ء	to hope	ء/م/ل
to be fed up	س/ء/م	to be brave/dare	ج/ر/ء
		to fill	م/ل/ء

EXERCISE
1·9

Write the hamzated *root that conveys these general meanings.*

EXAMPLE   ء/م/ل to hope

١ to be fed up _____

٢ to read _____

٣ to begin _____

٤ to fill _____

10   Roots, nonverbal sentences, and pronouns

_____ to ask ٥

_____ to command ٦

_____ to be slow ٧

_____ to take ٨

_____ to eat ٩

_____ to be brave/dare ١٠

EXERCISE

1·10

All the following verbs express something "we did," using the verb ending نا (-nā).
Decide the meaning of each verb, using the earlier list of hamzated roots to help you.

EXAMPLE   *we ate* أَكَلنا

_____ ١ أَخَذنا

_____ ٢ قَرَأنا

_____ ٣ أَمَلنا

_____ ٤ سَأَلنا

_____ ٥ بَدَأنا

_____ ٦ سَئِمنا

_____ ٧ أَمَرنا

_____ ٨ بَطُؤنا

_____ ٩ مَلَأنا

_____ ١٠ جَرُؤنا

4-letter (quadriliteral) roots

Although the vast majority of Arabic words are based on roots of three letters, there are a few four-letter roots, or quadriliterals. A quadriliteral root sequence can consist of four different root letters:

to translate	ت/ر/ج/م
to roll	د/ح/ر/ج
to adorn	ز/خ/ر/ف

It can consist of a repeated pair of consonants, often onomatopoeic (sounding as they mean):

to mutter	ت/م/ت/م
to gargle	غ/ر/غ/ر
to chatter	ث/ر/ث/ر
to hum	د/ن/د/ن
to crackle	ط/ق/ط/ق
to shake	ز/ل/ز/ل

EXERCISE 1·11

Give the general meaning for the following quadriliteral roots.

EXAMPLE   *to gargle* غ/ر/غ/ر

_____	١ ز/خ/ر/ف
_____	٢ ت/م/ت/م
_____	٣ ط/ق/ط/ق
_____	٤ د/ح/ر/ج
_____	٥ د/ن/د/ن
_____	٦ ز/ل/ز/ل
_____	٧ ث/ر/ث/ر
_____	٨ ت/ر/ج/م

EXERCISE 1·12

Follow the pattern in the example to produce similar quadriliteral verbs using the roots in the preceding list.

EXAMPLE   (*yudandin*) يُدَنْدِن he hums

_____	he translates ١
_____	he mutters ٢
_____	he shakes ٣
_____	he gargles ٤
_____	he rolls ٥
_____	he crackles ٦
_____	he chatters ٧
_____	he adorns ٨

Nonverbal sentences and pronouns

Expressing "to be" in the present tense

Every English sentence has a verb. There are many simple sentences in English that use the verb "to be" (*am*, *are*, *is*) that often do not require a verb at all in Arabic. This type of sentence is referred to as جُملة اِسميّة (*nominal* or *nonverbal*):

I (am) in the garden.	أنا في الحَديقة.
Shukri (is) with me.	شُكري مَعي.

In addition, there is no direct equivalent of the indefinite article (*a/an*), turning an English sentence such as "I am an accountant" into simply "I accountant":

I (am an) accountant.	أنا مُحاسِب.
Nadia (is an) engineer.	نادية مُهَندِسة.

The word هُناك (*there*) can also be used in nonverbal sentences to mean "there is" or "there are":

There (is an) airplane on the runway.	هُناكَ طائِرة عَلى المَهبَط.
There (are) clothes in the drawer.	هُناكَ مَلابِس في الدُّرج.

EXERCISE

2·1

Use the following words to create nonverbal sentences that match the English prompts.

Nadia نادية	we نَحنُ	I أنا
books كُتُب	a chair كُرسيّ	Shukri شُكري
school مَدرَسة	my house بَيتي	car سَيّارة
town مَدينة	garden حَديقة	mosque جامِع
in في	there هُناكَ	America أمريكا
next to بِجانِب	under تَحت	on عَلَى
		in front of أمام

EXAMPLE نَحنُ في المَدرَسة. We are in the school.

_____ We are in the garden. ١

_____ Nadia is in America. ٢

_____ Shukri is in my house. ٣

_____ There is a mosque in the town. ٤

_____ The school is next to the mosque. ٥

_____ I am in the school. ٦

_____ There is a chair in the garden. ٧

_____ The books are on the chair. ٨

_____ My house is in America. ٩

_____ Shukri is in front of the car. ١٠

_____ There are books in the car. ١١

_____ I am next to Shukri. ١٢

EXERCISE
2·2

Your Arabic-speaking friends are giving you inaccurate information, so each time you have to correct their statements. Follow the prompts to give the corrected statement. Pay attention to which part of the information (in parentheses) needs correcting.

EXAMPLE

شكري في الحَديقة. (نادية) لا، نادية في الحَديقة.

شكري في الحَديقة. (مَدرَسة) لا، شكري في المدرَسة.

١ نادية في البيت. (شكري) _____

٢ نادية في البيت. (الجامِع) _____

٣ الكُتُب في السيّارة. (المَلابِس) _____

٤ الكُتُب في السيّارة. (تَحت) _____

٥ هُناكَ مَلابِس على الكرسيّ. (كُتُب) _____

٦ هُناكَ مَلابِس على الكرسيّ. (تَحت) _____

٧ نادية في أمريكا. (أنا) _____

٨ نادية في أمريكا. (الكُوَيْت) _____

٩ نحن أمام الجامِع. (المدرسة) _____

١٠ نحن أمام الجامِع. (بجانب) _____

١١ الملابس على الكرسيّ. (تَحت) _____

١٢ المَلابس على الكرسيّ. (بجانب) _____

١٣ هُناك كرسيّ في الحديقة. (مَلابِس) _____

١٤ هُناك كرسيّ في الحديقة. (السيّارة) _____

Gender

Arabic has masculine and feminine gender. Nouns referring to females or those ending with the special feminine ending *tā' marbūṭa* (ة) are almost always feminine. Other nouns are almost always masculine. The *tā' marbūṭa* is pronounced "-a": مَدينة (*madīna*, city), or "-at" when followed directly by another noun with the meaning "of": مَدينة بَيروت (*madīnat bayrūt*, the city of Beirut).

Adjectives (for example, large, slow, short, expensive, tall) and descriptions (for example, jobs) change when referring to feminine people or things, also usually by adding *tā' marbūṭa*: مُهَندِس (*muhandis*, male engineer)/ مُهَندِسة (*muhandisa*, female engineer).

Shukri is an engineer.	شُكري مُهَندِس.
Nadia is an engineer.	نادية مُهَندِسة.
My father is tall.	أَبي طَويل.
My mother is tall.	أُمّي طَويلة.

Common adjectives include:

small	صَغير	large/big	كَبير
short	قَصير	tall/long	طَويل
old	قَديم	new	جَديد
light	خَفيف	heavy	ثَقيل
fast	سَريع	slow	بَطيء
closed	مَقفول	open	مَفتوح
broken	مَكسور	strange	غَريب
clean	نَظيف	beautiful	جَميل

EXERCISE
2·3

Write the feminine form and the meaning of the adjectives listed.

EXAMPLE   سَريع سَريعة *fast*

١ ثَقيل _____

٢ مَقفول _____

٣ صَغير _____

٤ جَديد _____

٥ قَصير _____

٦ غَريب _____

٧ كَبير _____

٨ قَديم ــ

٩ مَفتوح ــ

١٠ نَظيف ــ

١١ جَميل ــ

١٢ طَويل ــ

١٣ خَفيف ــ

١٤ بَطيء ــ

١٥ مَكسور ــ

EXERCISE 2·4

You find some assorted items in a drawer. Describe the items you find, following the prompts and making the adjective feminine, if necessary.

EXAMPLE   كِتاب (book) / ثقيل

هناك كتاب ثقيل في الدُّرج. (There's a heavy book in the drawer.)

١ مِفتاح (key) / صغير ــ

٢ مَحفَظة (wallet) / خفيف ــ

٣ قَلَم (pen) / قصير ــ

٤ مِسطَرة (ruler) / طويل ــ

٥ خاتِم (ring) / جميل ــ

٦ نَظّارة (pair of glasses) / قديم ــــــــــــــــــــــــــــــــــ

٧ صورة (picture) / كبير ــ

٨ ساعة (clock, watch) / مكسور ــــــــــــــــــــــــــــــــ

٩ قُفّاز (glove) / نظيف ــ

١٠ حَشَرة (insect) / غريب ــ

Here are some more adjectives that can be applied to people:

busy	مَشغول
energetic	نَشيط
clever	ذَكيّ
hard-working	مُجتَهِد
nervous	عَصَبيّ
afraid (of)	خائِف مِن
patient	صَبور

Nadia is Shukri's twin. They look alike and share the same characteristics and profession.
Rewrite the sentences about Shukri to refer to Nadia.

EXAMPLE   شُكري طويل. <u>نادية طويلة.</u>

_____ ١ شُكري نَشيط.

_____ ٢ شُكري سَريع.

_____ ("light of weight") ٣ شُكري خفيف الوَزن.

_____ ٤ شُكري مَشغول دائماً.

_____ ٥ شُكري ذَكيّ جِدّاً.

_____ ٦ شُكري مُهَندِس.

_____ ٧ شُكري مُجتَهِد في العَمَل.

_____ ٨ شُكري عَصَبيّ.

_____ ٩ شُكري خائِف من الحَشَرات.

_____ ١٠ شُكري صَبور مع الأطفال.

Subject pronouns

A pronoun can take the place of a person, a thing, or an idea. A subject pronoun is the equivalent of the English "I, he, we" (as opposed to the object pronouns like me, him, us, etc.). There are 12 subject pronouns in Arabic, with separate pronouns for masculine, feminine, singular, plural, and dual (used when referring to two people), giving a total of five equivalents of the English "you" and three equivalents of "they."

The singular and plural subject pronouns are:

Singular		Plural	
I	أَنا	we	نَحْنُ
you (masc.)	أَنْتَ	you (masc. pl.)	أَنْتُمْ
you (fem.)	أَنْتِ	you (fem. pl.)	أَنْتُنَّ
he/it (masc.)	هُوَ	they (masc.)	هُمْ
she/it (fem.)	هِيَ	they (fem.)	هُنَّ

Note that all the people in a group need to be female to use the plural feminine. If the group is mixed gender, then the masculine is used. (The dual is covered separately later in this chapter.)

Give the plural of these singular pronouns.

EXAMPLE   أنا نَحنُ

_____ هِيَ ١

_____ أنتِ ٢

_____ هُوَ ٣

_____ أنتَ ٤

Give the singular of these plural pronouns.

EXAMPLE   هُمْ هُوَ

_____ أنتُم ٥

_____ نحنُ ٦

_____ هُنَّ ٧

_____ أنتُنَّ ٨

Change the subjects in these sentences to a suitable pronoun.

EXAMPLE   شكري خائِف من الحَشَرات. هُوَ خائِف من الحَشَرات.

_____ نادية مشغولة دائماً. ١

_____ الأطفال في البيت. ٢

_____ أبي مهندس. ٣

_____ السيّارة بجانب البيت. ٤

_____ الجامع في وَسَط (center of) المدينة. ٥

_____ أُمّي طويلة وجميلة. ٦

_____ أنا وأبي في الحديقة. ٧

_____ المَمَرّ طَويل. ٨

_____ نادية وسامية وسميرة في المدرسة. ٩

_____ أَبي وأُمّي وأخي في أمريكا. ١٠

Sometimes a noun and a pronoun are used together for clarity:

Ahmed (he) is my father.	أحمد هو أبي.
This woman (she) is my sister.	هذه المَرأة هي أُختي.
This is my house.	هذا هو بَيتي.

EXERCISE
2·8

Fill in the correct pronouns in these sentences.

EXAMPLE شكري ‎ هو ‎ أَخي.

١ نادية _____ أُختي.

٢ سَمير _____ أبي.

٣ هذا الرَجُل _____ المُدير.

٤ ابنة أحمد _____ المهندسة.

٥ هذه المَرأة _____ أُمّي.

٦ شكري ونادية وسارة _____ أطفال سَمير.

٧ هذا _____ بيت أُمّي.

٨ هذه _____ سيّارة المُدير.

٩ الأطفال _____ في الحَديقة.

١٠ البَنات (the girls) _____ في المَدرَسة.

The dual

The dual is particular to Arabic and expresses the concept of "you two" or "they both." Whenever two people or things are referred to, a dual pronoun, noun, or verb should be used rather than the singular or plural. In general, the dual is characterized by a final ا (-ā) or ان (-ān). The exception is نَحنُ (we) and its relevant verb parts, which don't change with the dual.

Dual nouns and adjectives

Nouns and adjectives are made dual by adding ان (-ān) to the singular:

a boy	وَلَد
two boys	وَلَدان
a tall boy	وَلَد طَويل
two tall boys	وَلَدان طَويلان
the bag	الحقيبة
the two bags	الحقيبَتان
the large bag	الحقيبة الكبيرة
the two large bags	الحقيبَتان الكبيرتان

Make these nouns and adjectives dual.

EXAMPLE المَدينة المَدينَتان

_____ خاتِم ١

_____ المهندس ٢

_____ المهندس المشغول ٣

_____ جامع ٤

_____ جامع كبير ٥

_____ مَمَرّ طويل ٦

_____ القلم الجديد ٧

_____ الحديقة الجميلة ٨

Dual pronouns

Dual pronouns are formed by adding *alif* (ا) to the masculine plural and are used to refer to two people or things (of any gender):

you (two) أَنْتُما

they (both) هُما

Change these sentences to refer to two people or things.

EXAMPLE هو مهندس. هما مهندسان.

_____ هي مشغولة. ١

_____ أنتَ مُجتَهِد. ٢

_____ هي طويلة وجميلة. ٣

_____ هو خائِف من الحَشَرات. ٤

_____ أنتِ بِنت ذَكِيّة. ٥

_____ أنتَ وَلَد طَويل. ٦

_____ هو بيت قديم. ٧

_____ هي سيّارة سريعة. ٨

Plural of nonhumans

Arabic plurals are categorized as:

- *Human* (for example, أطفال [*children*], مُهَندِسون [*engineers*]), or
- *Nonhuman*, anything else: things, ideas, and so on (for example, كُتُب [*books*], سيّارات [*cars*], أَسباب [*reasons*]).

Nonhuman plurals are *grammatically feminine singular* in Arabic. This is very important in terms of Arabic grammar. Every time you refer to a nonhuman plural, you need to think of it as a feminine singular. It does not matter if the original nonhuman singular word was masculine or feminine, the plural will *always* be grammatically feminine singular. The plurals are reserved for humans only. It is as if in English we referred to children or engineers as they, but books or ideas as she.

Nonhuman plurals use:

- *Feminine singular pronouns*: الكُتُب (هي) على الكرسيّ. (The books [they] are on the chair.)
- *Feminine singular adjectives*: الـمَلابِس نظيفة. (The clothes are clean.)
- *Feminine singular demonstratives* (this/that): هذِهِ السيّارات سريعة. (These cars are fast.)
- *Feminine singular verbs*: رَجَعَتْ الشاحِنات إلى الـمَصنَع. (The trucks returned to the factory.)

EXERCISE
2·11

Change the sentences to refer to the plural, using the following list of plural nouns to help you.

picture/pictures صورة/صُوَر	book/books كِتاب/كُتُب
clock/clocks ساعة/ساعات	key/keys مِفتاح/مَفاتيح
insect/insects حَشَرة/حَشَرات	bag/bags حَقيبة/حَقائِب
town/towns مَدينة/مُدُن	pen/pens قَلَم/أقلام
house/houses بَيت/بُيوت	ring/rings خاتِم/خَواتِم

EXAMPLE   هذا الكِتاب ثَقيل. <u>هذه الكُتُب ثَقيلة.</u>

١ الخاتِم جَميل. _____

٢ المَدينة مَشهورة. _____

٣ هذِهِ السيّارة جَديدة. _____

٤ الحَشَرة صَغيرة وسَريعة. _____

٥ هذا البيت قَديم. _____

٦ المفتاح الصغير تحت الملابس. _____

٧ هذه الحَقيبة مَفتوحة. _____

٨ هناك مدينة كبيرة في الجَنوب (the south). _____

٩ هذا هو المفتاح. _____

١٠ هذه هي الحَقيبة. ــ

١١ هذا هو قَلَم شكري. ــ

١٢ هذه هي ساعة أُمّي. ـــ

Write these sentences in Arabic.

EXAMPLE الصُّوَر قديمة. The pictures are old.

The houses are beautiful. ١

_____

The keys are heavy. ٢

_____

The pictures are large. ٣

_____

These bags are light. ٤

_____

These clocks are old. ٥

_____

These are the houses. ٦

_____

These are the pens. ٧

_____

These are my mother's rings. ٨

_____

These are Shukri's keys. ٩

_____

The towns are small in the south. ١٠

_____

The cars are new in this street. ١١

_____

There are beautiful pictures in my house. ١٢

_____

There are old houses in this town. ١٣

_____

There are strange insects in the drawer. ١٤

_____

Attached pronouns

Arabic attached pronouns are the equivalent of both the English object pronouns (*me, him, us,* etc.) and also of the possessive pronouns (*my, his, our,* etc.). As the name suggests, they "attach" themselves to the end of a noun or verb, rather than being separate words like the subject pronouns.

I ate the fish.	أَكَلْتُ السَّمَك.
I ate it.	أَكَلْتُهُ.
This is Salma's house.	هذا هو بيت سَلمَى.
This is her house.	هذا هو بيتها.
We heard the boys.	سَمِعنا الأوْلاد.
We heard them.	سَمِعناهُم.

The attached pronoun meaning "my" is ـِي (*-ī*). This changes to ـني (*-nī*) when attached to a verb with the meaning "me":

house/my house	بَيت/بَيتي
pens/my pens	أَقلام/أَقلامي
he heard/he heard me	سَمِعَ/سَمِعَني
she mentioned/she mentioned me	ذَكَرَتْ/ذَكَرَتْني

All the other attached pronouns remain the same whether attached to a verb or a noun.

The singular and plural attached pronouns are:

Singular		**Plural**	
my/me	ـِي، ـني	our/us	ـنا
your/you (masc.)	ـكَ	your/you (pl. masc.)	ـكُم
your/you (fem.)	ـكِ	your/you (pl. fem.)	ـكُنَّ
his/him/its/it (masc.)	ـهُ	their/them (masc.)	ـهُم
her/its/it (fem.)	ـها	their/them (fem.)	ـهُنَّ

As with the subject pronouns, dual attached pronouns are formed by adding *alif* (ا) to the masculine plural and are used to refer to two people (of any gender):

your/you (two)	ـكُما
their/them (both)	ـهُما

Write the verbs and nouns with the correct attached pronouns.

EXAMPLE   سَمِعَ (he heard) + ...

هي = سَمِعَها (he heard her/it)

أنتَ = سَمِعَكَ (he heard you)

بيت (house) + ...

أنا = بَيتي (my house)

نحن = بَيتُنا (our house)

Note: Except for "my," a final vowel, in this case *ḍamma*, is included on the noun before the attached pronoun: بَيتي = my house; بَيتُهُ = his house; بَيتُنا = our house.

فَهِمَتْ (she understood) + ...

١ نحن = _____

٢ هم = _____

٣ أنتِ = _____

٤ هو = _____

٥ أنتم = _____

٦ هما = _____

٧ أنا = _____

٨ هنَّ = _____

مِفتاح (key) + ...

٩ أنا = _____

١٠ أنتِ = _____

١١ هنَّ = _____

١٢ هي = _____

١٣ هو = _____

١٤ هم = _____

١٥ أنتم = _____

١٦ نحن = _____

سَمِعتُ (I heard) + ...

١٧ هو = _____

١٨ أنتِ = _____

١٩ هم = _____

٢٠ هي = _____

٢١ أنتَ = _____

٢٢ هنَّ = _____

٢٣ أنتم = _____

٢٤ أنتما = _____

شاحنات (trucks) + ...

٢٥ هي = _____

٢٦ أنتم = _____

٢٧ هم = _____

٢٨ نحن = _____

٢٩ أنتَ = _____

٣٠ أنا = _____

٣١ هما = _____

٣٢ هنَّ = _____

EXERCISE 2·14

Shorten the following sentences, using an attached pronoun. (Remember that nonhuman plurals are feminine singular.)

EXAMPLE   I ate the apple. أَكَلتُ التُّفّاحة.

(I ate it.) أَكَلتُها.

١ أَكَلنا السَّمَك. We ate the fish.

_____

٢ طَبَختَ الأُرُزِّ. You (masc.) cooked the rice.

_____

٣ بَدَأَت العَمَل. She started the work.

_____

Nonverbal sentences and pronouns   **25**

٤ سَمِعَ الصَّوت. He heard the sound.

_____

٥ مَسَكْتِ الأقلام. You (fem.) held the pens.

_____

٦ غَسَلتُ المَلابِس. I washed the clothes.

_____

٧ قَفَلْنَ الباب. They (fem.) closed the door.

_____

٨ فَهِمتُ المُدَرِّسين. I understood the teachers.

_____

٩ دَرستُم اللُّغة العربيّة. You (masc. pl.) studied the Arabic language.

_____

١٠ وَجَدَ المَفاتيح. He found the keys.

_____

١١ سَمِعَت البَنات. She heard the girls.

_____

١٢ تَبِعنا شكري ونادية. We followed Shukri and Nadia.

_____

Expressing "to have"

Arabic does not have a direct equivalent of the verb "to have." The prepositions لِ (*to/for*) or عِندَ (*at*) are two of several prepositions used to express the concept, and a verb is not necessarily needed at all.

Shukri has a new washing machine.	لِشُكري غَسّالة جديدة.
"to Shukri (is a) new washing machine"	
My friend has a house in America.	عِندَ صَديقي بيت في أمريكا.
"at my friend (is a) house in America"	
The children have many books.	للأطفال كُتُب كَثيرة.
"to the children (are) many books"	
The grocer has fresh figs today.	عِندَ البَقّال تين طازِج اليَوم.
"at the grocer (are) fresh figs today"	

Note: Arabic words such as لِ consisting of a single consonant are always written joined to the following word. In addition, when لِ is joined to الـ (*al-*), the combination becomes لِلـ (*lil-*).

Describe what everyone has by using the prompts with the preposition لِ or عِندَ.

EXAMPLE   شُكري/بَيت صغير/الجنوب

<u>لِشكري بيت صغير في الجَنوب. / عِندَ شكري بيت صغير في الجَنوب.</u>

١ نادية/بيت جميل/المدينة

_____

٢ أمّي/خَواتِم كثيرة/الدُرج

_____

٣ صَديقي/سيّارة سريعة/الشارع

_____

٤ المُدَرِّسة/مَكتَب صَغير/المدرسة

_____

٥ اِبن أُختي/شَجَرة (tree) طويلة /الحَديقة

_____

٦ البِنت/ملابس نَظيفة/الدرج

_____

٧ أحمَد/صَديق/أمريكا

_____

٨ المُدير/صورة جميلة/المكتَب

_____

٩ الرَّجُل/نَظّارة/السيّارة

_____

١٠ المَلِك/طائِرة كبيرة/المَطار (airport)

_____

١١ الرَّسّام/ساعة قديمة/الصالة (hall)

_____

١٢ هذا الوَلَد/حَشَرة غريبة/الصَندوق (box)

_____

عِندَ/لِ + attached pronouns

Attached pronouns, as discussed earlier in this chapter, can be added to لِ or عِندَ, to produce the meanings such as "I have," "you have," and "he has." The final *fatḥa* of عند is removed when the attached pronoun ـي is added:

I have a pain in my leg.	عِندي أَلَم في رِجلي.
He has a brother in Kuwait.	عِندَهُ أَخ في الكُوَيت.
We have fresh figs today.	عِندَنا تين طازِج اليوم.

EXERCISE

2·16

Write the combinations and say what they mean.

EXAMPLE   عِندَ + نحن = عِندَنا *we have*

= عِندَ + هي ١	_____
= عِندَ + هم ٢	_____
= عِندَ + أَنتِ ٣	_____
= عِندَ + هو ٤	_____
= عِندَ + أَنتم ٥	_____
= عِندَ + أَنتَ ٦	_____
= عِندَ + أَنا ٧	_____
= عِندَ + هنَّ ٨	_____
= عِندَ + هما ٩	_____
= عِندَ + أَنتنّ ١٠	_____

The construction عِندَ + *attached pronoun* is commonly used even when the subject is mentioned:

Salma has ("Salma, at her") an apartment in Beirut.	سَلمَى عِندَها شَقّة في بيروت.
The children have ("the children, at them") a large room.	الأطفال عِندَهُم غُرفة كَبيرة.

Fill in عِنْدَ *with the correct attached pronoun to complete these sentences.*

EXAMPLE   أَحْمَد عِنْدَهُ شَقّة في لُندُن.

١ نادية _____ ثَلاثة أطفال.

٢ سَمير _____ أَلَم في رِجله.

٣ أخي _____ بيت بِجانِب النَّهر.

٤ المُدَرِّسون _____ غُرفة خاصّة (private) في المَدرَسة.

٥ البَقّال _____ تين طازِج اليوم.

٦ أبي وأُمّي _____ سيّارة قَديمة.

٧ المُديرة _____ مَكتَب خاصّ.

٨ البَنات _____ دَرّاجات جَديدة.

The preposition لِ becomes لي (*lī*) when the attached pronoun ـي is added:

I have a small apartment.	لي شَقّة صغيرة.
I have a sister in Beirut.	لي أُخت في بَيروت.

When the other attached pronouns are added, the vowel changes from *kasra* to *fatḥa* (from *li-* to *la-*):

They have three dogs.	لَهُم ثَلاثة كِلاب.
She has a gold ring.	لَها خاتِم ذَهَبيّ.
You (masc.) have a broken bicycle.	لَكَ دَرّاجة مَكسورة.
We have a son whose name ("his name") is Hatim.	لَنا ابن اسمُهُ حاتِم.

Write the combinations and say what they mean.

EXAMPLE   لِ + نحن = لَنا *we have*

١ لِ + هي = _____

٢ لِ + هم = _____

٣ لِ + أنتِ = _____

٤ لِ + هو = _____

٥ لِ + أنتم = _____

Nonverbal sentences and pronouns   **29**

$$٦ \quad لِ + أَنتَ =$$ _____

$$٧ \quad لِ + أَنا =$$ _____

$$٨ \quad لِ + هُنَّ =$$ _____

$$٩ \quad لِ + هما =$$ _____

$$١٠ \quad لِ + أَنتنّ =$$ _____

EXERCISE
2·19

How do you express these in Arabic using the preposition لِ?

EXAMPLE   We have three children. لَنا ثلاثة أطفال.

They (masc.) have three houses. ١

_____

I have a sister in America. ٢

_____

You (fem.) have a beautiful garden. ٣

_____

We have a broken watch in the drawer. ٤

_____

She has a brother whose name is Shukri. ٥

_____

He has a sister whose name is Nadia. ٦

_____

They (masc.) have a strange picture in the hall. ٧

_____

They (dual) have a large apartment. ٨

_____

You (masc.) have a fast car. ٩

_____

I have a very slow car. ١٠

_____

They (fem.) have a small office in the school. ١١

_____

You (dual) have a clever son! ١٢

_____

Other ways of expressing "to have"

Other prepositions used to express "to have" are:

- ◆ لَدَى (ladā) "at/by": when attached pronouns are added to لَدَى, the combination starts with لَدَيـ (laday-).

    We have a small problem. لَدَينا مُشكِلة صغيرة.

- ◆ مَعَ (maعa) "with": usually used to talk about things you have *with* you.

    She has candles and matches (with her). مَعَها شُموع وكَبريت.

EXERCISE

2·20

Rewrite the sentences to refer to the subject in parentheses.

EXAMPLE مَعَهُ مِفتاح السيّارة. (نحن) مَعَنا مفتاح السيّارة.

١ مَعَهُ كِتاب نادية. (أنت)

_____

٢ لَدَينا تين طازِج اليوم. (أنتُم)

_____

٣ لَدَيها مَكتَب صَغير في المَصنَع. (نَحنُ)

_____

٤ مَعَهُم شُموع كثيرة. (هو)

_____

٥ لَدَيها شَقّة جميلة في وَسَط المدينة. (أنتِ)

_____

٦ مَعي مِفتاح الشقّة. (هنّ)

_____

٧ مَعَهُ ثلاث دولارات. (أنا)

_____

٨ لَدَيكَ اِبنة ذَكِيّة ومُجتَهِدة. (أنتما)

_____

٩ لَدَيكم خَواتِم جميلة. (هي)

_____

١٠ مَعَكِ الأقلام والكُتُب. (أنتم)

_____

·3· Forming questions

Yes/no questions

In English, verbs change when put into a question: "*She went* to the bank." but "*Did she go* to the bank?" In Arabic there is no such change. Verbs do not have a question form.

The marker هَل can be put in front of a statement to make it into a question (with the answer yes [نَعَم] or no [لا]):

She went to the bank.	ذَهَبَتْ إلى البنك.
Did she go to the bank?	هَل ذَهَبَتْ إلى البنك؟
The mosque is close to the airport.	الجامِع قَريب من المَطار.
Is the mosque close to the airport?	هَل الجامِع قَريب من المَطار؟
He lives in Beirut.	يَسكُن في بيروت.
Does he live in Beirut?	هَل يَسكُن في بيروت؟

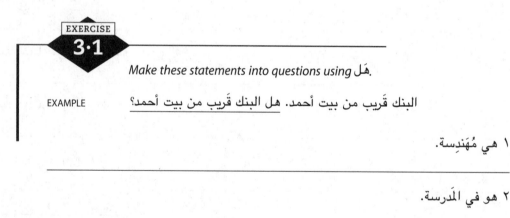

EXERCISE
3·1

Make these statements into questions using هَل.

EXAMPLE البنك قَريب من بيت أحمد. هل البنك قَريب من بيت أحمد؟

١ هي مُهَندِسة.

_____

٢ هو في المَدرسة.

_____

٣ الكُرسيّ في الحَمّام.

_____

٤ لِشَريف سيّارة جديدة.

_____

٥ الأقلام بِجانِب الكُتُب.

_____

٦ المُدير في المَكتَب.

_____

٧ هي مُهَندِسة.

_____

٨ هُناكَ حَديقة جميلة في وَسَط المدينة.

_____

٩ وَجَدَتْ نادية المفتاح.

_____

١٠ عِندَهُم أطفال.

_____

١١ أَكَلَ شكري السَّمَك.

_____

١٢ يَسكُن شَريف في شَقّة صغيرة.

_____

EXERCISE
3·2

Your friend is telling you about her son, who has just moved and found a new job.
You are very curious and are interrogating her about all the details. Ask questions following
the prompts.

EXAMPLE   هل لَهُ مَكتَب كَبير؟ has large office?

lives near your house? ١

_____

has small apartment? ٢

_____

the apartment new? ٣

_____

has children? ٤

_____

has car? ٥

_____

has garden? ٦

_____

apartment near office? ٧

_____

office in center of town? ٨

_____

your son engineer? ٩

_____

hardworking? ١٠

_____

always very busy? ١١

_____

his manager patient? ١٢

_____

An alternative question marker is أ. This is written joined to the following word:

He is a grocer.	هو بَقّال.
Is he a grocer?	أهو بَقّال؟
The city is far from here.	المَدينة بَعيدة من هنا.
Is it far from here?	أهِيَ بَعيدة من هنا؟

The question marker أ rather than هَل should be used for negative questions:

He doesn't live in Damascus.	لا يَسكُن في دِمشَق.
Doesn't he live in Damascus?	ألا يَسكُن في دِمشَق؟

EXERCISE
3·3

Make these statements into questions using أ.

EXAMPLE   هذا القَلَم مكسور. <u>أهذا القَلَم مكسور؟</u>

_____ ١ أنتَ المُهندِس الجديد.

_____ ٢ هُنَّ مُمَرِّضات.

_____ ٣ هي في الحديقة.

_____ ٤ لا يسكُن في بيروت.

_____ .ه أنتِ مَعي

_____ ٦ هذا بيتك.

_____ ٧ هذه الحقيبة ثقيلة.

_____ ٨ أنتُم مُحاسِبون.

Question words

Question words usually come first in Arabic, as they do in English.

Where do you (masc.) live?	أَين تَسكُن؟
How did she find the apartment?	كَيفَ وَجَدَت الشقّة؟
Why did you (fem.) go to the school?	لِماذا ذَهَبتِ إلى المدرسة؟

where?	أَين؟
when?	مَتَى؟
how?	كَيفَ؟
why?	لِماذا؟
who?	مَن؟
what? + noun	ما؟
what? + verb	ماذا؟
which? masc./fem.	أَيّ/أَيّة؟

EXERCISE

3·4

Ask questions following the prompts.

EXAMPLE ذَهَبَ شكري إلى الجامِعة. (Shukri went to the university.)

لِماذا ذَهَبَ إلى الجامِعة؟ why

كَيفَ ذَهَبَ إلى الجامِعة؟ how

وَجَدَتْ نادية خاتِمها. (Nadia found her ring.)

_____ where ١

_____ how ٢

_____ when ٣

فَتَحوا الصَّندوق. (They opened the box.)

_____ how ٤

_____ why ٥

_____ where ٦

يَدرُس شَريف التاريخ. (Sharif is studying history.)

7 why _____

8 in which university _____

أَكَلَ أحمد في مَطعَم. (Ahmed ate in a restaurant.)

9 what _____

10 when _____

11 where _____

12 with whom (masc.) _____

Decide on the correct question word to fill each gap. You will need to look at the answer following the question to confirm.

EXAMPLE   أَينَ ذَهَبتَ؟ ذَهَبتُ إلى السّوق.

١ _____ هذا؟ هذا كتاب.

٢ _____ هذا الوَلَد؟ هذا أخي.

٣ _____ ذَهَبَ أحمد إلى وسط المدينة؟ ذَهَبَ بالسيّارة.

٤ _____ الأولاد؟ هم في الحديقة.

٥ أنتَ من _____ بَلَد؟ أنا من سوريا.

٦ من _____ مدينة؟ من دِمَشق.

٧ _____ أنت مُهندس؟ لا، أنا مُدرِّس.

٨ _____ أَكَلَ شكري صَباحاً؟ أَكَلَ الخُبز والفول.

٩ _____ رَجَعَتْ نادية من أمريكا؟ رَجَعَتْ أمس مساءً.

١٠ _____ يَسكُن هنا؟ لأنّ الشقّة قريبة من وسط المدينة.

PAST TENSE

Arabic has only two main tenses:

- ◆ Past (or perfect) tense: الماضي
- ◆ Present/future (or imperfect) tense: المُضارِع

Other verbal moods and time references are formed with modifications and additional markers, or with a combination of the two main tenses. It can be easier to study the past tense first, since it shows the root of the verb more clearly.*

---

*In Part I of this book, Arabic words used in the exercises were translated. In Part II and subsequent parts, it is not possible to include a translation for all the additional words. You may sometimes need to use a dictionary. However, we have strived to use high-frequency vocabulary that should be largely familiar to those learning Arabic.

Regular basic verbs and sentence structure

Strictly speaking, the Arabic language does not have "regular" and "irregular" verbs, just many different categories of verb that largely behave predictably within their type. However, Arabic verbs based on roots of three different, stable consonants are generally called "regular," with other types termed "irregular."

Past tense formation and uses

Basic verbs (also called form I) constructed from regular roots are the simplest type of verb. Nonbasic or "derived" forms of the verb are covered in Part IV of this book.

The past tense is formed by adding subject endings to a past tense "stem." The past tense stem of basic regular verbs is formed with the three root letters, usually separated by *fatḥa(a)*:

sat	جَلَس
washed	غَسَل
went out	خَرَج

Some past tense stems have *kasra* as the second vowel:

drank	شَرِب
understood	فَهِم
played	لَعِب

and a few have *ḍamma* as the second vowel:

was/became large	كَبُر
was/became small	صَغُر

Endings are added to the stem to show the subject of the verb. The simplest of the endings is a final *fatḥa* showing that the subject is هُوَ (*he/it*, or third person masculine singular): جَلَسَ (*he sat*); فَهِمَ (*he understood*). The other singular and plural past tense endings are shown in the following table. The subject endings for the dual are covered in Chapter 8.

PAST TENSE ENDING		EXAMPLE	
SINGULAR			
I أنا	ـتُ	جَلَسْتُ	I sat
you (masc.) أنتَ	ـتَ	جَلَسْتَ	you (masc.) sat
you (fem.) أنتِ	ـتِ	جَلَسْتِ	you (fem.) sat
he/it (masc.) هُوَ	ـَ	جَلَسَ	he/it (masc.) sat
she/it (fem.) هِيَ	ـَتْ	جَلَسَتْ	she/it (fem.) sat
PLURAL			
we نَحنُ	ـنا	جَلَسْنا	we sat
you (masc. pl.) أنتُم	ـتُمْ	جَلَسْتُمْ	you (masc. pl.) sat
you (fem. pl.) أنتُنَّ	ـتُنَّ	جَلَسْتُنَّ	you (fem. pl.) sat
they (masc.) هُمْ	ـوا*	جَلَسوا	they (masc.) sat
they (fem.) هُنَّ	ـنَ	جَلَسْنَ	they (fem.) sat

*Pronounced -ū, for example جَلَسوا *jalasū*. The final *alif* is a spelling convention and is silent.

The past tense is used to talk about completed actions. خَرَجَ means both "he went out" and "he has gone out"; كَتَبْتُ means "I wrote" and "I have written." In other words, there is no equivalent of the English "has/have gone out," "has/have written," or "has/have washed."

Separate pronouns are not usually needed with an Arabic verb since the ending indicates the subject. However, pronouns are sometimes used for clarity or emphasis.

We washed the clothes yesterday.	غَسَلْنا المَلابِس أمس.
She cooked lunch for us.	طَبَخَت الغَداء لَنا.
Have you (masc.) understood the instructions?	هل فَهِمْتَ التَعليمات؟
Did they carry the bags?	هل حَمَلوا الحَقائِب؟
No, we carried them.	لا، نَحنُ حَمَلْناها.
Did Sami drink the juice?	هل شَرِبَ سامي العَصير؟
Sami went out so *I* drank all the juice.	خَرَجَ سامي فَشَرِبْتُ أنا كُلّ العَصير.

Write the correct part of the verb in the past tense to match the subject in parentheses,
and add its meaning in English.

EXAMPLE   جَلَس (نحن) جَلَسْنا _we sat_

_____ ١ جَلَس (أنا)

_____ ٢ غَسَل (نحن)

_____ ٣ فَهِم (هو)

_____ ٤ كَتَب (أنتِ)

_____ ٥ حَمَل (أنتنّ)

_____ ٦ خَرَج (هم)

_____ ٧ كَبُر (هي)

_____ ٨ لَعِب (أنتَ)

_____ ٩ طَبَخ (أنتم)

_____ ١٠ فَهِم (هنّ)

Write the correct Arabic verb to match the English.

EXAMPLE   خَرَجْتَ you (masc.) went out

_____ I went out ١

_____ he cooked ٢

_____ you (masc.) washed ٣

_____ you (fem.) carried ٤

_____ we understood ٥

_____ she drank ٦

_____ they (fem.) sat ٧

_____ you (masc. pl.) wrote ٨

_____ they (masc.) became bigger ٩

_____ you (fem. pl.) played ١٠

At a party, everyone drank something different. Write sentences using the prompts and the following additional vocabulary.

فِنجان شاي a cup of tea   فِنجان قَهوة a cup of coffee

كوب حَليب a glass of milk   كوب ماء a glass of water

عَصير بُرتُقال orange juice   عَصير تُفّاح apple juice

عَصير لَيمون lemon juice   عَصير رُمّان pomegranate juice

                                               كولا cola

EXAMPLE   I/cup of coffee شَرِبْتُ فِنجان قَهوة. (I drank a cup of coffee.)

he/glass of milk ١

_____

you (masc.)/cup of tea ٢

_____

she/pomegranate juice ٣

_____

we/apple juice ٤

_____

you (fem.)/a glass of water ٥

_____

they (masc.)/cola ٦

_____

they (fem.)/lemon juice ٧

_____

you (masc. pl.)/orange juice ٨

_____

Past tense stems of regular roots

Here are the past tense stems of regular roots introduced in Part I. Pay special attention to those that have *kasra* as the second vowel of the stem.

left	تَرَك	followed	تَبَع	searched	بَحَث
reserved	حَجَز	gathered	جَمَع	sat	جَلَس
attended	حَضَر	burned	حَرَق	happened	حَدَث
went out	خَرَج	carried	حَمَل	saved/memorized	حَفِظ

pushed/paid	دَفَع	studied	دَرَس	came in	دَخَل
returned	رَجَع	went	ذَهَب	mentioned	ذَكَر
rode	رِكِب	danced	رَقَص	drew	رَسَم
fell	سَقَط	stole	سَرَق	planted	زَرَع
drank	شَرِب	heard	سَمِع	resided	سَكَن
hit	ضَرَب	laughed	ضَحِك	made	صَنَع
appeared	ظَهَر	requested	طَلَب	cooked	طَبَخ
worked	عَمِل	learned/found out	عَلِم	knew	عَرَف
did	فَعَل	opened	فَتَح	washed	غَسَل
cut	قَطَع	killed	قَتَل	understood	فَهِم
wrote	كَتَب	closed	قَفَل	jumped	قَفَز
wore	لَبِس	broke	كَسَر	hated	كَرِه
went down	نَزَل	held	مَسَك	played	لَعِب
escaped	هَرَب	descended	هَبَط	looked	نَظَر

EXERCISE

4·4

What do these Arabic verbs mean?

EXAMPLE   <u>*they looked*</u>   نَظَروا

١ ضَرَبْتُ _____

٢ لَبِسَتْ _____

٣ نَزَلْنا _____

٤ بَحَثَ _____

٥ قَفَزْتُم _____

٦ تَرَكْنَ _____

٧ سَرَقوا _____

٨ كَرِهْتَ _____

٩ هَرَبْنا _____

١٠ ضَحِكْتِ _____

١١ فَعَلْتُ _____

١٢ هَبَطَ _____

١٣ مَسَكْتْ _____

١٤ طَلَبْتُنَّ _____

١٥ حَجَزْتُم _____

Leila had a busy day yesterday. What did she do? Write sentences using the prompts.

EXAMPLE   drank/orange juice شَرِبَتْ عَصير بُرتُقال. (She drank orange juice.)

_____ drank/a cup of coffee ١

_____ washed/the clothes ٢

_____ drew/a picture ٣

_____ cooked/the lunch ٤

_____ played/tennis ٥

_____ wrote/an e-mail ٦

_____ rode/her bicycle ٧

_____ went/the park ٨

Now pretend you are Leila, and write the sentences from Exercise 4.5 again.

EXAMPLE   شَرِبتُ عَصير بُرتُقال. (I drank orange juice.)

_____ ١

_____ ٢

_____ ٣

_____ ٤

_____ ٥

_____ ٦

_____ ٧

_____ ٨

Write the correct Arabic verb to match the English.

EXAMPLE   لَعِبْتُ I played

_____ they (masc.) drank ١

_____ she rode ٢

_____	I requested ٣
_____	you (fem.) sat ٤
_____	we entered ٥
_____	he fell ٦
_____	she carried ٧
_____	he stole ٨
_____	you (masc.) returned ٩
_____	he resided ١٠
_____	they (fem.) danced ١١
_____	you (masc. pl.) reserved ١٢

EXERCISE

4·8

Now choose one of the verbs you created in Exercise 4.7 to fill in the blanks in the following sentences.

EXAMPLE لَعِبْتُ التَنِس مَعَ صَديقي.

١ _____ القَصر من الباب الأماميّ.

٢ مَتى _____ من المطعم؟

٣ _____ أُختي دَرّاجتها الجَديدة.

٤ _____ على المَسرَح الكبير.

٥ الأولاد _____ عصير البرتقال.

٦ _____ الخَيمة على ظَهرها.

٧ _____ المَفاتيح من المُدير.

٨ هل _____ لنا ثلاثة مقاعد؟

٩ _____ أخي من فَوق الحِصان.

١٠ _____ اللِصّ ساعَتي الذَهَبِيّة.

١١ _____ الوَزير في الشَقّة الواسِعة.

١٢ هل _____ في الحديقة بَعدَ الظُّهر يا نادية؟

Attached pronouns with verbs

There are few things to note when adding attached pronouns to verbs, or *verb + preposition* combinations:

1. The final silent *alif* of the masculine plural is not included before an attached pronoun:

They (masc.) drank the juice.	شَرِبوا العَصير.
They (masc.) drank it.	شَرِبوهُ.
They (masc.) reserved the seats.	حَجَزوا المَقاعِد.
They (masc.) reserved them.	حَجَزوها.

2. In a *verb + preposition* combination, the attached pronoun should be added to the preposition and not to the verb itself:

We returned from the restaurant.	رَجَعْنا مِن المَطعَم.
We returned from it.	رَجَعْنا مِنهُ.
I searched for the boys.	بَحَثْتُ عَن الأولاد.
I searched for them.	بَحَثْتُ عَنْهُم.

    The prepositions إلى *ilā* (*to*) and على *alā* (*on*) become إلَيـ *ilay-* and عَلَيـ *alay-* before an attached pronoun:

I went to the school.	ذَهَبْتُ إلى المَدرَسة.
I went to it.	ذَهَبْتُ إلَيها.
Nadia sat on her spectacles.	جَلَسَتْ نادية على نَظّارَتِها.
Nadia sat on them.	جَلَسَتْ نادية عَلَيها.

3. The *ḍamma* of the attached pronouns هُ, هُمْ, and هُنَّ changes to *kasra* when following the sound *i*, *ī* or *ay*:

We danced in the street.	رَقَصنا في الشارع.
We danced in it.	رَقَصنا فيهِ.
Did you (fem.) drink the juice?	هل شَرِبْتِ العَصير؟
Did you drink it?	هل شَرِبْتِهِ؟
I sat on the chair.	جَلَستُ على الكُرسيّ.
I sat on it.	جَلَستُ عَلَيهِ.
The teacher looked at the boys.	نَظَرَ المُدَرِّس إلى الأولاد.
The teacher looked at them.	نَظَرَ المُدَرِّس إلَيهِم.

    (**Note:** Refer to the section "Attached pronouns" in Chapter 2 for more explanation.)

Shorten these sentences using attached pronouns.

EXAMPLE   لَعِبْتُ مَعَ صَديقي. لَعِبْتُ مَعَهُ.

١ دَخَلوا القَصر. _____

٢ بَحَثْنا عَن المَفاتيح. _____

٣ سَرَقوا ساعَتي الذَهَبِيّة. _____

٤ ذَهَبْنا إلى المَكتَب. _____

٥ رَقَصْتُ على المَسرَح الكبير. _____

٦ الأولاد شَرِبوا عصير البرتقال. _____

٧ مَتى رَجَعْتُمْ مِن المطعم؟ _____

٨ هل جَلَسْتِ على النَّظارة؟ _____

٩ خَرَجَت الحَشَرات مِن الشَّجَرة. _____

١٠ خَرَجوا من البيت. _____

١١ رَجَعْتُ إلى أَصدِقائي. _____

١٢ جَلَسوا على الأرض. _____

١٣ نَظَرْتُ إلى البَنات. _____

١٤ رَسَموا هذه الصورة الجميلة. _____

١٥ سَمِعْنا عَن هذا الشَخص. _____

١٦ الرجال حَمَلوا الحَقيبة الثَّقيلة. _____

Word order and singular/plural agreement

In Arabic the verb can come before or after the subject. This is largely a matter of emphasis and/or formality. If the subject is first, it is often preceded by إِنَّ in written Arabic. إِنَّ is not directly translatable, but comes close to the archaic English "verily."

My sister rode her bicycle.	رَكِبَت أُختي دَرّاجتها./(إِنَّ) أُختي رَكِبَت دَرّاجتها.
The thief stole my watch.	سَرَقَ اللِّصّ ساعتي./(إِنَّ) اللِّصّ سَرَقَ ساعتي.
Mona cooked the vegetables.	طَبَخَت منى الخُضار./(إِنَّ) منى طَبَخَت الخُضار.

EXERCISE 4·10

Rewrite the sentences using إِنَّ.

EXAMPLE
كَسَرَ الوَلَد ساعتي. إِنَّ الوَلَد كَسَرَ ساعتي.

١ دَخَلَ شكري الغُرفة.

_____

٢ دَفَعَت أُمّي ثَمَن الفستان.

_____

٣ قَفَزَ الحِصان مِن فَوقَ السِّياج (the fence).

_____

٤ دَرَسَت ابنتي اللُّغة العربيّة.

_____

٥ شَرِبَ الوَلَد عصير البرتقال.

_____

٦ خَرَجَت الحَشرات من الشَّجَرة.

_____

٧ ذَهَبَ المُدير إلى مَكتَبه.

_____

٨ طَبَخَت لَيلَى الغَداء.

_____

٩ سَرَقَ اللِّصّ الحَقيبة.

_____

١٠ تَرَكَت نادية المَفاتيح على المائِدة.

_____

If a verb comes after a plural subject, it will also be plural:

The boys drank the orange juice.	(إِنَّ) الأولاد شَرِبوا عَصير البُرتُقال.
The thieves stole my watch.	(إِنَّ) اللُّصوص سَرَقوا ساعتي.
The (female) nurses entered the hospital.	(إِنَّ) المَرِّضات دَخَلْنَ المُستَشفَى.

However, if the verb is placed *before* a plural subject, it will be *singular*. Look again at the preceding sentences, this time with the verb placed first:

شَرِبَ الأولاد عَصير البُرتُقال.

سَرَقَ اللُّصوص ساعتي.

دَخَلَت المَرِّضات المُستَشفَى.

The verb is now either masculine or feminine singular, depending on the gender of the subject, but not plural.

Change these sentences to put the verb first.

EXAMPLE   إنّ الأولاد دَخَلوا الغرفة. <u>دَخَلَ الأولاد الغرفة.</u>

١ إنّ الأولاد شَرِبوا العصير.

_____

٢ إنّ البَنات خَرَجْنَ من البيت.

_____

٣ اللُّصوص فَتَحوا الشُّباك.

_____

٤ كُلّ أصدِقائي (my friends) رَقَصوا في الحَفلة.

_____

٥ إنّ المُدَرِّسات حَضَرْنَ الاجتِماع.

_____

٦ الأطفال رَسَموا صورة جميلة للمدرّسة.

_____

٧ الطالِبات (female students) دَخَلْنَ الجامِعة.

_____

٨ إنّ الرِجال عَمِلوا حَتَّى الساعة التاسِعة مساء.

_____

Any second or subsequent verb after the subject will be plural:

singular verb + subject + plural verb

The actors went in and sat down in the theater.   دَخَلَ المُمَثِّلون وجَلَسوا في المَسرَح.

The girls opened the door and looked at the plane.   فَتَحَت البَنات الباب ونَظَرْنَ إلى الطائِرة.

Write the correct part of the past tense verb in parentheses to complete the sentences.

EXAMPLE   حَمَلَ (حمل) الرِجال الكُتُب الثقيلة <u>وذَهَبوا</u> (ذهب) إلى المَكتَبة.

١ _____ (جلس) المُمَثِّلون و _____ (حفظ) المَسرَحيّة.

٢ _____ (خرج) البَنات و _____ (لعب) في الحديقة.

٣ _____ (سمع) أصدِقائي قِصّتي و _____ (ضحك).

٤ _____ (فتح) اللُّصوص الشُّبّاك و _____ (سرق) الأموال كُلّها.

٥ _____ (ركب) الطالِبات القِطار و _____ (ذهب) إلى الجامِعة.

٦ _____ (سقط) الأولاد من السِّياج و _____ (جرح) رُؤوسهُم (their heads).

٧ _____ (ذهب) اللاعبون إلى المَلعَب و _____ (لبس) الشورت.

٨ _____ (دفع) الأطفال ثَمَن اللُّعَب و _____ (رجع) بها إلى البيت.

٩ _____ (دخل) الجارات (female neighbors) المَطبَخ و _____ (طبخ) الغَداء مَعاً.

١٠ _____ (ترك) الناس الفُندُق و _____ (رقص) في الشارِع.

Forming the past tense negative with ما

There are two ways of forming a past tense negative:

1. ما + past tense verb

2. لَم + modified present tense verb

The second method will be covered in Chapter 20 in the section "Past tense negative with لَم."

The simplest way of expressing a past tense negative is by adding ما (*not*) directly in front of a past tense verb. This produces the meaning of "didn't . . ." or "hasn't/haven't . . .":

I didn't drink/haven't drunk the juice.	ما شَرِبْتُ العصير.
We didn't hear/haven't heard about this person here.	ما سَمِعْنا عن هذا الشَّخص هُنا.
Nadia didn't cook/hasn't cooked the vegetables.	ما طَبَخَتْ نادية الخُضار.

EXERCISE

4·13

Make these sentences and questions negative using ما.

EXAMPLE   فَهِمتُ التَّعليمات. ما فهمتُ التَّعليمات.

١ رَكِبْتُ الطائِرة أَمس.

_____

٢ سَمِعْنا عن هذه المدينة.

_____

٣ لماذا حَضَرْتَ هذا الاجتِماع؟

_____

٤ حَفِظْنا المَسرَحيّة كلّها.

_____

٥ خَرَجَتْ أُمّي من غُرفتها اليوم.

_____

٦ إنَّ الطالِبات دَرَسْنَ الفَرَنسيّة السَّنة الماضية.

_____

٧ حَرَقَت الخِطابات والصُّوَر.

_____

٨ لِماذا تَرَكتُم المَطعَم؟

_____

٩ طَلَبْتُ فِنجان قَهوة.

_____

١٠ الأولاد جَلَسوا على الأرض.

_____

EXERCISE
4·14

Everyone is trying to help organize a family reunion, but only some things have been completed. Use the additional vocabulary and the prompts to make sentences.

flowers زُهور	invitations دَعوات	hall صالة	menu قائِمة
band فِرقة	falafel فَلافِل	suit بَذلة	bread خُبز

EXAMPLE   Nadia: reserve hall ✓/write invitations ✗ حجزَتْ نادية الصالة ولكِن ما كتبَت الدَّعوات.

(Nadia reserved the hall but she didn't write the invitations.)

١ Shukri: reserve band ✓/search for his suit ✗

_____

٢ Nadia's mother: go to market ✓/cook falafel ✗

_____

٣ Nadia's father: wash car ✓/pay for (the price of) the flowers ✗

_____

٤ Nadia's uncle (عَمّ): write menu ✓/order (request) bread ✗

_____

٥ The children: draw the pictures ✓/memorize their play ✗

_____

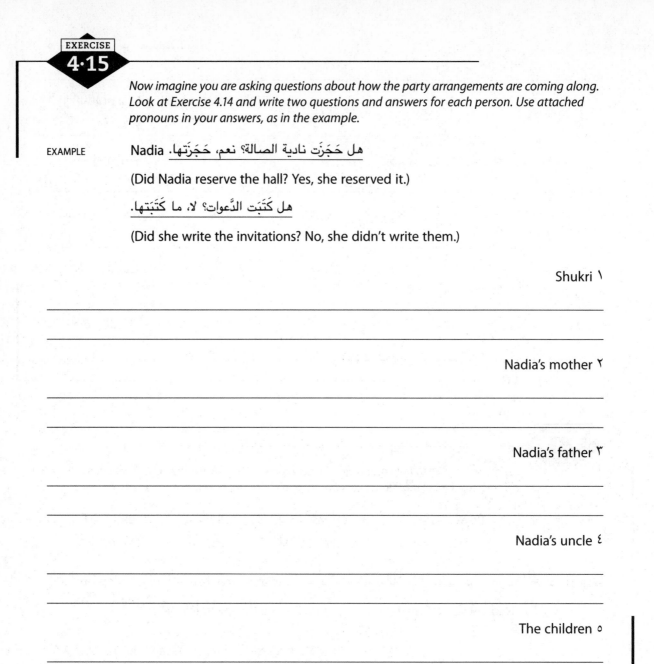

Now imagine you are asking questions about how the party arrangements are coming along. Look at Exercise 4.14 and write two questions and answers for each person. Use attached pronouns in your answers, as in the example.

EXAMPLE   Nadia. هل حَجَزَت نادية الصالة؟ نعم، حَجَزَتها.

(Did Nadia reserve the hall? Yes, she reserved it.)

هل كَتَبَت الدَّعوات؟ لا، ما كَتَبَتها.

(Did she write the invitations? No, she didn't write them.)

Shukri ١

_____

_____

Nadia's mother ٢

_____

_____

Nadia's father ٣

_____

_____

Nadia's uncle ٤

_____

_____

The children ٥

_____

_____

Changes to the object of verbs

Arabic has a system of grammatical case endings, largely confined to formal, religious and literary Arabic. Generally these case endings are written as additional final vowel marks and can stay on the peripheries of awareness, at least until the fundamentals are well established. However, from time to time the case endings affect the main spelling, and these instances need to be registered at an earlier stage. One of these instances concerns the *object* of verbs. The *subject* (الفاعل) of a verb is the person or thing that carries out an action and the *object* (المفعول به) is the person or thing that "receives" the action of a verb. In the sentence "Adel drank the juice," "Adel" is the subject and "the juice" is the object.

Alif tanwīn

The object of a verb is grammatically *accusative*. If an Arabic noun is *accusative indefinite* (i.e., meaning *a/an* or *some*) and does not end in *tā' marbūṭa* (ة), it will usually be written with an additional *alif tanwīn* (اً pronounced *-an*). Compare the same sentences with definite and indefinite objects:

I wrote a letter to my mother.	كَتَبْتُ خِطاباً لِأُمّي.
I wrote the letter to my mother.	كَتَبْتُ الخِطاب لِأُمّي.
We didn't attend a meeting in the school yesterday.	ما حَضَرْنا اِجتِماعاً في المدرسة أمس.
We didn't attend the school meeting yesterday	ما حَضَرْنا اِجتِماع المدرسة أمس.
The children drew (some) pictures for the party	رَسَمَ الأطفال صُوَراً للحَفلة.
The children drew their pictures for the party.	رَسَمَ الأطفال صُوَرهُم للحَفلة.
Sameh cooked (some) delicious fish.	طَبَخَ سامح سمكاً لَذيذاً.
Sameh cooked the delicious fish.	طَبَخَ سامح السمك اللَذيذ.

EXERCISE
4·16

Translate the English into Arabic, using alif tanwīn *where necessary.*

EXAMPLE   حَجَزْتُ مِقعَداً. I reserved a seat.

                حَجَزْتُ المِقعَد. I reserved the seat.

Did you (masc.) reserve a seat on the train? ١

_____

My son drank (some) milk. ٢

_____

The thieves stole my bag... ٣

_____

...and they stole a beautiful ring. ٤

_____

Sameh carried a large bag. ٥

_____

I carried the heavy books. ٦

_____

We ordered (some) bread... ٧

_____

...but we didn't order the fish. ٨

_____

Sound masculine plural as the object of a verb

The sound masculine plural (SMP) is used for some groups of males (or of mixed gender). It is generally formed by adding ون to the singular word: مُهَندِس/مُهَندِسون (engineer/engineers). This ending changes to ين when the SMP is the *object* of a verb whether definite or indefinite:

The engineers (subject) went to the tower.	ذَهَبَ المهندسون إلى البُرج.
We followed the engineers (object) to the tower.	تَبَعْنا المهندسين إلى البرج.
Some clowns (subject) jumped onto the stage.	قَفَزَ مُهَرِّجون على المَسرَح.
The boy drew some clowns (object) in his picture.	إنّ الوَلَد رَسَمَ مُهَرِّجين في صورته.

EXERCISE
4·17

Put these sentences in the correct order.

EXAMPLE   إلى/المهندسون/المَصنَع/ذَهَبَ <u>ذَهَبَ المهندسون إلى المَصنَع.</u>

(The engineers went to the factory.)

١ القطار/رَكِبَ/المُسافِرون

_____

٢ في/اللاعبين/سَمِعْنا/الحديقة

_____

٣ صالة/دَخَل/الوُصول/الطيّارون

_____

٤ المُمَثِّلين/خِطابي/ذَكَرْتُ/في

_____

٥ الغداء/تَرَكْتَ/بَعدَ/هل/الطبّاخين؟

_____

٦ سوق/البَقّالون/خَرَجَ/الخُضار/مِن

_____

٧ الدَّرس/جَلَسَ/بَعد/المدرِّسون

_____

٨ المُدَرِّبين/لِماذا/شَكَرَ/ما/اللاعبون؟

_____

Doubled verbs in the past tense

Past tense formation

Doubled verbs have the same second and third root letters. There is a straightforward rule that you can apply to doubled verbs in all tenses to know whether second and third letters are written separately, or written together with a *shadda* (ّ):

* If the pattern for regular verbs requires a *sukūn* (ْ) over the third root letter, the doubled root letters are written separately:

(regular verb) I went	ذَهَبْتُ	
(doubled verb) I answered/replied	رَدَدْتُ	

* If the pattern for regular verbs requires a *vowel* over the third root letter, the doubled root letters are written together:

(regular verb) he went	ذَهَبَ	
(doubled verb) he answered/replied	رَدَّ	

The following table shows the complete past tense for the doubled verb رَدَّ (*replied*):

PAST TENSE ENDING		EXAMPLE	
SINGULAR			
I أَنا	رَدَدْتُ	ـتُ	I answered/replied
you (masc.) أَنتَ	رَدَدْتَ	ـتَ	you (masc.) answered/replied
you (fem.) أَنتِ	رَدَدْتِ	ـتِ	you (fem.) answered/replied
he/it (masc.) هُوَ	رَدَّ	ـَ	he/it (masc.) answered/replied
she/it (fem.) هِيَ	رَدَّتْ	ـَتْ	she/it (fem.) answered/replied
PLURAL			
we نَحنُ	رَدَدْنا	ـنا	we answered/replied
you (masc. pl.) أَنتُم	رَدَدْتُمْ	ـتُمْ	you (masc. pl.) answered/replied
you (fem. pl.) أَنتنَّ	رَدَدْتُـنَّ	ـتُـنَّ	you (fem. pl.) answered/replied
they (masc.) هُمْ	رَدّوا	ـوا	they (masc.) answered/replied
they (fem.) هُنَّ	رَدَدْنَ	ـنَ	they (fem.) answered/replied

EXERCISE

5·1

Translate these questions and sentences into Arabic.
(Notice that "I answered/replied <u>to</u>" is رَدَدْتُ على.)

EXAMPLE   رَدَدْتُ على رِسالَتَك. I answered your letter.

Did you (masc.) answer the telephone? ١

_____

He answered his mother. ٢

_____

We replied to the letter. ٣

_____

Why didn't she answer yesterday? ٤

_____

Did you (masc. pl.) reply to the invitation? ٥

_____

When did you (fem.) reply to the manager? ٦

_____

I replied yesterday. ٧

_____

They (fem.) didn't answer the (female) teacher. ٨

_____

Common basic doubled verbs

Common basic doubled verbs include:

believed/thought	ظَنَّ	broadcast/spread	بَثَّ
replied/answered	رَدَّ	proved/guided	دَلَّ
had suspicions/doubted	شَكَّ	finished/was completed	تَمَّ
included/joined	ضَمَّ	smelled	شَمَّ
cut	قَصَّ	counted	عَدَّ
stretched/extended	مَدَّ	went around/wrapped	لَفَّ
		passed	مَرَّ

When the doubled root is written separately in the past, the vowel over the second root letter is usually *fatḥa*, but can be *kasra* (as it can be for regular verbs). All of the verbs in the preceding list are voweled with *fatḥa* except شَمَّ (*smelled*):

I replied	رَدَدْتُ
I counted	عَدَدْتُ
I smelled	شَمِمْتُ

EXERCISE
5·2

Write the correct Arabic verb to match the English.

EXAMPLE   ظَنَنْتُ I believed

_____ they (masc.) counted ١

_____ he cut ٢

_____ I had suspicions ٣

_____ it (masc.) finished/was completed ٤

_____ she went around ٥

_____ it (masc.) broadcast ٦

_____ we smelled ٧

_____ you (masc.) guided/proved ٨

_____ they (fem.) included ٩

_____ you (fem.) believed ١٠

_____ I extended ١١

_____ you (fem. pl.) passed ١٢

EXERCISE
5·3

Fill in the correct Arabic verb to match the English translation.

EXAMPLE   شَمِمْنا رائِحة الزُّهور. We smelled the scent of the flowers.

The fox smelled the scent of the barbecue. الثَّعلَب رائِحة الشِّواء. _____ ١

The building of the tower was completed a year ago. بِناء البُرج مُنذُ عام. _____ ٢

The queen cut the red ribbon. المَلِكة الشَريط الأحمر. _____ ٣

٤ هل ـــــــــــــ المال في مكتب المدير؟ Did you (masc.) count the money in the manager's office?

٥ ـــــــــــــ لي يَدَهُ. He extended his hand to me.

٦ ـــــــــــــ إلى المَعْبَد. We guided her to the temple.

٧ ـــــــــــــ في هذا الصَّرّاف مُنذُ سِنين.

They (fem.) have had suspicions about this cashier for years.

٨ في البِداية ـــــــــــــ أنَّني سائِح. In the beginning they (masc.) thought that I was a tourist.

٩ لِماذا ـــــــــــــ حَولَ المَيدان ثلاث مَرّات؟ Why did you (masc. pl.) go around the square three times?

١٠ ما ـــــــــــــ على الهاتف. I didn't answer the phone.

١١ ما ـــــــــــــ المُدَرِّب لِلفَريق. The coach didn't include me in the team.

١٢ ـــــــــــــ الضُيوف على المطعم و ـــــــــــــ رائِحة الطَّعام.

The guests passed by the restaurant and smelled the food.

EXERCISE
5·4

Make the subject plural in these sentences and adjust the verb if necessary. (Remember that the verb remains singular if it comes before a plural subject.)

EXAMPLE   الضَّيف شَمَّ رائِحة الطعام. الضُّيوف شَمّوا رائِحة الطعام.

١ المُهندس مَرَّ على البُرج. ـــــــــــــــــــــــــــــــــــــــ

٢ لِماذا ما رَدَدْتَ؟ ـــــــــــــــــــــــــــــــــــــــ

٣ بَثَّت المَحَطّة هذا الخَبَر أمس. ـــــــــــــــــــــــــــــــــــــــ

٤ هل شَكَكْتِ في الطبّاخ؟ ـــــــــــــــــــــــــــــــــــــــ

٥ قَصَّت البِنت الزُهور في الحديقة. ـــــــــــــــــــــــــــــــــــــــ

٦ ما مَرَّت الطائِرة فوق أسبانيا. ـــــــــــــــــــــــــــــــــــــــ

٧ عَدَدْتُ الضُّيوف عِندَ الباب. ـــــــــــــــــــــــــــــــــــــــ

٨ لَفَّ الولد حَولَ الحديقة وعَدَّ الشَجَر. ـــــــــــــــــــــــــــــــــــــــ

EXERCISE
5·5

Fawzi Abu Sha'ra is the king's barber. The strange story of how he became a barber was broadcast yesterday. Underline all the doubled verbs you can find in the text.

EXAMPLE

بَثَّ التليفِزيون أمس حِواراً.

بَثَّ التليفِزيون أمس حِواراً (an interview) مع فوزي أبو شعرة حَلاّق المَلِك:

"قِصّتي هي أنني شَكَكْتُ وأنا طِفل أن عندي مَرَض خَطير (a serious illness) لأنّني في يَوم من الأيّام شَمِمْتُ رائحة غَريبة على وِسادَتي (my pillow) في الصَّباح، ثُمَّ وَجَدْتُ شَعري كلّه على الوِسادة وفي رأسي عَدَدْتُ ثلاث شَعرات فَقَط. أنا عَدَدْتُها بِنَفسي!

مَرَرْتُ مع أبي على المُستَشفِيات ولَفَفْتُ مع أمّي على كلّ الأَطِبّاء (the doctors) ولكنّهم رَدّوا "لا أَمَل!" ظَنَنْتُ أَنّني سَأعيش حياتي (I would live my life) كلّها بِثلاث شَعرات فقط.

وَجَدَني المَلِك وأنا تحت شَجَرة في الحَديقة فمَدَّ يَدهُ نحوي، ونَذَهَبْنا إلى القصر وضَمّني الى العُمّال (workers). ثم قَصَصْتُ شَعر المَلِك مَرّة وبعد ذلك أَصبَحتُ (I became) حلاّقهُ الخاصّ. قِصّتي هي دَليل على أن الحَياة غَريبة!"

EXERCISE
5·6

قِصَّتي *You are telling a friend about Fawzi's story. Change the text in Exercise 5.5 from* قِصَّتي *(my story) to* قِصّتهُ *(his story).*

EXAMPLE

بَثَّ التليفِزيون أمس حِواراً مع فوزي أبو شعرة حلاّق المَلِك. قِصّتهُ هي أنّهُ شَكَّ وهو طِفل...

_____

_____

_____

_____

_____

_____

_____

_____

_____

_____

Doubled verbs in the past tense   **59**

·6·

Weak verbs in the past tense

Weak verbs are those that have either و or ي as one of their root letters. In Arabic, these two letters are unstable, sometimes representing the consonant sounds *w* and *y*, and sometimes the long vowel sounds *oo* and *ee*. It is this tendency to transform from a consonant to a vowel sound that makes these letters unstable or "weak."

When و or ي appear as one of the root letters of a verb, the consonant sound can change to a long vowel in some patterns, to a short vowel in others, and occasionally drop out altogether.

Weak verbs are divided into three main categories, depending on which root letter is weak:

- *Assimilated*: the first root is weak; for example و/ص/ل (*to arrive*)
- *Hollow*: the second root is weak; for example ق/و/ل (*to say*)
- *Defective*: the third root is weak; for example م/ش/ي (*to walk*)

Some of the most common Arabic verbs are weak, and so it is important to master the various patterns.

Assimilated verbs

Assimilated verbs have و or ي appearing as their first root letter. In practice, the overwhelming majority of assimilated verbs have و as their first root letter, with only a couple of common verbs having ي as the first root.

In the past tense, basic (form I) assimilated verbs behave entirely regularly because the weak letter is the initial sound of the verb and so keeps its full consonantal value:

they found	وَجَدوا	he arrived	وَصَلَ
		we described	وَصَفْنا

Common basic assimilated verbs in the past tense include:

promised	وَعَد	arrived	وَصَل
fell	وَقَع	described	وَصَف
stood up	وَقَف	found	وَجَد
gave birth	وَلَد	put/placed	وَضَع
was/became dry	يَبِس	jumped	وَثَب
was/became certain	يَقِن	inherited	وَرِث
		weighed	وَزَن

EXERCISE
6·1

Write the correct Arabic verb to match the English.

EXAMPLE   وَرِثوا they (masc.) inherited

_____ they (masc.) described ١

_____ I promised ٢

_____ she gave birth ٣

_____ you (masc.) arrived ٤

_____ we weighed ٥

_____ he fell ٦

_____ she stood up ٧

_____ you (fem.) put ٨

_____ they (fem.) jumped ٩

_____ it (fem.) became dry ١٠

_____ we arrived ١١

_____ you (masc. pl.) inherited ١٢

EXERCISE
6·2

What has everyone found? Your entire family has been searching for your house keys.
Everyone has found something. Fill in the blanks with the correct part of the verb وَجَد.

EXAMPLE   وَجَدَتْ أمي كتابي. (My mother found my book.)

١ _____ أبي قلمي.

٢ _____ أُختي خاتِمي.

٣ _____ أخي ساعتي.

٤ _____ جَدّتي قِلادتي.

٥ _____ كلبي جَوربي.

٦ أطفالي _____ مِعطَفي وقُبّعتي وحِزامي.

٧ بنات عَمّي _____ حقيبتي.

٨ أنا _____ مَفاتيحي!

Fill in the correct Arabic verb to match the English translation.

EXAMPLE   وَصَلَ القِطار في مَوعده. The train arrived on time.

١ ــــــــــــــــــــ البَقّال الجُبن والزَّيتون. The grocer weighed the cheese and olives.

٢ هل ــــــــــــــــــــ الخاتِم الذَهَبيّ؟ Did you (masc.) find the gold ring?

٣ ــــــــــــــــــــ جَدَّتها بِهَدِية غالية. Her grandmother promised her an expensive present.

٤ ــــــــــــــــــــ هذه المَزرَعة عن أبي. I inherited this farm from my father.

٥ ــــــــــــــــــــ الفارِس من فَوقَ الحِصان. The rider fell off the horse.

٦ ــــــــــــــــــــ الزهور في الشَّمس. The flowers became dry in the sun.

٧ إنّ الأولاد ــــــــــــــــــــ مَلامِح اللصّ. The boys described the features of the thief.

٨ ــــــــــــــــــــ أمامَ شُبّاك التَذاكِر. We stood in front of the ticket window.

٩ أين ــــــــــــــــــــ تَذكِرتي؟ Where did you (fem.) put my ticket?

١٠ ما ــــــــــــــــــــ بَقَرتي عجلاً اليوم. My cow didn't give birth to a calf today.

Hollow verbs

Hollow verbs have و or ي as their second, or middle, root letter. Hollow verbs often seem to have only two root letters, but this is because the middle root has changed into a long or short vowel, creating a "hollow" center.

he said	قالَ
I sold	بِعتُ

In the past tense, basic hollow verbs follow rules similar to those for doubled verbs:

◆ If the pattern for regular verbs requires a vowel over the third root letter, as with "he," "she," and "they" (masc.), a long ا (*aa*) appears instead of the middle root letter.

he said	قالَ
she visited	زارَتْ
they sold	باعوا

◆ If the pattern for regular verbs requires a *sukūn* (°) over the third root letter, the middle root letter changes to a short vowel in hollow verbs; almost always to *u* (´) for verbs with و as the second root and *i* (   ) for verbs with ي.

I said	قُلْتُ
we visited	زُرْنا
you (masc. pl.) sold	بِعْتُم

	root = ب/ي/ع		root = ق/و/ل
he sold	باعَ	he said	قالَ
she sold	باعَتْ	she said	قالَتْ
they (masc.) sold	باعوا	they (masc.) said	قالوا
I sold	بِعْتُ	I said	قُـلْتُ
you (masc.) sold	بِعْتَ	you (masc.) said	قُـلْتَ
you (fem.) sold	بِعْتِ	you (fem.) said	قُـلْتِ
we sold	بِعْنا	we said	قُـلْـنا
you (masc. pl.) sold	بِعْـتُم	you (masc. pl.) said	قُـلْـتُم
you (fem. pl.) sold	بِعْـتُـنَّ	you (fem. pl.) said	قُـلْـتُـنَّ
they (fem.) sold	بِعْنَ	they (fem.) said	قُـلْنَ

EXERCISE

6·4

Write out the past tense conjugation for these hollow verbs, following the two preceding examples.

EXAMPLE   *he visited* زارَ

root = ز/و/ر (visit) ١

_____

_____

_____

_____

_____

_____

_____

_____

_____

Weak verbs in the past tense   **63**

_____
_____
_____
_____
_____
_____
_____
_____
_____
_____

Common hollow verbs in the past tense

Basic hollow verbs in the past tense with و as the second root letter include:

said	قال
visited	زار
returned	عاد
fasted	صام
stood up	قام
went round/turned	دار
melted	ذاب
wandered	طاف

Basic hollow verbs with ي as the second root letter include:

sold	باع
shouted	صاح
flew	طار
inclined/leaned	مال
increased	زاد
became	صار

Fill in the gaps with the correct part of the past tense hollow verb.

EXAMPLE   نحن عُدنا (عاد) من رحلَتنا أمس.

١ أنا _____ (قال) هذا الكَلام أكثر من مَرّة.

٢ _____ (ذاب) الثَلج في الرَّبيع.

٣ يا نادية، هل _____ (زار) أُمّك في المُستَشفى؟

٤ _____ (طار) الحَمامة فوق البُحَيرة.

٥ _____ (زار) المَلِك المَصنَع الجديد.

٦ إنّ الدُيوك _____ (صاح) فَجر اليوم.

٧ المُسلِمون _____ (صام) في شَهر رَمَضان.

٨ هل أنتُم _____ (باع) السيّارة؟

٩ إنّ الأسعار _____ (زاد) هذا العام.

١٠ الطالِبات _____ (قام) حينَ دَخَلَت المُدَرِّسة.

Noura has written you an e-mail telling you about her vacation with her friends. Yesterday they visited the old city, and she bought a small rug (بساط صغير) in a carpet shop.

تحياتي من هذه المدينة الجميلة!

زُرْنا صباح أمس المدينة القديمة. طُفْنا حول أسوارها ودُرْنا حتّى وَصَلْنا إلى باب السوق.

وَجَدْنا بساطاً صغيراً في دُكّان. أنا كان عِندي بساط مِثله ولكنني بِعْتُهُ لابنة عمّي.

فَمِلْتُ على البائِع وقُلْتُ لَهُ "ما ثَمَن البساط؟". قالَ البائِع "مِئة جُنيه" ولكن بَعد ساعة باعَ البَساط لَنا بخَمسين.

عُدْنا إلى الفُندق في المَساء وقُلْنا للمدير إننا زِدْنا شَخصاً لأنَّ أخي وَصَلَ إلى الفندق وصِرْنا الآن سِتّة بَدَلاً من خمسة.

مع حُبّي،

نورا.

Imagine you are forwarding the e-mail to another friend. Rewrite it, changing it from the first person ("I" and "we") to the third person ("she" and "they").

_____

_____

_____

_____

_____

_____

_____

_____

_____

_____

كان (was/were)

Probably the most important hollow verb is the verb "to be." Although it is not usually necessary in Arabic to include the verb "to be" in simple present tense sentences, a verb *is* required in the past tense:

Nadia is busy.	نادية مَشغولة.
Nadia was busy.	كانَتْ نادية مَشغولة.
I am in Ahmed's house.	أنا في بيت أحمد.
I was in Ahmed's house.	كُنتُ في بيت أحمد.
Is my son with you?	هل اِبني مَعكُم؟
Was my son with you?	هل كان اِبني معكم؟

The root of the verb is ك/و/ن so it behaves like the hollow verb ق/و/ل (*to say*):

root = ك/و/ن

he was	كانَ
she was	كانَتْ
they (masc.) were	كانوا
I was	كُنْتُ
you (masc.) were	كُنْتَ
you (fem.) were	كُنْتِ

we were	كُنّا
you (masc. pl.) were	كُنْتُم
you (fem. pl.) were	كُنْتُنَّ
they (fem.) were	كُنَّ

Notice that "we" and "they (fem.)" are written with a *shadda* over the *nūn*:

$$كُن + نا = كُنّا$$

$$كُن + نَ = كُنَّ$$

Put these sentences into the past tense.

EXAMPLE   أَنا في وَسَط المدينة. <u>كُنْتُ في وَسَط المَدينة.</u>

_____ ١ نَحنُ في مِصر.

_____ ٢ شُكري في المَكتَبة.

_____ ٣ سَميرة في بيتها.

_____ ٤ أنا أمامَ البنك.

_____ ٥ هل أنتِ مَشغولة؟

_____ ٦ هم مع المُدرّس.

_____ ٧ الفِئران تَحت المائِدة.

_____ ٨ هُنَّ في الحَديقة.

_____ ٩ البُحيرة هادئة.

_____ ١٠ أنتَ المدير.

_____ ١١ الرسالة طويلة.

_____ ١٢ السيّارات في الشارع.

_____ ١٣ أين أنتُم؟

_____ ١٤ البقّالون في سوق الخُضار.

_____ ١٥ هل أنتنَّ في المدرسة؟

When كان is followed by information (الخَبَر [news], grammatically called the predicate), this is treated as if it were the object (see the section "Changes to the object of verbs" in Chapter 4.) In other words, if the predicate is indefinite and does not end in *tā' marbūṭa* (ة), it will need to be written with the additional *alif tanwīn* (ا).

He is a cook.	هو طَبّاخ.
He was a cook.	كانَ طَبّاخاً.
The door is open.	الباب مَفتوح.
The door was open.	كانَ الباب مَفتوحاً.
Are you (masc.) busy?	هل أنتَ مَشغول؟
Were you busy?	هل كُنْتَ مَشغولاً؟

Likewise, the sound masculine plural will change from ون to ين:

We are cooks.	نَحنُ طَبّاخون.
We were cooks.	كُنّا طَبّاخين.
They are engineers in Iraq.	هم مهندسون في العراق.
They were engineers in Iraq.	كانوا مهندسين في العراق.

EXERCISE
6·8

You are asking your friend a lot of questions about his recent vacation. Follow the prompts and form the questions, agreeing the adjective or adding alif tanwīn *if necessary.*

EXAMPLE   (Was the apartment large?) الشَّقّة/كبير هل كانَت الشَّقّة كبيرة؟

١ الشَّقّة/جديد

_____

٢ الرِّحلة/قصير

_____

٣ السيّارة/سريع

_____

٤ المَنظَر/جميل

_____

٥ حَقيبَتك/خفيف

_____

٦ أنتُم/أمامَ البحر

_____

٧ ابنك/صَبور

_____

٨ البَحر/هادِئ

_____

٩ الطَّقس/حارّ

_____

١٠ أنتَ/سَعيد

_____

EXERCISE
6·9

Now your friend is answering all your questions in Exercise 6.8, but he's not very happy.
Every answer is negative! Write your friend's answers to the questions.

EXAMPLE   لا، ما كانَت الشقّة كبيرة إطلاقاً! (No, the apartment wasn't large at all!)

١ _____

٢ _____

٣ _____

٤ _____

٥ _____

٦ _____

٧ _____

٨ _____

٩ _____

١٠ _____

Using كان to express "there was/were"

The verb كان (or the feminine كانَتْ) can be placed in front of the phrase هناك (*there is/are*) to express "there was" or "there used to be":

There is a dog in the garden.	هناك كلب في الحديقة.
There was a dog in the garden.	كان هناك كلب في الحديقة.
There is a school near the river.	هناك مَدرَسة بجانب النَّهر.
There was a school near the river.	كانَتْ هناك مَدرَسة بجانب النَّهر.
There are many problems with this project.	هناك مَشاكِل كَثيرة في هذا المَشروع.
There were many problems with this project.	كانت هناك مَشاكِل كَثيرة في هذا المَشروع.

EXERCISE
6·10

You visited a small town yesterday. What was it like? Describe the town using the prompts.

EXAMPLE   حديقة ✓ / مَتحَف ✗

<u>كانَتْ هناك حديقة ولكن ما كان هناك مَتحَف.</u>

(There was a park but there wasn't a museum.)

١ سينما ✓ / مَسرَح ✗

_____

٢ بنك ✓ / مَكتَب البَريد ✗

_____

٣ مَحَلات كَثيرة ✓ / سوق ✗

_____

٤ جامِع ✓ / كَنيسة ✗

_____

٥ مَدرَسة ✓ / جامِعة ✗

_____

٦ مَحَطّة أُتوبيس ✓ / مَحَطّة قِطار ✗

_____

Using كان to express "had/used to have"

The verb كان can also be placed in front of the phrases used to express "to have," producing a past tense meaning:

I have a pain in my leg.	عِندي أَلَم في رِجلي.
I had a pain in my leg.	كان عِندي أَلَم في رِجلي.
We have a house in the Red Sea.	لَدَينا بيت في البحر الأحمر.
We used to have a house in the Red Sea.	كان لَدَينا بيت في البحر الأحمر.
They have three dogs.	لَهُم ثَلاثة كِلاب.
They used to have three dogs.	كان لَهُم ثَلاثة كِلاب.
The grocer has fresh figs today.	عِندَ البَقّال تين طازِج اليَوم.
The grocer had fresh figs yesterday.	كان عِندَ البَقّال تين طازِج أمس.
He has (with him) the key to the car.	مَعَهُ مِفتاح السيّارة.
He had (with him) the key to the car.	كان مَعَهُ مِفتاح السيّارة.

EXERCISE 6·11

Your friend is asking questions about you and your family, but his information is completely out of date. Correct your friend, using the prompts.

EXAMPLE
هل عِندكُم شَقّة في القاهرة؟ (السَّنة الماضية) <u>لا، كان عِندنا شقّة في القاهرة السَّنة الماضية.</u>

١ هل عِندكُم كِلاب؟ (السَّنة الماضية)

_____

٢ هل لَدَيكُم دَرّاجة مَكسورة؟ (الشَهر الماضي)

_____

٣ هل عندك ألم في رِجلك؟ (الأُسبوع الماضي)

_____

٤ هل عِندَ البقّال تين طازِج؟ (يَوم السَّبت الماضي)

_____

٥ هل لَكُم سيّارة سريعة؟ (مُنذُ سَنة)

_____

٦ هل لِصَديقِك بَيت في البَحر الأحمَر؟ (مُنذُ سَنَتَين)

_____

٧ هل لَدى أمِّك شجرة طويلة في الحديقة؟ (مُنذُ ثلاث سِنين)

_____

٨ هل مَعَك صُوَر اليَوم؟ (أمس)

_____

Defective verbs

Defective verbs have و or ي as their third or final root letter. Basic (form I) defective verbs fall into one of three models, depending on the root and the voweling of the verbal stem.

- *Model 1*: و as the final root letter
- *Model 2*: ي as the final root letter and *fatḥa* as the second vowel of the past tense stem
- *Model 3*: ي as the final root letter and *kasra* as the second vowel of the past tense stem

Many common verbs are defective and so it is important to master the different models.

Defective verbs: Model 1

In the past tense, defective verbs with و often behave regularly. The main exceptions are the parts of the verb for هو (*he/it*), هي (*she/it*), and هم (*they*).

		root = ش/ك/و
he complained		شَكا
she complained		شَكَتْ
they (masc.) complained		شَكَوْا
I complained		شَكَوْتُ
you (masc.) complained		شَكَوْتَ
you (fem.) complained		شَكَوْتِ
we complained		شَكَوْنا
you (masc. pl.) complained		شَكَوْتُمْ
you (fem. pl.) complained		شَكَوْتُنَّ
they (fem.) complained		شَكَوْنَ

Write out the past tense conjugation for these verbs, following the preceding example.

EXAMPLE   <u>*he requested*</u> رَجَا

١ (to request) ر/ج/و = root

_____

_____

_____

_____

_____

_____

_____

_____

_____

٢ (to invite/to summon) د/ع/و = root

_____

_____

_____

_____

_____

_____

_____

_____

_____

Another verb that follows the same pattern is بَدَا (*appeared/seemed*; root = ب/د/و).

Fill in the blanks with the correct verb in the past tense.

EXAMPLE   أنا شَكَوْتُ (شكا) من الخَدمة.

١ نَحنُ _____ (دعا) صَديقنا على العَشاء.

٢ هل أنتُم _____ (شكا) للمُدير؟

٣ أنا _____ (رَجا) من النُّزَلاء الامِتناع من التَدخين (refrain from smoking).

٤ _____ (بدا) علَيهم التَّعب من العَمَل.

٥ هُم _____ (شكا) من حَرارة المَكتَب.

٦ لِماذا ما _____ (دعا) المُدير للحَفلة يا نادية؟

٧ _____ (رَجا) المُدرِّسة من الأولاد السُكوت في الفَصل.

٨ إنّ المُمَرِّضات _____ (شكا) للطَبيب.

٩ _____ (بدا) على أبي عَلامات الغَضَب (signs of anger).

١٠ _____ (دعا) الطبّاخون أصدِقائهم على الغَداء.

Defective verbs: Model 2

Model 2 defective verbs have ي as the final root letter and *fatḥa* as the second vowel of the past tense stem. They are similar to model 1, except the part of the verb for هو (*he/it*) is written with a final *alif maqṣūra* (ى) and the و is replaced with ي in the regular parts of the verb.

root = م/ش/ي	
he walked	مَشَى
she walked	مَشَت
they (masc.) walked	مَشَوْا
I walked	مَشَيْتُ
you (masc.) walked	مَشَيْتَ
you (fem.) walked	مَشَيْتِ
we walked	مَشَيْنا
you (masc. pl.) walked	مَشَيْتُم
you (fem. pl.) walked	مَشَيْتُنَّ
they (fem.) walked	مَشَيْنَ

Write out the past tense conjugation for these verbs, following the preceding example.

EXAMPLE   <u>*he threw* رَمَى</u>

root = ر/م/ي (to throw) ١

_____

_____

_____

_____

_____

_____

_____

_____

_____

root = ب/ك/ي (to cry/to weep) ٢

_____

_____

_____

_____

_____

_____

_____

_____

_____

Write the correct part of the past tense verb in parentheses to complete the sentences.

EXAMPLE   نحن جَرَيْنا (جرى) إلى الحديقة.

١ أنا ــــــــــــــــــــــــــــــ (مشى) فوق الجِسر.

٢ لِماذا أنتم ــــــــــــــــــــــــــــــ (جرى) من البيت؟

٣ ما ــــــــــــــــــــــــــــــ (رمى) أحمد القميص القديم.

٤ لِماذا ــــــــــــــــــــــــــــــ (بكى) في المدرسة يا سَميرة؟

٥ ــــــــــــــــــــــــــــــ (رمى) القُرود (the monkeys) المَوز و ــــــــــــــــــــــــ (جرى) إلى الشجرة.

٦ ما ــــــــــــــــــــــــــــــ (جرى) نادية في سِباق الأُمَّهات (the mothers' race).

٧ نحن ــــــــــــــــــــــــــــــ (بكى) في نِهاية الفيلم.

٨ هم ــــــــــــــــــــــــــــــ (مشى) في الصَّحراء لِمُدّة طويلة.

٩ الأُمَّهات ــــــــــــــــــــــــــــــ (بكى) في المطار.

١٠ ــــــــــــــــــــــــــــــ (جرى) الأولاد وراء السيّارة و ــــــــــــــــــــــــ (رمى) علَيها الزُّهور.

Defective verbs: Model 3

Model 3 defective verbs have ي as the final root letter but *kasra* as the second vowel of the past tense stem. This affects the way the past tense is conjugated. Although the pattern is largely regular, take note of how the ي drops out in the part of the verb for هـم (*they*).

root = ن/س/ي

he forgot	نَسِيَ
she forgot	نَسِيَتْ
they (masc.) forgot	نَسُوا
I forgot	نَسِيتُ
you (masc.) forgot	نَسِيتَ
you (fem.) forgot	نَسِيتِ
we forgot	نَسِينا
you (masc. pl.) forgot	نَسِيتُمْ
you (fem. pl.) forgot	نَسِيتُنَّ
they (fem.) forgot	نَسِينَ

Write out the past tense conjugation for these verbs, following the preceding example.

EXAMPLE   <u>he met لَقِيَ</u>

١ (to meet) ل/ق/ي = root

_____

_____

_____

_____

_____

_____

_____

_____

٢ (to be pleased with) ر/ض/ي = root

_____

_____

_____

_____

_____

_____

_____

_____

Weak verbs in the past tense   **77**

Use the verbs from Exercise 6.16 to translate the following into Arabic.

EXAMPLE   نَسينا الزهور. We forgot the flowers.

١. I forgot his name.

_____

٢. Did you (fem.) forget my name?

_____

٣. We met my mother in the market.

_____

٤. Were you (masc.) pleased with (about) the workers?

_____

٥. Nadia met Shukri in front of the cinema.

_____

٦. Shukri forgot his ticket.

_____

٧. Did Nadia forget her ticket?

_____

٨. The engineers were pleased with the project.

_____

٩. When did you (masc. pl.) meet the minister?

_____

١٠. We met him yesterday.

_____

Hamzated verbs in the past tense

·7·

General rules for writing *hamza*

Hamzated verbs have the "half-letter" *hamza* (ء) as one of the root letters. *Hamzated* verbs behave largely regularly. The main consideration concerns how to write the *hamza*. The general rules for writing *hamza* are as follows:

1. If the *hamza* is at the beginning of the verb, it is written on an *alif* (أ).

2. Otherwise, the letter carrying the *hamza* tends to relate to the vowel before the *hamza*:

   - *fatḥa* before *hamza* = *hamza* written on *alif* (أ)
   - *ḍamma* before *hamza* = *hamza* written on *wāw* (ؤ)
   - *kasra* before *hamza* = *hamza* written on *yā'* without dots (ئ or ئـ)

3. If the *hamza* has no vowel before it (i.e., the letter before is written with a *sukūn*), then the preceding rules default to the vowel over the *hamza* itself.

4. If a pattern means you would need to write two *alifs*, these are combined as one with a *madda* sign above (آ), pronounced *ā*.

Past tense formation

Since the past tense of basic verbs is largely voweled with *fatḥa*, the majority of basic (form I) *hamzated* verbs are written with the *hamza* on an *alif*:

he ate	أَكَلَ
they asked	سَأَلوا
we took	أَخَذْنا
I read	قَرَأْتُ

The main exceptions are the few *hamzated* verbs that have *ḍamma* or *kasra* as the second vowel on the past tense stem:

we slowed down/became slow	بَطُؤْنا
she dared	جَرُؤَتْ
I was fed up	سَئِمْتُ

Common *hamzated* verbs in the past tense

Basic *hamzated* verbs with *hamza* as the first root letter include:

ate	أَكَل
took	أَخَذ
ordered/commanded	أَمَر
apologized	أَسِف
hoped	أَمَل
permitted	أَذَن

Verbs with *hamza* as the second root letter include:

asked	سَأَل
was/became fed up	سَئِم

Verbs with *hamza* as the third root letter include:

began	بَدَأ
read	قَرَأ
slowed down/became slow	بَطُؤ
was brave/dared	جَرُؤ
filled	مَلَأ

EXERCISE

7·1

Write the correct Arabic verb to match the English.

EXAMPLE   قَرَأْنا we read

_____ you (masc.) began ١

_____ I asked ٢

_____ she filled ٣

_____ he was fed up ٤

_____ we permitted ٥

_____ they (fem.) took ٦

_____ you (fem.) dared ٧

_____ you (masc. pl.) ate ٨

_____ they (masc.) commanded/ordered ٩

_____ we were bored ١٠

_____ I apologized ١١

_____ you (fem. pl.) read ١٢

Use the verbs from Exercise 7.1 to translate these sentences into Arabic.

EXAMPLE We were fed up by the repetition in the meeting. سَئِمْنا مِن التِكرار في الاِجتِماع.

١. I asked the manager about (عَن) the project.

_____

٢. They (masc.) took the train to Cairo.

_____

٣. When did you (fem. pl.) read these books?

_____

٤. Samira filled the bottle with juice.

_____

٥. Why did you (masc.) begin (in) this research?

_____

٦. I apologized for (على) my lateness (تَأخيري) yesterday.

_____

٧. Ahmed was fed up of the repetition in the film.

_____

٨. Did you (masc. pl.) eat the chocolate?

_____

Nadir made a list of everything he wanted to do yesterday and pinned it on his wall. His friend has just seen the list and is quizzing him about what was actually achieved. Play the part of Nadir and answer the friend's questions according to the prompts.

EXAMPLE هل سَأَلْتَ أُمّك عن الحَفلة؟ نعم، سَأَلتُها.

(Did you ask your mother about the party? Yes, I asked her.)

هل بَدَأْتَ في الكَيّ؟ لا، ما بَدَأْتُ فيه.

(Did you start the ironing? No, I didn't start it.)

١ هل أَكَلْتَ الدَجاج؟ نعم، _____.

٢ هل أَكَلْتَ المَكَرونة؟ لا، _____.

٣ هل أَخَذْتَ الأولاد إلى المَدرسة؟ نعم، _____.

٤ هل أَخَذْتَ السيّارة إلى الميكانيكيّ؟ لا، _____.

٥ هل قَرَأْتَ الرسالة الإلكترونيّة من أُختك؟ نعم، _____.

٦ هل قَرَأْتَ رسالة المُدَرِّسة؟ لا، _____.

٧ هل مَلَأْتَ الزجاجة بالماء؟ نعم، _____.

٨ هل أَخَذَ شُكري كِتابه؟ نعم، _____.

٩ هل أَخَذَتْ نادية حَقيبتها؟ لا، _____.

١٠ هل الأولاد بَدَأُوا في المَشروع؟ نعم، _____.

EXERCISE
7·4

Fill in the correct Arabic verb to match the English translation.

EXAMPLE   Have you (masc.) read the newspaper? هل قَرَأْتَ الجَريدة؟

١ _____ الزُّجاجات من البِئر. We filled the bottles from the well.

٢ _____ المدرّس لَهُم بالخُروج. The teacher allowed them to go out.

٣ _____ في بِناء البُرج. They (masc.) began to build the tower.

٤ هل _____ السَمَك كلّه أمس؟ Did you (masc. pl.) eat all the fish yesterday?

٥ _____ الشُرطيّ عن الطَّريق. We asked the policeman about the way.

٦ ما _____ تَفاصيل العَقد. You (fem.) didn't read the details of the contract.

٧ _____ كلبي إلى الحديقة. I took my dog to the park.

٨ ما _____ من تِكرار هذه اللُّعبة. We didn't get bored of repeating this game.

٩ _____ أمّي لتأخِّرها عَن الحَفلة. My mother apologized for her lateness (in getting) to the party.

١٠ إنّ البنات ما _____ هواتفهنَّ معهنَّ. The girls didn't take their cellphones with them.

١١ _____ جَدّي بعد الجِراحة. My grandfather became slow after the surgery.

١٢ كيف _____ على مهاجمته؟ How did they (masc.) dare to face him?

١٣ _____ من وُعودكُم. I've become bored of your promises.

١٤ _____ أمّي أن أَظَلّ في حُجرَتي. My mother ordered me to stay in my room.

١٥ هل _____ عن الحفلة؟ Did you (masc.) ask them about the party?

Dual verbs in the past tense

Dual verbs are formed in the past tense by adding ا (-ā) to the verbs for هو (he), هي (she), and أنتُم (you, pl.):

they both (masc.) went	(هُما) ذَهَبا
they both (fem.) went	(هُما) ذَهَبَتا
you two (masc. or fem.) went	(أنتُما) ذَهَبْتُما
they both (masc.) were	(هُما) كانا
they both (fem.) were	(هُما) كانَتا
you two (masc. or fem.) were	(أنتُما) كُنْتُما
they both (masc.) threw	(هُما) رَمَيا
they both (fem.) threw	(هُما) رَمَتا
you two (masc. or fem.) threw	(أنتُما) رَمَيْتُما

EXERCISE

8·1

Change the subject of these sentences and questions from the singular to the dual.

EXAMPLE
المُدير ذَهَبَ إلى الاجتِماع. المُديران ذَهَبا إلى الاجتِماع.

١ اللِّصّ أخَذَ ساعتي.

_____

٢ أين كُنتِ أمس؟

_____

٣ الحارِس كان عند الباب.

_____

٤ هل نَسِيتَ مِفتاح السيّارة؟

_____

83

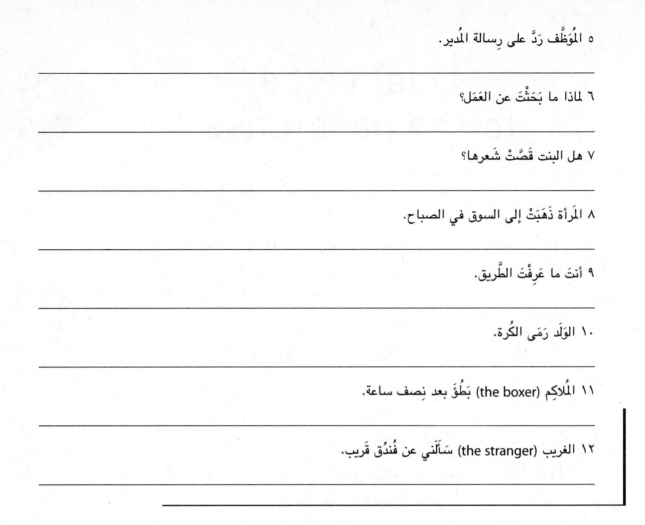

٥ المُوَظَّف رَدَّ على رِسالة المُدير.

_____

٦ لِماذا ما بَحَثْتَ عن العَمَل؟

_____

٧ هل البنت قَصَّتْ شَعرها؟

_____

٨ المَرأة ذَهَبَتْ إلى السوق في الصباح.

_____

٩ أنتَ ما عَرِفْتَ الطَّريق.

_____

١٠ الوَلَد رَمَى الكُرة.

_____

١١ المُلاكِم (the boxer) بَطُؤَ بعد نِصف ساعة.

_____

١٢ الغريب (the stranger) سَأَلَني عن فُندُق قَريب.

_____

Past tense verb and subject order with the dual

As with the plural, if the verb is placed *before* a dual subject, it will be singular (either masculine or feminine depending on the gender of the subject):

The two dogs ran behind the car.	جَرَى الكَلبان وَراءَ السيّارة.
The two (female) teachers were at the door.	كانَت المُدَرِّسَتان عند الباب.
The two correspondents returned and described the battle to us.	رَجَعَ المُراسِلان ووَصَفا لَنا المَعرِكة.

Notice in the last example that the first verb رَجَعَ (*returned*) is singular since it is before the subject المُراسِلان (*the correspondents*), but the second verb وَصَفا (*described*) is dual since it is after the subject.

Write the correct past tense verb in each blank to complete the sentences.

EXAMPLE خَرَجَ (خرج) الرَجُلان من المَحَطّة وَمَشَيا (مشى) إلى الفُندُق.

١ ـــــــــــــ (دفع) البنتان ثمن اللُعَب و ـــــــــــــ (رجع) بها إلى البيت.

٢ ـــــــــــــ (دخل) سميرة ونادية المَطبَخ و ـــــــــــــ (بدأ) في الطَّبخ.

٣ ـــــــــــــ (حجز) الصديقان المطعم ولكنّهما ـــــــــــــ (نسي) الزهور.

٤ ـــــــــــــ (ذهب) المُدرِّستان إلى الناظِر (the principal) و ـــــــــــــ (شكا) من حرارة الفَصل.

٥ ـــــــــــــ (جرى) الكلبان إلى الحديقة بَعدَ أن ـــــــــــــ (شمّ) رائِحة غريبة.

٦ ـــــــــــــ (سكن) أبي وأمي في الريف ولكِنَّهُما ـــــــــــــ (عمل) في وَسَط المدينة.

٧ ـــــــــــــ (جلس) نادية وسميرة في السينما و ـــــــــــــ (بكى) في نهاية الفيلم.

٨ ـــــــــــــ (أخذ) الولدان الحقيبة و ـــــــــــــ ها (حمل) إلى أمّهما.

The dual as the object or predicate of كان

The dual ending on nouns and adjectives changes from ان (-*ān*) to ـَين (-*ayn*) when it is the object of a verb or predicate of كان:

The team included two players from China.	الفَريق ضَمَّ لاعِبَين من الصين.
I carried the two large bags.	حَمَلْتُ الحَقيبَتَين الكبيرتَين.
Both the managers were busy.	المُديران كانا مَشغولَين.
Were you two nurses in Yemen?	هل كُنْتُما مُمَرِّضَتين في اليَمَن.

Translate these sentences and questions into Arabic.

EXAMPLE سَألنا مُديرَين عن العَقد. We asked two managers about the contract.

We carried the two heavy boxes. ١

_____

I asked the two boys (about) the way. ٢

_____

Did he read the two books? ٣

_____

They were both (male) engineers in Egypt. ٤

_____

The meeting included two managers from China. ٥

_____

They (fem.) were both tall and beautiful. ٦

_____

Did you two ride the two horses? ٧

_____

Were you two busy yesterday? ٨

_____

I attended the two meetings. ٩

_____

Nadia found two insects under the book. ١٠

_____

The thief stole two beautiful rings. ١١

_____

I threw (away) the two old shirts. ١٢

_____

PRESENT/FUTURE TENSE

The second of the two basic Arabic tenses is the present/future, or imperfect, known in Arabic as المُضارِع. This tense is used to talk about events or states happening in the present, or that will happen in the future.

As with the past tense (see Part II), present/future verbs are based on the root letters. However, the root is a little less obvious, and so it is often easier to study present/future verbs after gaining confidence with the basics of the past tense.

Regular basic verbs

The present (or imperfect) tense is used to express both the habitual ("I drink") or the continuous ("I am drinking"):

Every day I drink a cup of coffee after dinner.	كُلّ يَوم أَشرَب فِنجان قَهوة بعد العَشاء.
I am drinking a cup of coffee now.	أَشرَب فِنجان قَهوة الآن.

Present tense formation

As with the past tense, the present tense is formed by including additions on a verbal stem. These additions indicate the subject of the verb. The present tense stem is based on the root letters of the verb but displays a different voweling pattern from the past tense stem. In the present tense, the additions are generally prefixes (added to the front of the stem), but also sometimes suffixes (endings).

The present tense stem for basic (form I) regular verbs has a vowel over the middle root letter, but not over the first root letter:

drinks	شرَب
sits	جلِس
goes out	خرُج

The subject prefix for هو (he/it, third person masculine singular) is يَـ (ya-). When this is put in front of a present tense stem, for example شرَب (shrab), you create the verb meaning "he drinks/is drinking," يَشْرَب (yashrab):

he drinks/is drinking	يَشْرَب
he sits/is sitting	يَجْلِس
he goes out/is going out	يَخْرُج

Basic form I verbs that have a *kasra* as their middle vowel in the past tense (see "Past tense formation and uses" in Chapter 4), generally have *fatha* as the vowel on the present tense stem: شَرِب (*shariba*)/يَشْرَب (*yashrab*), "he drank/he drinks." However, for other form I regular verbs, there is no automatic way of knowing what the middle vowel of the present tense stem is. We will show the correct vowel over the present tense stem; dictionaries sometimes show it this way or show the voweling in brackets after the verb.

EXERCISE

9·1

Make verbs from the present tense stems using the subject prefix for هو. *Then give the meaning in English based on your knowledge of the root letters.*

EXAMPLE   <u>خرُج يَخْرُج *he goes out/is going out*</u>

‏_____ ١ غسِل

‏_____ ٢ ذهَب

‏_____ ٣ كتُب

‏_____ ٤ حمِل

‏_____ ٥ طبُخ

‏_____ ٦ فهَم

‏_____ ٧ ترُك

‏_____ ٨ رجِع

‏_____ ٩ رسُم

‏_____ ١٠ لعَب

‏_____ ١١ حرِق

‏_____ ١٢ ضحَك

All the singular and plural parts of the present tense verb are shown in the following table. The prefix يَ (*ya-*) is associated with the third person (he/they) and تَ (*ta-*) with the second person (you). Notice that أنتِ (feminine singular *you*) is the only singular part of the verb to have a suffix as well as a prefix, but that نَحنُ (*we*) is the only plural part that *does not* have a suffix.

	PREFIX/ SUFFIX	EXAMPLE	
SINGULAR			
I أنا	أَ	أَجْلِس*	I sit/am sitting
you (masc.) أنتَ	تَـ	تَـجْلِس*	you (masc.) sit/are sitting
you (fem.) أنتِ	تَـ/ـين	تَـجْلِسين	you (fem.) sit/are sitting
he/it (masc.) هُوَ	يَـ	يَجْلِس*	he/it (masc.) sits/is sitting
she/it (fem.) هِيَ	تَـ	تَـجْلِس*	she/it (fem.) sits/is sitting
PLURAL			
we نَحنُ	نَـ	نَـجْلِس*	we sit/are sitting
you (masc. pl.) أنتُم	تَـ/ـون	تَـجْلِسون	you (masc. pl.) sit/are sitting
you (fem. pl.) أنتُنَّ	تَـ/ـنَ	تَـجْلِسْن	you (fem. pl.) sit/are sitting
they (masc.) هُم	يَـ/ـون	يَجْلِسون	they (masc.) sit/are sitting
they (fem.) هُنَّ	يَـ/ـنَ	يَجْلِسْن	they (fem.) sit/are sitting

*These parts of the present tense verb include a final *ḍamma* (أَجْلِسُ *ajlisu*, I sit; يَشْرَبُ *yashrabu*, he drinks, etc.). However, this final vowel is only pronounced in more formal modern standard Arabic.

EXERCISE
9·2

Write out the conjugation for these present tense verbs, following the example in the preceding table.

EXAMPLE   <u>*I wash/am washing* أَغْسِل</u>

present tense stem = غسِل (washes) ١

_____

_____

_____

_____

_____

_____

_____

_____

_____

_____

present tense stem = خرُج (goes out) ٢

_____

_____

_____

_____

_____

_____

_____

_____

_____

_____

_____

Present tense stems of regular roots

Here are the present tense stems of regular roots introduced in Part I. The present tense stem is easier to remember if you include the prefix ـَ *ya-*.

leaves	يَتْرُك	follows	يَتْبَع	searches	يَبْحَث
reserves	يَحْجِز	gathers	يَجْمَع	sits	يَجْلِس
attends	يَحْضُر	burns	يَحْرِق	happens	يَحْدُث
goes out	يَخْرُج	carries	يَحْمِل	saves/memorizes	يَحْفَظ
pushes/pays	يَدْفَع	studies	يَدْرُس	comes in	يَدْخُل
returns	يَرْجِع	goes	يَذْهَب	mentions	يَذْكُر
rides	يَرْكَب	dances	يَرْقُص	draws	يَرْسُم
falls	يَسْقُط	steals	يَسْرِق	plants	يَزْرَع
drinks	يَشْرَب	hears	يَسْمَع	resides	يَسْكُن
hits	يَضْرِب	laughs	يَضْحَك	makes	يَصْنَع
appears	يَظْهُر	requests	يَطْلُب	cooks	يَطْبُخ
opens	يَفْتَح	learns	يَعْلَم	knows	يَعْرِف
kills	يَقْتُل	washes	يَغْسِل	works/functions	يَعْمَل
closes	يَقْفِل	understands	يَفْهَم	does	يَفْعَل
breaks	يَكْسِر	jumps	يَقْفِز	cuts	يَقْطَع
holds	يَمْسِك	hates	يَكْرَه	writes	يَكْتُب
descends	يَهْبُط	plays	يَلْعَب	wears	يَلْبَس
escapes	يَهْرُب	looks	يَنْظُر	goes down	يَنْزِل

EXERCISE

9·3

Write the correct part of the present tense verb based on the root letters, and then give the meaning in English.

EXAMPLE   *we sit/are sitting* نَجْلِس (نحن) جلس

١ نظر (أَنا) _____

٢ ضحك (نحن) _____

٣ سمع (هو) _____

٤ كتب (أَنتِ) _____

٥ جمع (أَنتنّ) _____

‏٦ طلب (هم) _____

‏٧ ترك (هي) _____

‏٨ لعب (أنتَ) _____

‏٩ حجز (أنتم) _____

‏١٠ فهم (هنّ) _____

EXERCISE 9·4

Write the correct Arabic verb to match the English.

EXAMPLE   تَذْهَب you (masc.) go/are going.

_____	‏١ I carry/am carrying
_____	‏٢ he drinks/is drinking
_____	‏٣ you (masc.) wash/are washing
_____	‏٤ you (fem.) mention/are mentioning
_____	‏٥ we study/are studying
_____	‏٦ she falls/is falling
_____	‏٧ they (fem.) search/are searching
_____	‏٨ you (masc. pl.) burn/are burning
_____	‏٩ they (masc.) dance/are dancing
_____	‏١٠ you (fem. pl.) ride/are riding

Important factors for sentence structure include:

◆ There is usually no need to include a separate subject pronoun with a verb.

We are looking for an apartment by the sea.	نَبْحَث عَن شَقّة على البَحر.
Every Saturday they (masc.) play football in the club.	كلّ يوم سَبت يَلعَبونَ كُرة القَدَم في النادي.

◆ A verb coming *before* a plural subject will be singular.

Every year the scientists attend the conference at the university.	كلّ سَنة يَحْضُر العُلَماء المُؤْتمَر في الجامِعة.
The pupils go out after the lesson and drink cola together	يَخرُج التَّلاميذ بَعدَ الدَّرس ويَشْرَبون كولا مَعاً.

◆ An indefinite object of a verb will be usually be written with an additional *alif tanwīn* (اً) if it does not end in *tā' marbūṭa* (ة).

I hear strange stories about this house.	أَسْمَع قِصَصاً غَريبة عَن هذا البيت.
In spring we plant flowers in the garden.	في الرَّبيع نَزْرَع زُهوراً في الحَديقة.

Note: See "Word order and singular/plural agreement" and "Changes to the object of verbs" in Chapter 4 for more details.

Zeinah has specific activities for each day of the week. Describe her week using the prompts.

EXAMPLE   Saturday/play football <u>تَلعَب رَينة كُرة القَدَم يوم السَّبت.</u>

Saturday/play tennis ١

_____

Sunday/go to the market ٢

_____

Monday/cook the falafel ٣

_____

Tuesday/ride her horse ٤

_____

Wednesday/wash the clothes ٥

_____

Thursday/study English (الإنجِليزيّة) ٦

_____

Friday/go to the cinema ٧

_____

Now imagine you are Zeinah, and write the sentences from Exercise 9.5 again.

EXAMPLE ألْعَب كُرة القَدَم يوم السَّبت.

١ _____

٢ _____

٣ _____

٤ _____

٥ _____

٦ _____

٧ _____

Choose a verb from the list to fill in the gaps in the sentences and questions. Then write the correct vowels on the verb.

أشرب   تترك   تضحكون   تغسلين   يحرق   نبحث
تذهبين   تسمع   يدرسون   يذهب   يجمعن

EXAMPLE هل تَذْهَبينَ إلى السوق كلّ يوم يا سميرة؟

١ لماذا _____ يا أولاد؟

٢ _____ الشاي بالحليب.

٣ هل _____ سيّارتك يوم السبت يا ليلى؟

٤ يا سمير، هل _____ الموسيقى قَبلَ النَّوم؟

٥ نادية دائماً _____ حقيبتها في وَسَط الغُرفة!

٦ العُلَماء _____ الحَشرات في الغابة.

٧ المُدَرِّسات _____ أوراق الامتِحان.

٨ الصَّيّاد _____ إلى النَّهر في الفَجر.

٩ _____ عن شقّة على البحر.

١٠ _____ الخَشَب في الشِّتاء.

Your mother has asked you to look after the house while she's away for a couple of months, but it seems she doesn't trust things to run smoothly in her absence. She is calling you to check on whether you have remembered everything. Answer her questions following the prompt. Use attached pronouns in your answers, as in the example.

EXAMPLE هل طَبَخْتَ الغَداء؟ (كلّ يوم) (?Did you cook lunch)

طَبعاً، أَطْبُخُهُ كلّ يوم. (.Of course, I cook it every day)

١ هل غَسَلْتَ الأطباق؟ (كلّ يوم) _____

٢ هل قَفَلْتُ الباب؟ (كلّ مَساء) _____

٣ هل حَضَرْتَ الاِجتِماع في المَدرسة؟ (كلّ أُسبوع) _____

٤ هل حَجَزْتَ تَذْكِرة القِطار؟ (كلّ يوم سَبت) _____

٥ هل ذَهَبْتَ إلى السوق. (كلّ يوم اثنين) _____

٦ هل دَفَعْتَ الإيجار (rent). (كلّ شَهر) _____

٧ هل كَتَبَتْ نادية دُروسها (her lessons)؟ (كلّ يوم أحد) _____

٨ هل الأولاد غَسَلوا السيّارة؟ (كلّ يوم جُمعة) _____

٩ هل البنات لَعِبْنَ التَنِس؟ (كلّ أُسبوع) _____

١٠ هل خَرَجْتُم مع الكلب؟ (كلّ صَباح) _____

١١ هل رَكِبْتُم دَرّاجاتكُم؟ (كلّ أُسبوع) _____

١٢ هل زَرَعْتُم الزهور في الحديقة؟ (كلّ رَبيع) _____

Forming the negative with لا

The present tense negative is formed by putting لا directly in front of the verb:

I don't drink tea with milk.	لا أشرَب الشاي بالحليب.
My father doesn't go to the center of town every day.	لا يَذهب أبي إلى وَسَط المدينة كلّ يوم.
Why don't you (masc.) collect stamps?	لماذا لا تجمَع طَوابِع البَريد؟

EXERCISE 9·9

Make these sentences and questions negative.

EXAMPLE   أَدرُس الفَرَنسيّة. لا أَدرُس الفَرَنسيّة.

١ أذهَب إلى هذا المطعم. _____

٢ نطلُب منكم شيئاً. _____

٣ يحجِز لي أحمَد مقعَداً بجانب الشُّبّاك. _____

٤ يركَب عَمّي الحِصان يوم الجُمعة. _____

٥ إنّها ترقُص في الأفراح. _____

٦ ندرُس الرِّياضيّات كلّ يوم. _____

٧ لِماذا تدفَعين الإيجار كلّ أسبوع؟ _____

٨ يسمَع التلاميذ الجَرَس فيجلِسون على الأرض. _____

٩ نشرَب القهوة بعد العشاء. _____

١٠ يزرَع المُزارِع (the farmer) هذا الحَقل في الصَّيف. _____

never لا . . . أَبَداً

The concept of "never" is expressed in Arabic by using a negative verb with أَبَداً. For example, لا أَطبُخ أَبَداً (*I never cook* [literally, *I don't cook ever*]):

I never drink tea with milk.	لا أشرَب الشاي بالحليب أَبَداً.
You (fem.) never leave your bag in the room.	لا تَترُكين حَقيبَتِك في الغُرفة أَبَداً.

EXERCISE 9·10

Munira works long hours and feels that her family and friends don't pull their weight. She is telling you about all the things they never do to help her. Use the prompts to make sentences.

EXAMPLE   Nadia: cook lunch لا تَطبُخ نادية الغداء أَبَداً!

Shukri: wash the car ١

_____

Zeinah: go to the market ٢

_____

My friend, Fatima: write to me ٣

_____

Samira: play with her sister ٤

_____

Ahmed: close the door ٥

_____

My husband, Anas: attend meetings at the school ٦

_____

the boys: ride their bicycles ٧

_____

the girls: wear their new clothes ٨

_____

The same structure can be used for a question, for example لِـماذا لا تَطبُخ أبداً؟ (*Why do you* [*masc.*] *never cook?* [or *Why don't you ever cook?*]).

EXERCISE
9·11

Bravely, you have decided to confront Munira's family and friends and ask them why they never do things to help her. Look at Exercise 9.10 and write a question for each person or group.

EXAMPLE   لِـماذا لا تَطبُخينَ الغداء أبداً، يا نادية؟

_____ ١

_____ ٢

_____ ٣

_____ ٤

_____ ٥

_____ ٦

_____ ٧

_____ ٨

Expressing the future

سَـ and سَوفَ

The present (or imperfect) tense can also be used to express the future, usually with the addition of the independent word سَوْفَ *sawfa* or its contracted equivalent سَـ *sa-*. These express the concept of both the English "will" and "is (am/are) going to":

We will go to the vegetable market tomorrow.	سَوْفَ نَذهَب إلى سوق الخُضار غَداً.
I'm going to play football in the club next Friday.	سَألعَب كُرة القَدَم في النادي يوم الجُمعة القادِم.
My son will leave school after the exams.	سَيَترُك ابني المدرسة بعد الامتِحانات.
Nadia is going to wear the red dress to the party.	سوف تَلبِس نادية الفُستان الأحمَر في الحَفلة.

EXERCISE
10·1

Fill in the correct future verb to match the English translation, using either سَـ or سَوْفَ.

EXAMPLE I will study Arabic next year. سَأَدرُس/سوف أدرُس العربيّة في العام القادِم.

١ We will enter through (from) this door. ـــــــــــــــ من هذا الباب.

٢ He's going to ride the horse tomorrow. ـــــــــــــــ الحِصان غَداً.

٣ سميرة ـــــــــــــــ لَهُ الثَّمَن المُناسِب. Samira will pay the right price for it.

٤ ـــــــــــــــ أبي تَحتَ الشِّجَرة و ـــــــــــــــ إلى المَنظَر.
My father will sit under the tree and look at the view.

٥ إن الأطفال ـــــــــــــــ تِمثالاً من هذه العُلَب.
The children are going to make a sculpture from these boxes.

٦ الكَنز مَدفون هُنا وأنا ـــــــــــــــ عَنهُ.
The treasure is buried here and I will search for it.

٧ ــــــــــــــــــــــــ مِنها قِصَصاً غَريبة. You (masc. pl.) will hear strange stories from her.

٨ ــــــــــــــــــــــــ الهَدِية بَعدَ العَشاء. I'll open the present after dinner.

٩ المُهَندِسون المُؤتَمَر و ــــــــــــــــــــــــ بَعدَ الظُّهر.
The engineers will attend the conference and will return in the afternoon.

١٠ ــــــــــــــــــــــــ البَنات صُوَراً وبعد ذلك ــــــــــــــــــــــــ في الحديقة.
The girls are going to draw pictures and after that they are going to play in the park.

EXERCISE 10·2

Nour is expecting a visit from three of his friends tomorrow. He is excited about their visit and has written them an e-mail with all the things he is planning. Read the e-mail and underline all the examples of verbs referring to the future.

EXAMPLE سوف تذهبون إلى وسط المدينة.

يا أصدِقائي،

الغَد هو يوم زِيارَتكُم!

سوف تذهبون إلى وسط المدينة بالباص، وستنزلون أمام البنك القَطَريّ. بيتنا قريب من هناك.
في البيت سنشرب قهوة وبعد ذلك سنخرج. أوَّلاً سنذهب إلى النادي، وأخي يوسُف سيَذهب معنا أيضاً. سنلعب
كرة القدم وكرة السَّلّة هناك وسوف نرجع في الساعة الواحدة للغداء. قالَتْ أمّي إنّها ستطبخ لَنا الغَداء.

بعد الظُّهر سوف نَحضُر حفلة موسيقيّة، وسنَسمَع المُغَنّي اللُّبناني المَشهور رَفيق خوري. حَجَزْتُ أربع تَذاكِر أمس،
ولكنّنا سندفع غَداً. أخيراً سوف أذهب معكم إلى محطّة الباص في المساء.

أنا في اِنتِظاركم!

صديقكُم نور

EXERCISE 10·3

Find these phrases in Nour's e-mail in Exercise 10.2.

EXAMPLE We will attend a music concert. سوف نَحضُر حفلة موسيقيّة.

١ After that we will go out.

_____

٢ We will pay tomorrow.

_____

٣ You will get off in front of the Qatari Bank.

_____

My brother, Yusuf, will go with us. ٤

_____

She will cook (the) lunch for us. ٥

_____

We will play football and basketball. ٦

_____

We will drink coffee. ٧

_____

We will hear the famous Lebanese singer. ٨

_____

We will return at one o'clock. ٩

_____

I will go with you to the bus station. ١٠

_____

We will go to the club. ١١

_____

Using your answers to Exercise 10.3 for reference, translate these phrases into Arabic.

EXAMPLE   <u>سوف أَحضُر حفلة موسيقيّة</u>. I will attend a music concert.

After that he will go out. ١

_____

They (masc.) will pay tomorrow. ٢

_____

You (fem.) will get off in front of the Qatari Bank. ٣

_____

My sister, Samira, will go with us. ٤

_____

They (fem.) will cook lunch for us. ٥

_____

I will play football and basketball. ٦

_____

You (masc.) will drink coffee. ٧

_____

You (masc. pl.) will hear the famous Lebanese singer. ٨

_____

She will return at one o'clock. ٩

_____

We will go with you to the bus station. ١٠

_____

You (fem. pl.) will go to the club. ١١

_____

Questions about the future

In general, سَ (*sa-*) rather than سَوْفَ (*sawfa*) is used when forming questions about the future:

Where will you (fem.) go after lunch?	أينَ سَتذهَبينَ بعد الغداء؟
Is Ahmed going to attend the meeting next Saturday?	هل سَيحضُر أحمد الإجتِماع يوم السَّبت القادِم؟
How are they (masc.) going to break the lock?	كَيف سَيَكسِرون القَفل؟

EXERCISE
10·5

Translate these questions into Arabic.

EXAMPLE   هل سَتَذهب معي إلى مَحطّة الباص؟ Will you (masc.) go with me to the bus station?

Is Samira going to cook the fish? ١

_____

Where will you (fem.) play basketball? ٢

_____

How am I going to pay? ٣

_____

Will they (masc.) carry the bag? ٤

_____

When will the manager return? ٥

_____

What are we going to drink? ٦

_____

Where will you (masc. pl.) leave my books? ٧

_____

Are the new (female) teachers going to work tomorrow? ٨

_____

What is going to happen next Saturday? ٩

_____

When will you (masc.) reserve the tickets? ١٠

_____

Doubled verbs in the present tense

Present tense formation

The rules for writing the doubled root letters in verbs apply to the present tense as well as the past tense:

◆ If the pattern for regular verbs requires a *sukūn* (°) over the third root letter, the doubled root letters are written separately
◆ If the pattern for regular verbs requires a vowel over the third root letter, the doubled root letters are written together with a *shadda* (˝)

Any final *ḍamma* in the present tense (e.g., يَشْرَبُ *yashrabu*) must be taken into account when the rules for doubled verbs are applied. This leaves only the relatively uncommon feminine plurals requiring a *sukūn* over the third root letter in the present tense pattern for regular verbs (see the table in "Present tense formation," Chapter 9), and effectively means that the doubled root is almost always written together with a *shadda* (˝).

(regular verb) he goes	يَذْهَب
(doubled verb) he answers	يَرُدّ
(regular verb) we jump	نَقْفِز
(doubled verb) we doubt	نَشُكّ
(regular verb) they (fem.) play	يَلعَبْنَ
(doubled verb) they (fem.) cut	يَقْصُصْنَ

The following table shows the complete present tense for the doubled verb يَشُكّ (*doubt/have suspicions about*).

	PREFIX/ SUFFIX	EXAMPLE	
SINGULAR			
I أنا	أَ	أَشُكّ	I doubt
you (masc.) أنتَ	تَـ	تَـشُكّ	you (masc.) doubt
you (fem.) أنتِ	تَـ/ينَ	تَـشُكّينَ	you (fem.) doubt
he/it (masc.) هُوَ	يَـ	يَشُكّ	he doubts
she/it (fem.) هِيَ	تَـ	تَشُكّ	she doubts

	PREFIX/ SUFFIX	EXAMPLE	
PLURAL			
نَحنُ we	نَـ	نَشُكّ	we doubt
أنتُم you (masc. pl.)	تَـ/ونَ	تَشُكّونَ	you (masc. pl.) doubt
أنتُنَّ you (fem. pl.)	تَـ/نَ	تَشْكُكْنَ	you (fem. pl.) doubt
هُم they (masc.)	يَـ/ونَ	يَشُكّونَ	they (masc.) doubt
هُنَّ they (fem.)	يَـ/نَ	يَشْكُكْنَ	they (fem.) doubt

EXERCISE

11·1

Your family is reading an article about a high-profile murder of a billionaire in his mansion. You all have suspicions about who murdered him. Make sentences showing these suspicions, using the prompts.

EXAMPLE   أمّي – الطَّباخ أُمّي تَشُكّ في الطَّباخ. (My mother suspects the cook.)

١ أبي – الابنة

_____

٢ أُختي – السائِق

_____

٣ أخي – الزَّوجة

_____

٤ جَدّي – الابن

_____

٥ جَدَّتي – المُمَرِّضة

_____

٦ أولاد أختي – المُحاسِب

_____

٧ بنات أخي – البُستانيّ (the gardener)

_____

٨ أنا – عامِل النَّظافة (the cleaner)

_____

Common basic doubled verbs

Common basic doubled verbs in the present tense include:

believes/thinks	يَظُنّ	broadcasts/spreads	يَبُثّ
replies/answers	يَرُدّ	proves/indicates	يَدُلّ
smells	يَشُمّ	has suspicions/doubts	يَشُكّ
counts	يَعُدّ	includes/joins	يَضُمّ
goes around/wraps	يَلُفّ	cuts	يَقُصّ
passes	يَمُرّ	stretches/extends	يَمُدّ

The most common middle vowel for doubled verbs is *ḍamma* but this can vary:

wants	يَوَدّ	is completed/is finished	يَتِمّ

EXERCISE

11·2

Write the present tense or future tense verb to match the English.

EXAMPLE   <u>تَقُصّ</u> she cuts

_____ they (masc.) believe ١

_____ I will prove ٢

_____ we wrap ٣

_____ you (fem.) pass ٤

_____ she doesn't answer ٥

_____ we broadcast ٦

_____ it (masc.) doesn't include ٧

_____ you (masc.) don't want ٨

_____ they (fem.) will count ٩

_____ you (masc. pl.) smell ١٠

_____ it (fem.) will be finished ١١

_____ you (fem. pl.) doubt ١٢

Change these sentences and questions to match the new subject in parentheses, adjusting the verbs as necessary.

EXAMPLE   لا يَرُدّ على السُّؤال. (هي) <u>لا تَرُدّ على السُّؤال.</u>

١ يَقُصّون الصُّوَر من المَجَلّات. (نحن) _____

٢ هل تشكّ في الأسعار؟ (أنتم) _____

٣ نمرّ على هذه اللافِتة (this sign) كلّ يوم. (أنا) _____

٤ أبُثّ مُدَوَّنَتي (my blog) على الإنترنت. (هو) _____

٥ سوف يشمّون رائحة السمك. (هنّ) _____

٦ إنّهم لا يظنّون أن هناك أَمَل. (هي) _____

٧ سوف أدلّكَ على الطَّريق. (هم) _____

٨ ألا تدلّون الضُّيوف إلى مقاعدهم؟ (أنتِ) _____

Fill in the correct Arabic verb to match the English translation.

EXAMPLE   We will show the guests to their seats. سوف <u>نَدُلّ/سنَدُلّ</u> الضُّيوف إلى مقاعدهم.

١ _____ الضُّيوف عند الباب. .I will count the guests at the door

٢ إنّ المُوَظَّفين _____ على الهاتِف. .The employees don't answer the telephone

٣ _____ أن نَذهَب إلى الاجتماع. .We want to go to the meeting

٤ هل _____ أن هذا الرَّجُل جاسوس؟ ?Do you (masc.) think that this man is a spy

٥ _____ على الرسالة الإلكترونيّة غداً. .I will answer the e-mail tomorrow

٦ إنها _____ بِسَبَب الزُّكام. .She can't (does not) smell because of (her) congestion

٧ _____ الطَّبيب في نَتيجة التَّحليل. .The doctor doesn't doubt the result of the analysis

٨ هذه القَناة _____ البَرامِج الرِّياضيّة. .This channel doesn't broadcast sports programs

٩ _____ بفَترة انتِعاش اقتِصاديّ. .We are passing through a period of economic recovery

١٠ لِماذا _____ المِنشَفة حَولَ رأسِك؟ ?Why don't you (fem.) wrap the towel around your head

Weak verbs in the present tense

Weak verbs are those that have either و or ي as one of their root letters. As with the past tense (see Part II), these two letters are unstable in the present tense, sometimes representing the consonant sounds *w* and *y*, sometimes representing vowel sounds, and occasionally disappearing altogether.

Assimilated verbs

Assimilated verbs have و or ي as their first root letter. In the past tense, basic (form I) assimilated verbs behave entirely regularly (see Chapter 6, "Weak verbs in the past tense"). However, in the present tense the initial و drops out:

he arrived	وَصَلَ
he arrives/is arriving	يَصِل
we put/placed	وَضَعْنا
we put/are putting	نَضَع
they found	وَجَدوا
they find/are finding	يَجِدونَ

The exception is doubled verbs that also have و as their first root letter. These verbs follow the pattern for doubled verbs (see Chapter 11):

he wanted	وَدَّ
he wants	يَوَدّ

The (uncommon) assimilated verbs with ي as the initial root letter are regular in both the past and the present tenses:

it was/became dry	يَبِسَ
it is/becomes dry	يَيْبَس

Common basic assimilated verbs in the present tense

Assimilated verbs tend to have *kasra* as the middle vowel, but some have *fatḥa*:

describes	يَصِف	arrives	يَصِل
puts/places	يَضَع	finds	يَجِد
leaves/lets	يَدَع	jumps	يَثِب
weighs	يَزِن	inherits	يَرِث
falls	يَقَع	promises	يَعِد
gives (fem.) birth	تَلِد	stops/stands	يَقِف
		is/becomes dry	يَيْبَس

Write the present tense or future tense verb to match the English.

EXAMPLE   سوف نَصِل/سَنَصِل we will arrive

_____	I weigh ١
_____	he will find ٢
_____	we are not describing ٣
_____	you (masc.) put ٤
_____	she is standing ٥
_____	we will inherit ٦
_____	they (masc.) are not jumping ٧
_____	it (masc.) will become dry ٨
_____	you (fem.) let/leave ٩
_____	you (masc. pl.) don't promise ١٠
_____	she gives birth ١١
_____	you (fem. pl.) will fall ١٢

Change these sentences and questions from the past tense to the present tense.

EXAMPLE ما وَصَلَ القِطار قبل الساعة الواحدة. <u>لا يَصِل القِطار قبل الساعة الواحدة.</u>

١ وَزَنَ البَقّال الجُبن والزَّيتون.

_____

٢ وَجَدْتُ صُوَراً كثيرة على الإنترنت.

_____

٣ وَعَدَت جَدَّتها بِهَدِية غالية.

_____

٤ وَقَفَ القِطار في قَرْيَتِنا.

_____

٥ وَصَفْنا السِّباق في الراديو.

_____

٦ إنّ الأولاد وَصَفوا مَلامِح اللصّ.

_____

٧ وَقَفْنا أَمامَ شُبّاك التَذاكِر.

_____

٨ يَبِسَت الزُّهور بِسَبَب حَرارة الشَّمس.

_____

٩ هل وَضَعْتِ البيتزا في الفُرن صباحاً؟

_____

١٠ لِماذا ما وَثِبْتُم من فوق السور؟

_____

EXERCISE

12·3

Nadia went out for the morning and was expecting a number of things to happen. But when she returns nothing seems to have changed. She asks her mother, who assures Nadia that everything will happen in the afternoon. Answer Nadia's questions.

EXAMPLE هل وَضَعتِ الغَسيل في الغَسّالة؟ <u>لا، سـأَضَعهُ في الغسالة بعد الظُّهر.</u>

١ هل وَجَدْتِ مِفتاح السيّارة؟

_____

٢ هل وَزَنْتِ الأَرُزّ؟

_____

٣ هل وَضَعْتِ الأوراق في الدُّرج؟

_____

٤ هل وَعَدْتِ سميرة بِدرّاجة جديدة؟

_____

٥ هل وَضَعَتْ سميرة مَلابِسها في غُرفَتها؟

_____

٦ هل وَصَلَ البَريد؟

_____

٧ هل الأولاد وَصَلوا من المَدرسة؟

_____

٨ هل وَصَفَ أحمد الحقيبة المفقودة للشُّرطة؟

_____

Hollow verbs

Hollow verbs have و or ي as their second or middle root letter. In the present tense, hollow verbs also follow the same general rules as for the past tense (see Chapter 6).

- If the pattern for regular verbs requires a *vowel* over the third root letter, a long vowel appears instead of the middle root letter.
- If the pattern for regular verbs requires a *sukūn* (˚) over the third root letter, the middle root letter changes to a short vowel in hollow verbs: almost always *u* (´) for verbs with و as the second root and *i* (ِ) for verbs with ي.

As for doubled verbs, any final *ḍamma* in the present tense (e.g., يَشْرَبُ *yashrabu*) must be taken into account when the rules are applied. Effectively this means that all parts of present tense hollow verbs, except the relatively uncommon feminine plurals, are characterized by a long vowel in the place of the second root letter. In the past tense the long vowel in the middle is always

Weak verbs in the present tense **111**

a long *ā*. However, in the present tense it is a long *ī* if the second root letter is ي, and usually a long *ū* if the second root letter is و:

he says	يَقول
I visit	أزور
they wander	يَطوفونَ
he flies	يَطير
we shout	نَصيح
they sell	يَبيعونَ

The following table shows the complete present tense for the two common hollow verb types.

	TO FLY (ط/ي/ر)	TO SAY (ق/و/ل)
SINGULAR		
I أنا	أَطير	أَقول
you (masc.) أنتَ	تَطير	تَقول
you (fem.) أنتِ	تَطيرينَ	تَقولينَ
he/it (masc.) هُوَ	يَطير	يَقول
she/it (fem.) هِيَ	تَطير	تَقول
PLURAL		
we نَحنُ	نَطير	نَقول
you (masc. pl.) أنتُم	تَطيرونَ	تَقولون
you (fem. pl.) أنتُنَّ	تَطِرْنَ	تَقُلْنَ
they (masc.) هُم	يَطيرونَ	يَقولون
they (fem.) هُنَّ	يَطِرْنَ	يَقُلْنَ

EXERCISE 12·4

Write out the present tense conjugation for these hollow verbs, following the two preceding examples.

EXAMPLE *I return/am returning.* أعود

١ (to return) ع/و/د = root

_____

_____

_____

_____

٢) (to sell) ب/ي/ع = root

_____

_____

_____

_____

_____

_____

_____

_____

_____

_____

_____

_____

_____

Common hollow verbs in the present tense

The present tense of basic hollow verbs with و as the second root letter include:

says	يَقول
visits	يَزور
returns	يَعود
fasts	يَصوم
stands up	يَقوم
goes round/turns	يَدور
melts/dissolves	يَذوب
walks around/wanders	يَطوف

The present tense of basic hollow verbs with ي as the second root letter include:

sells	يَبيع
shouts	يَصيح
flies	يَطير
inclines/leans	يَميل
increases	يَزيد
becomes	يَصير

Fill in the correct Arabic verb to match the English translation.

EXAMPLE   I visit my mother every day. أَزورُ أُمّي كلّ يوم.

١   _____ هذا الصَّحَفيّ الحَقيقة. This journalist is telling (is saying) the truth.

٢   _____ فاطمة ثلاثة أَيّام كلّ شَهر. Fatima fasts three days every month.

٣   _____ من مِقعَدي بِصُعوبة. I get up from my seat with difficulty.

٤   المِلح _____ في الماء. Salt dissolves in water.

٥   _____ حَولَ الكَعبة أَثناء الحَجّ.
They (masc.) walk around the Ka'aba during the pilgrimage.

٦   المُحَرِّكات والمَصنَع يَعمَل _____. The engines turn and the factory operates.

٧   إنّ السُّوّاح _____ المَعابِد الأَثَرِيّة في الأقصُر.
The tourists visit the ancient temples in Luxor.

٨   عَدَدنا كلّ يوم _____. Our number increases every day.

٩   الدُّيوك في الفَجر _____. The roosters crow (shout) at dawn.

١٠   البُرج إلى اليَمين _____. The tower leans to the right.

١١   الآن إلى المَوضوع الأصليّ _____. We are returning now to the original subject.

١٢   الحَمامات حَولَ الحَقل _____. The pigeons are flying around the field.

١٣   أَفضَل أَنواع الصابون _____. They (fem.) sell the best types of soap.

Now use the vocabulary in Exercise 12.5 to help you translate these sentences and questions into Arabic.

EXAMPLE   متى سيَعودون إلى البُرج؟ When will they (masc.) return to the tower?

1. This house leans to the left.

_____

2. Why are you (fem.) shouting?

_____

3. The engine turns with difficulty.

_____

4. They (masc.) sell the best types of salt.

_____

Roosters don't fly. ٥

_____

Samira always visits her mother on Saturday. ٦

_____

The number of tourists increases every year. ٧

_____

Does soap dissolve in water? ٨

_____

I don't fast because of my illness. ٩

_____

When will you (masc.) tell me the truth? ١٠

_____

How will you (masc. pl.) return to the factory? ١١

_____

They (fem.) are walking around the tower. ١٢

_____

Hollow verbs such as نام/ينام (to sleep)

There is a third category of hollow verbs that behaves unusually. Although the verbs have و as the second root letter, in the past tense they behave like verbs that have ي as a middle root, and in the present tense they display the long vowel ā in the middle (rather than ū as might be expected). Although this category is relatively uncommon, it does contain some high-frequency verbs, notably م/و/ن (to sleep) and خ/و/ف (to fear/to be afraid).

The following table shows the complete past and present tenses for the verb م/و/ن (to sleep).

	PAST TENSE	PRESENT TENSE
SINGULAR		
I أنا	نِـمْتُ	أَنام
you (masc.) أنتَ	نِـمْتَ	تَنام
you (fem.) أنتِ	نِـمْتِ	تَنامينَ
he/it (masc.) هُوَ	نامَ	يَنام
she/it (fem.) هِيَ	نامَتْ	تَنام

(continued)

	PAST TENSE	PRESENT TENSE
PLURAL		
we نَحنُ	نِـمْنا	نَنام
you (masc. pl.) أنتُم	نِـمْتُم	تَنامونَ
you (fem. pl.) أنتنَّ	نِـمْتُـنَّ	تَنَمْنَ
they (masc.) هُـم	ناموا	يَنامونَ
they (fem.) هُـنَّ	نِـمْنَ	يَنَمْنَ

Samira is having a large number of house guests to stay for a family wedding. The sleeping arrangements are complicated, and guests have to be moved around, as do the family pets. Describe where everyone slept yesterday; and where they will be sleeping tonight using the prompts. (Remember the rules about plural subjects. See "Word order and singular/plural agreement" in Chapter 4.)

EXAMPLE

الخال سامي/غُرفة أحمد/غرفة الجُلوس

أمس نامَ الخال سامي في غُرفة أحمد ولكنّه سَينام الليلة في غرفة الجُلوس.

(Yesterday Uncle Sami slept in Ahmed's room, but he will be sleeping tonight in the sitting room.)

١ الخالة فاطِمة/غُرفة سارة/غرفة ماري

_____

٢ أبو سميرة/فُنْدُق/غُرفة أحمد

_____

٣ سميرة/غُرفتها/غُرفة سارة

_____

٤ أطفال سميرة/غرفة الجُلوس/غرفة الطَّعام

_____

٥ بَنات سامي/غرفة ماري/المَكتَب

_____

٦ أولاد فاطِمة/المَكتَب/خَيمة في الحَديقة

_____

٧ البَبَغاء (the parrot)/الحَمّام/المَطبَخ

_____

٨ الكِلاب/المَطبَخ/الجَراج

_____

سَيَكُون (will be)

Although it is not usually necessary in Arabic to include the verb "to be" in simple present tense sentences, a verb is required in the future, as it is in the past tense. The root of "to be" is ك/و/ن. It follows the same pattern as the hollow verb ق/و/ل (*to say*) as discussed earlier in this chapter, and is generally characterized by a long *ū* in the present/future tense:

Nadia is busy.	نادية مَشغولة.
Nadia will be busy.	سَتَكُون نادية مَشغولة.
I am in Ahmed's house.	أنا في بيت أحمد.
I will be in Ahmed's house.	سوف أكون في بيت أحمد.
Is my son with you?	هل ابني مَعَكُم؟
Will my son be with you?	هل سَيكون ابني معكم؟

Remember that the feminine plurals of the present tense are the exception and are characterized by a *short* vowel:

The mothers will be in the school tomorrow.	إنّ الأُمَّهات سوف يَكُنَّ في المدرسة غداً.
Girls! Will you be in the library this afternoon?	يا بنات! هل سَتَكُنَّ في المَكتَبة بعد الظُّهر؟

As with كان, when the verb يكون is followed by an indefinite predicate that does not end in *tā' marbūṭa* (ة), it will need to be written with the additional *alif tanwīn* (ا). In addition, a sound masculine plural predicate will change from ون to بين:

He is a cook in the new restaurant.	هو طَبّاخ في المَطعَم الجديد.
He will be a cook in the new restaurant.	سَيكون طَبّاخاً في المَطعَم الجديد.
They are engineers.	هم مهندسون.
They will be engineers.	سوف يَكُونَ مهندسين.

Note: For more details, see the section "كان (*was/were*)" in Chapter 6.

EXERCISE

12·8

Rewrite these sentences in the future tense.

EXAMPLE   أنا في الحَديقة. <u>سوف أكون/سأكون في الحديقة.</u>

١ نَحنُ في مِصر. _____

٢ شُكري في المَكتَبة. _____

٣ سَميرة في بيتها. _____

٤ أنا أمامَ البنك. _____

٥ هل أنتِ مَشغولة؟ _____

٦ هم مع المُدرِّس. _____

٧ الكِلاب في الحديقة. _____

٨ هُنَّ في العراق. _____

٩ الكتاب ثقيل. _____

١٠ أنتَ المدير. _____

١١ الرِّحلة طويلة. _____

١٢ السيّارات أمام المَدخَل. _____

١٣ البقّالون في سوق الخُضار. _____

١٤ هل أنتُم في المدرسة؟ _____

Fill in the blanks with the correct part of the verb يكون.

EXAMPLE   المُدير سَيكون هنا الساعة التاسعة.

١ نَحن سَ _____ في المَكتَبة لِمُدّة ثلاث ساعات.

٢ أنا سوف _____ في مِصر الأُسبوع القادِم.

٣ يا سَميرة، هل سَ _____ في الاجتماع غداً؟

٤ ابنة عَمّتي سوف _____ طَبيبة عُيون.

٥ هذا الطِّفل مَوهوب وسوف _____ شَهيراً في المُستَقبَل.

٦ خَمس مُمَرِّضات سَ _____ موجودات للجِراحة (for the surgery).

٧ يا سَمير، هل سَ _____ مَسؤولاً عَن هذا المَشروع؟

٨ إنّ الأولاد سوف _____ أصدِقاء بعد اليوم.

٩ يا شَباب، هل سَ _____ مَشغولين يوم الجُمعة؟

١٠ يا بنات، هل سَ _____ مَعنا غَداً؟

Using سوف يَكون/سَيَكون to express "there will be" or "will have"

The verb سوف يَكون or سَيَكون can be placed in front of هناك to express "there will be":

There will be dancers at the wedding party.   سَيكون هناك راقِصون في حَفل الزِّفاف.

There will be a new school here.   سوف تكون هناك مَدرَسة جديدة هنا.

Nadia is getting married and there is a big wedding party (حَفل الزِّفاف) planned.
Describe what all there will be at the party using سَيكون هناك *or* سوف يكون هناك.

EXAMPLE   راقِصون dancers سوف يكون/سَيكون هناك راقِصون في حَفل الزِّفاف.

(There will be dancers at the wedding party).

١ فِرقة كبيرة a large band

_____

٢ مُطرِب شَهير a famous singer

_____

٣ ألعاب ناريّة fireworks

_____

٤ نافورة شوكولاتة a chocolate fountain

_____

٥ حَمام doves

_____

٦ ضُيوف من كُلّ العالَم guests from all (over) the world

_____

٧ زُهور على كلّ مائِدة flowers on every table

_____

٨ هَديّة لِكلّ ضَيف a present for every guest

_____

In addition, سوف يكون or سَيكون can be placed in front of the various prepositions expressing "have/has" (see the section "Expressing 'to have'" in Chapter 2), changing the meaning to "will have":

She will have an office on the first floor.	سوف يكون لَدَيها مَكتَب في الطابِق الأوَّل.
We will have a large wing at the exhibition.	سوف يكون لَنا جَناح كبير في المَعرَض.
The grocer will have fresh dates tomorrow.	سوف يكون عِندَ البَقّال تَمر طازِج غَداً
Will he have the papers with him?	هل سَتكون الأوراق مَعَهُ
I will have a lot of money in the future!	سوف يكون عِندي مال كثير في المُستَقبَل!

Weak verbs in the present tense   119

Translate these sentences and questions into Arabic using عِندَ.

EXAMPLE سَيَكون عِندَهُ غُرَف كَثيرة في بيته الجَديد. He will have a lot of rooms in his new house.

I will have an office on the fifth floor. ١

_____

We will have a car next year. ٢

_____

The grocer will have figs next week. ٣

_____

She will have a headache (صُداع) in the morning. ٤

_____

They (masc.) will have six seats in their new car. ٥

_____

Translate these sentences into Arabic using لِ.

My sister will have a new refrigerator. ٦

_____

The engineers will have a private restaurant. ٧

_____

We will have a small kitchen in the new apartment. ٨

_____

I will have a big part (دور) in the film. ٩

_____

Will you (fem.) have a lot of pictures in the magazine? ١٠

_____

Translate these sentences into Arabic using مَعَ.

I will have the key (with me). ١١

_____

Will you (masc.) have a pen (with you)? ١٢

_____

Will you (fem.) have my book (with you)? ١٣

_____

They (masc.) will have their mother (with them). ١٤

_____

Will you (masc. pl.) have the dog (with you)? ١٥

_____

Translate these sentences into Arabic using لَدَى.

We will have a meeting on Saturday. ١٦

_____

The town will have a new theater next year. ١٧

_____

He will have a lot of bags. ١٨

_____

They (masc.) will have a large wing in the museum. ١٩

_____

Will you (fem. pl.) have time? ٢٠

_____

Defective verbs

Defective verbs have و or ي as their third, or final, root letter. Basic (form I) defective verbs fall into one of three models, depending on the root and the voweling of the verbal stem.

- ◆ *Model 1:* و as the final root letter
- ◆ *Model 2:* ي as the final root letter and *fatḥa* as the second vowel of the past tense stem
- ◆ *Model 3:* ي as the final root letter and *kasra* as the second vowel of the past tense stem

The three models behave differently in both tenses.

Defective verbs: Model 1

In the present tense, the third root و generally becomes a long *ū,* but drops out altogether when the endings ينَ (-*īna*) or ونَ (-*ūna*) are added.

The following table shows the complete present tense for the common defective verb يَشْكو from the root ش/ك/و (*to complain*). (Notice that because the long *ū* drops out before the masculine plural ending وﻥَ [-ūna], the masculine and feminine plurals are the same for this type of defective verb in the present tense.)

	PREFIX/ SUFFIX	EXAMPLE	
SINGULAR			
أنا I	أَ	أشْكو	I complain/am complaining
you (masc.) أنتَ	تَـ	تَشْكو	you (masc.) complain/are complaining
you (fem.) أنتِ	تَـ/ينَ	تَشْكينَ	you (fem.) complain/are complaining
he/it (masc.) هُوَ	يَـ	يَشْكو	he/it (masc.) complains/is complaining
she/it (fem.) هِيَ	تَـ	تَشْكو	she/it (fem.) complains/is complaining
PLURAL			
we نَحنُ	نَـ	نَـشْكو	we complain/are complaining
you (masc. pl.) أنتُم	تَـ/ونَ	تَشْكونَ	you (masc. pl.) complain/are complaining
you (fem. pl.) أنتنَّ	تَـ/نَ	تَشْكونَ	you (fem. pl.) complain/are complaining
they (masc.) هُم	يَـ/ونَ	يَشْكونَ	they (masc.) complain/are complaining
they (fem.) هُنَّ	يَـ/نَ	يَشْكونَ	they (fem.) complain/are complaining

**EXERCISE
12·12**

You work at a hotel and everything is going wrong today. There are a lot of people complaining at customer services. Your manager has arrived and is asking you about everyone's complaints.

Explain their complaints to the manager, following the prompts. (Notice that "complain about" is يَشكو مِن.)

EXAMPLE

هذا الرَّجُل/حَجم الغُرفة <u>هذا الرَّجُل يَشْكو من حَجم الغُرفة.</u>

(This man is complaining about the size of the room.)

١ هذه المَرأة/حَجم الحَمّام _____

٢ هذا الوَلد/التليفزيون المَكسور _____

٣ هذه الشابّة/حَجم السَرير _____

٤ هؤُلاء الرِّجال/عَدَم وُجود الماء الساخِن (lack of hot water) _____

٥ هؤُلاء النِّساء/الموسيقَى الصاخِبة _____

٦ هذا الشابّ/تكييف الهَواء (air conditioning) _____

٧ هؤُلاء الأطفال/حمّام السِّباحة المَقفول _____

٨ أنا/كلّ هذه المَشاكِل! _____

Other verbs following the same pattern as يَشْكو are:

requests	يَرْجو
invites/summons	يَدْعو
appears	يَبْدو

The verb يَرْجو is commonly used as a formal way of saying "please":

Please don't wait (I request you the lack of waiting) here.	أَرجوك عَدَم الانتِظار هُنا.
Please pay attention (we request you to pay attention to these instructions).	نَرجوكُم الانتِباه لهذه التعليمات.

The verb يَبْدو is often followed by أَن (that), to mean "it appears that":

It appears that he is a stranger and lost.	يَبدو أنَّهُ غَريب وتائِه.
It appears that they have gone out.	يَبدو أنَّهُم خَرَجوا.

EXERCISE
12·13

Choose the correct part of the verb from the parentheses to fill the gap.

EXAMPLE   إنَّها تَشكو (يَشكو، تَشكو، نَشكو) من مَشاكِل كَثيرة.

١ نَحنُ لا ــــــــــــــــــــــــ (نَدعو، يَدعونَ، تَدعونَ) الرِّجال لاجتِماعِنا.

٢ ــــــــــــــــــــــــ (أشكو، يَشكو، تَشكو) سَميرة من أمِّها لأبيها.

٣ إنَّهُم ــــــــــــــــــــــــ (يَدعو، تدعو، يَدعونَ) الوَزير لِقَصِّ الشَّريط.

٤ ــــــــــــــــــــــــ (يَرجو، تَرجو، يَرجونَ) المدرِّسون مِنّا أن نَذهَب إلى المدرسة فَوراً.

٥ ــــــــــــــــــــــــ (يَبدو، تَبدو، يَبدونَ) أنَّهم باعوا البيت.

٦ لِماذا لا ــــــــــــــــــــــــ (تَشكو، تَشكينَ، تَشكونَ) للمُدير يا نادية؟

٧ نَحنُ ــــــــــــــــــــــــ (أرجوكُم، نَرجوكُم، يَرجوكُم) عَدَم التَدخين هُنا.

٨ ــــــــــــــــــــــــ (يَبدو، تَبدو، يَبدونَ) السَّعادة عَلَى وَجه الولد.

٩ إنِّي ــــــــــــــــــــــــ (سَأَدعو، سَيَدعو، سَنَدعو) ثَلاثة أصدِقاء.

١٠ ــــــــــــــــــــــــ (تَشكو، يَشكونَ، تَشكونَ) البنات من مُدَرِّسة الرِّياضيّات.

Defective verbs: Model 2

Model 2 defective verbs (with ي as the final root letter and *fatḥa* as the second vowel of the past tense stem) are similar to model 1, except the third root ي becomes a long *ī*. This final long vowel drops out when the endings ينَ (-*īna*) or ونَ (-*ūna*) are added.

The following table shows the complete present tense for the common defective verb يَـمْشي, from the root م/ش/ي (*to walk*).

	PREFIX/ SUFFIX	EXAMPLE	
SINGULAR			
I أنا	أَ	أَمْشي	I walk/am walking
you (masc.) أنتَ	تَـ	تَـمْشي	you (masc.) walk/are walking
you (fem.) أنتِ	تَـ/ـينَ	تَـمْشينَ	you (fem.) walk/are walking
he/it (masc.) هُوَ	يَـ	يَـمْشي	he/it (masc.) walks/is walking
she/it (fem.) هِيَ	تَـ	تَـمْشي	she/it (fem.) walks/is walking
PLURAL			
we نَحنُ	نَـ	نَـمْشي	we walk/are walking
you (masc. pl.) أنتُم	تَـ/ـونَ	تَـمْشونَ	you (masc. pl.) walk/are walking
you (fem. pl.) أنتنَّ	تَـ/ـنَ	تَـمْشينَ	you (fem. pl.) walk/are walking
they (masc.) هُم	يَـ/ـونَ	يَـمْشونَ	they (masc.) walk/are walking
they (fem.) هُنَّ	يَـ/ـنَ	يَـمْشينَ	they (fem.) walk/are walking

EXERCISE

12·14

Change the past tense verb to the equivalent present tense.

EXAMPLE   مَشَيْنا (we walked) نَمْشي (we walk/are walking)

١ مَشَى _____

٢ مَشَيْتُ _____

٣ مَشَيْتُم _____

٤ مَشَيْتِ _____

٥ مَشَيْنَ _____

٦ مَشَتْ _____

٧ مَشَيْتَ _____

٨ مَشوا _____

٩ مَشَيْتنَّ _____

Other verbs following the same pattern are:

runs	يَجْري
throws	يَرْمي
cries/weeps	يَبْكي

EXERCISE 12·15

Fill in the correct Arabic verb to match the English translation.

EXAMPLE We walk to the station every day. نَـمْشي إلى المَحَطّة كلّ يوم.

١ _____ ثلاثة أميال كلّ صَباح. I run three miles every morning.

٢ _____ في الشارِع. They (masc.) are walking in the street.

٣ _____ من بيتنا إلى السوق. We will walk from our house to the market.

٤ لِماذا _____؟ Why is he crying?

٥ هل _____ النُّقود في النافورة؟ Will you (fem.) throw the money in the fountain?

٦ _____ النِّساء إلى النَّهر. The women are walking to the river.

٧ _____ الأطفال كلّ يوم في وَقت النَوم. The children cry every day at bedtime.

٨ أشعُر أنّني _____ على السَّحاب. I feel that I am walking on the clouds.

٩ _____ هذا الطِفل الطَّعام على الأرض دائِماً.
This child always throws the food on the floor.

١٠ إنّ البنات _____ الخُبز للبَطّ. The girls are throwing bread for the ducks.

Defective verbs: Model 3

Model 3 defective verbs have ى as the final root letter but *kasra* as the second vowel of the past tense stem. In the present tense they are distinguished by a final *alif maqsūra* (ā ى) which changes to a diphthong (*ay* or *aw*) when subject endings are added:

ā ى + *īna* ينَ or *na* نَ = *ayna* ـَيْنَ

ā ى + *ūna* ونَ = *awna* ـَوْنَ

The following table shows the complete present tense for the defective verb يَنْسَى, from the root ي/س/ن (to forget).

	PREFIX/SUFFIX	EXAMPLE	
SINGULAR			
I أنا	أَ	أَنْسَى	I forget/am forgetting
you (masc.) أنتَ	تَـ	تَنْسَى	you (masc.) forget/are forgetting
you (fem.) أنتِ	تَـ/ينَ	تَنْسَيْنَ	you (fem.) forget/are forgetting
he/it (masc.) هُوَ	يَـ	يَنْسَى	he/it (masc.) forgets/is forgetting
she/it (fem.) هِيَ	تَـ	تَنْسَى	she/it (fem.) forgets/is forgetting
PLURAL			
we نَحنُ	نَـ	نَنْسَى	we forget/are forgetting
you (masc. pl.) أنتُم	تَـ/ونَ	تَنْسَوْنَ	you (masc. pl.) forget/are forgetting
you (fem. pl.) أنتُنَّ	تَـ/نَ	تَنْسَيْنَ	you (fem. pl.) forget/are forgetting
they (masc.) هُم	يَـ/ونَ	يَنْسَوْنَ	they (masc.) forget/are forgetting
they (fem.) هُنَّ	يَـ/نَ	يَنْسَيْنَ	they (fem.) forget/are forgetting

EXERCISE 12·16

Write out the present tense for these verbs that follow the same pattern as يَنْسَى.

EXAMPLE   _ألْقَى I meet_

root = ل/ق/ي (to meet) ١

٢ (to be pleased with) ر/ض/ي = root

_____

_____

_____

_____

_____

_____

_____

_____

_____

EXERCISE

12·17

Rewrite these sentences in the present tense and add دائماً *(always).*

EXAMPLE نَسِيَ أحمد الزُّهور. يَنْسَى أحمد الزُّهور دائماً.

١ نَسَيْتُ اسمها. _____

٢ لَقَيْنا أُمّنا في السوق. _____

٣ رَضوا عَن العُمَّال. _____

٤ لَقِيَ شُكري نادية أمام السينما. _____

٥ نَسِيَ شُكري تَذكِرَته. _____

٦ هل لَقَيْتُنَّ سميرة في النادي؟ _____

٧ نَسيتِ كِتابكِ. _____

٨ نَسِيَتْ نادية مِفتاح الصُّندوق. _____

٩ هل لَقَيْتَ الوزير في مَكتَبه؟ _____

١٠ إنَّ المُهنْدِسات رَضينَ عن المَشروع. _____

When an attached pronoun is added to a defective verb, the final *alif maqsūra* (ى) changes to a regular *alif* (ا):

I never forget my book.	لا أنسى كِتابي أبداً.
I never forget it.	لا أنساهُ أبداً.
We meet our friends after school.	نَلقَى أصدِقاءنا بعد المَدرَسة.
We meet them after school.	نَلقَاهُم بعد المَدرَسة.

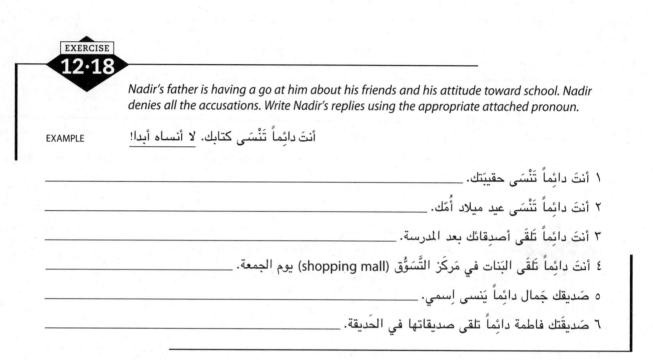

EXERCISE
12·18

Nadir's father is having a go at him about his friends and his attitude toward school. Nadir denies all the accusations. Write Nadir's replies using the appropriate attached pronoun.

EXAMPLE   أنتَ دائِماً تَنْسَى كتابك. <u>لا أنساه أبدا!</u>

١ أنتَ دائِماً تَنْسَى حقيبَتك. _____

٢ أنتَ دائِماً تَنْسَى عيد ميلاد أُمّك. _____

٣ أنتَ دائِماً تَلقَى أصدِقائك بعد المدرسة. _____

٤ أنتَ دائِماً تَلقَى البَنات في مَركَز التَّسَوُّق (shopping mall) يوم الجمعة. _____

٥ صَديقك جَمال دائِماً يَنسى اِسمي. _____

٦ صَديقَتك فاطمة دائِماً تلقى صديقاتها في الحَديقة. _____

Hamzated verbs in the present tense

Present tense formation

As with the past tense, verbs with *hamza* (ء) as one of the root letters behave largely regularly in the present tense; the main consideration is where to put the *hamza*. (The general rules for writing *hamza* are given in Chapter 1 under "*Hamzated* roots.")

For basic (form I) present tense verbs, the *hamza* (or *madda*) is usually written on an *alif*:

she apologizes	تَأْسِف
I eat	آكل
they take	يَأْخُذونَ
we read	نَقْرَأً

The main exception is when *hamza* is the final root letter and the middle vowel of the present tense is *not fatḥa*, although this is relatively uncommon:

he is slow/slows down	يَبْطُؤَ
we dare	نَجْرُؤُ

Common *hamzated* verbs in the present tense

Basic *hamzated* verbs with *hamza* as the first root letter include:

eats	يَأْكُل
takes	يَأْخُذ
orders/commands	يَأْمُر
apologizes	يَأْسِف
permits/allows	يَأْذَن

Verbs with *hamza* as the second root letter include:

asks	يَسْأَل
is/becomes fed up	يَسْأَم

129

Verbs with *hamza* as the third root letter include:

begins	يَبْدَأ
reads	يَقْرَأ
fills	يَمْلَأ
is/becomes slow	يَبْطُؤ
is brave/dares	يَجْرُؤ

EXERCISE

13·1

Complete the English translation to match the Arabic.

EXAMPLE   سَتَأْكُل نانسي في مَطْعَم إيطاليّ. Nancy will *eat* in an Italian *restaurant*. _____

١ لا تَقْرَأ سوزي قبل أن تَنام.

Suzy doesn't _____ before she _____.

٢ آسِف عَن تَأْخيري.

I _____ for my _____.

٣ سَتَقرَأون عَني في الجَريدة غَداً.

_____ will read about me in the _____ tomorrow.

٤ لِماذا تَأْكُلين كَعكة أُختك؟

Why are you _____ your sister's _____?

٥ يَبدو أنّها تَقرَأ عن المَوضوع.

It appears that she is _____ about the _____.

٦ سوف يَأْخُذون المَشروبات إلى الشاطِئ.

They _____ take the _____ to the beach.

٧ لا أَسأَم من سَماعها أبداً.

I _____ get _____ of hearing it.

٨ هل تَأْذَنون لي بالخُروج الآن؟

Will you allow _____ to go out _____?

٩ إنّ المُمَرِّضات يَملأْنَ قُلوبنا بالأَمَل.

The nurses _____ our hearts with _____.

١٠ نَبدَأ الآن في تَرتيب أُمورنا.

We're _____ now to organize _____ affairs.

١١ يَسْأَم المُشاهِدون من هذه البَرامِج.

The _____ are fed up of _____ programs.

١٢ أنا لا أجرُؤ على النَظَر في المِرآة.

I don't _____ look _____ the mirror.

١٣ يَأْخُذ السِنجاب اللَّوزة من يَدي.

The squirrel _____ the nut from my _____.

١٤ يَأكُل الأطفال الحُلوَى ويَشعُرون بالنَّشاط.

The _____ eat candy and _____ energetic.

EXERCISE
13·2

Use the sentences in Exercise 13.1 to translate the following English sentences, changing the subject accordingly.

EXAMPLE   سَنَأكُل في مَطعَم إيطاليّ. We will eat in an Italian restaurant.

_____ Samir doesn't read before he sleeps. ١

_____ We apologize for our lateness. ٢

_____ We will read about him in the paper tomorrow. ٣

_____ Why is he eating his sister's cake? ٤

_____ It appears that you (masc.) read about the subject. ٥

_____ They will (fem.) take the drinks to the beach. ٦

_____ Suzy never gets fed up of hearing it. ٧

_____ Will he allow you (masc. pl.) to go out now? ٨

_____ The children fill our hearts with hope. ٩

_____ I am starting now to organize my affairs. ١٠

_____ Are you (fem.) getting fed up with these programs? ١١

_____ My mother doesn't dare to look in the mirror. ١٢

_____ The pigeon takes the nut from her hand. ١٣

_____ We eat candy and feel energetic. ١٤

Hamzated verbs in the present tense   **131**

Dual verbs
in the present tense

Dual verbs are formed in the present tense by adding ان (-āni) to the verbs for
هو (he), هي (she), and أنتُم (you, pl.):

they both (masc.) go/are going	(هُما) يَذْهَبانِ
they both (fem.) go/are going	(هُما) تَذْهَبانِ
you two (masc. or fem.) go/are going	(أنتُما) تَذْهَبانِ
they both (masc.) eat/are eating	(هُما) يَأْكُلانِ
they both (fem.) eat/are eating	(هُما) تَأْكُلانِ
you two (masc. or fem.) eat/are eating	(أنتُما) تَأْكُلانِ
they both (masc.) walk/are walking	(هُما) يَـمْشيانِ
they both (fem.) walk/are walking	(هُما) تَـمْشيانِ
you two (masc. or fem.) walk/are walking	(أنتُما) تَـمْشيانِ

EXERCISE
14·1

Complete the sentences with the correct dual verb in the present tense.

EXAMPLE الوَلَدان يَذهَبانِ (go) إلى المدرسة بالقِطار.

١ يا أحمد ونادِر، هل _____ (know) الطريق؟

٢ الرَّجُلان _____ (run) نحو المطعم.

٣ أنوَر وحَسَن دائماً _____ (forget) مَوعِد القِطار.

٤ أنتُما لا _____ (say/tell) القِصّة كلّها.

٥ أبي وأمّي _____ (live/reside) الآن في هذه المَدينة.

٦ أُختي وأمّي _____ (drink) الشاي بَعد الغَداء.

٧ البِنتان لا _____ (hear) صَوت الجَرَس.

٨ المُهَندِسان _____ (attend) كلّ الاجتِماعات مَعاً.

٩ أنتُما سَوف _____ (inherit) بيت جَدّكُما.

١٠ يا سمير ونادية، لِماذا لا _____ (search) عن عَمَل؟

132

Referring to couples

The dual is often naturally used when talking about a couple within the family such as parents, spouses, two children, or siblings.

My mother and father eat breakfast in the garden.

أَبي وأُمّي يَأْكُلانِ الإفطار في الحَديقة.

We have two children and they (both) go to school by train.

عِندَنا طِفلان وهُما يَذْهَبانِ إلى المدرسة بالقطار.

Samira's parents are creatures of habit. Every day they follow exactly the same routine. Describe their routine using the prompts provided.

EXAMPLE   eat/breakfast/kitchen كُلّ يوم يَأْكُلان الإفطار في المَطبخ.

_____ read/newspaper/after breakfast ١

_____ go/market/10 o'clock ٢

_____ drink/coffee/market ٣

_____ meet their friends/park ٤

_____ eat lunch/Italian restaurant ٥

_____ sleep/for an hour/after lunch ٦

_____ visit/library/3 o'clock ٧

_____ carry books/house ٨

_____ play chess (الشَّطرَنج)/before dinner ٩

_____ eat/dinner/7 o'clock ١٠

_____ write/letters/after dinner ١١

_____ sleep/half past 10 ١٢

Present tense verb and subject order with the dual

Remember that if a verb is placed *before* a dual subject, it will be singular (either masculine or feminine depending on the gender of the subject):

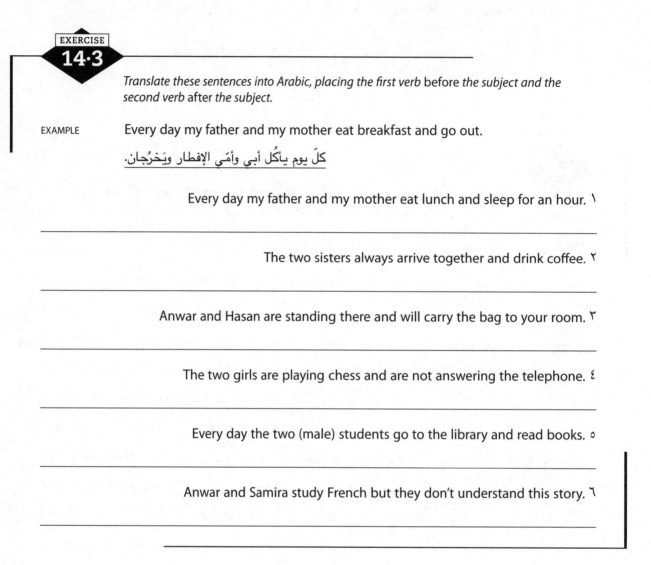

EXERCISE
14·3

Translate these sentences into Arabic, placing the first verb before *the subject and the second verb* after *the subject.*

EXAMPLE   Every day my father and my mother eat breakfast and go out.

كلّ يوم يأكُل أبي وأمّي الإفطار ويَخرُجان.

Every day my father and my mother eat lunch and sleep for an hour. ١

_____

The two sisters always arrive together and drink coffee. ٢

_____

Anwar and Hasan are standing there and will carry the bag to your room. ٣

_____

The two girls are playing chess and are not answering the telephone. ٤

_____

Every day the two (male) students go to the library and read books. ٥

_____

Anwar and Samira study French but they don't understand this story. ٦

_____

FORMS OF THE VERB

All of the verbs practiced in Parts I, II, and III are "basic," or form I, verbs. Basic verbs display the three-consonant root of the verb most clearly. In addition there are a large number of "derived" verbs. These derived forms of the verb have additional letters before and/or between the original root letters, producing a modified meaning. Each form has particular meaning patterns associated with it. There are ten forms used in modern Arabic, including the basic form I. By convention, they are referred to using the Roman numerals I to X or, by Arab linguists, using the present tense pattern with the root represented by the three letters ف/ع/ل.

Most roots have some derived forms in common circulation, but few have all. In addition, for some roots derived verbal forms are in common circulation while the basic form I is not.

The existence of derived forms may at first seem to complicate the picture for a learner. However, these forms are in fact more predictable than the basic verb, and linked meanings from a shared root helps expand vocabulary.

The derived forms divide themselves into three groups that share characteristics:

◆ Forms II, III, and IV (يُفَعِّل/يُفاعِل/يُفعِل)

◆ Forms V and VI (يَتَفَعَّل/يَتَفاعَل)

◆ Forms VII, VIII, and X (يَنْفَعِل/يَفْتَعِل/يَسْتَفْعِل)

(Form IX is very uncommon in modern standard Arabic.)

Forms II, III, and IV

Form II يُفَعِّل

Form II is formed by doubling the middle root letter, and often has a causative meaning (i.e., causing someone to be or do something).

Form I: to be good	حَسُنَ/يَحْسُن
Form II: to cause to be good, (i.e., to improve)	حَسَّنَ/يُحَسِّن
Form I: to study	دَرَسَ/يَدْرُس
Form II: to cause to study, (i.e., to teach)	دَرَّسَ/يُدَرِّس

Form II also occasionally carries an intensive meaning (i.e., carrying out an action with intensity).

Form I: to break	كَسَرَ/يَكْسِر
Form II: to break with intensity, (i.e., to smash to pieces, to shatter)	كَسَّرَ/يُكَسِّر

In the past tense, form II is voweled with *fathas*, and the present tense with *damma/fatha/kasra*. Unlike form I verbs where the middle vowel can vary, the derived forms have consistent voweling. The past and present tense subject endings and prefixes remain the same (see "Past tense formation and uses" in Chapter 4 and "Present tense formation" in Chapter 9), except that the vowel on the present tense prefix changes from *fatha* to *damma*.

I teach the Arabic language.	أُدَرِّس اللُّغة العربيّة.
The thief shattered the glass of the window.	كَسَّرَ اللِّصّ زُجاج الشُّبّاك.
Did they improve the road to the city?	هل حَسَّنوا الطَّريق إلى المدينة؟

The following table shows the conjugations for past and present tenses of the form II verb دَرَّس/يُدَرِّس (*to teach*):

	PAST TENSE	PRESENT TENSE
SINGULAR		
I أنا	دَرَّسْتُ	أُدَرِّس
you (masc.) أنتَ	دَرَّسْتَ	تُدَرِّس
you (fem.) أنتِ	دَرَّسْتِ	تُدَرِّسينَ
he/it (masc.) هُوَ	دَرَّسَ	يُدَرِّس
she/it (fem.) هِيَ	دَرَّسَتْ	تُدَرِّس

(continued)

	PAST TENSE	PRESENT TENSE
PLURAL		
we نَحنُ	دَرَّسْنا	نُدَرِّس
you (masc. pl.) أَنتُم	دَرَّسْتُم	تُدَرِّسونَ
you (fem. pl.) أَنتُنَّ	دَرَّسْتُنَّ	تُدَرِّسْنَ
they (masc.) هُم	دَرَّسوا	يُدَرِّسونَ
they (fem.) هُنَّ	دَرَّسْنَ	يُدَرِّسْنَ

EXERCISE 15·1

Write out the past tense and present tense conjugations and their meanings for these form II verbs, following the example in the preceding table.

EXAMPLE   أَحَسِّن   حَسَّنْتُ   أنا /

to improve ١

to shatter ٢

What do these sentences and questions mean?

EXAMPLE   <u>Who smashed the glass?</u> مَنْ كَسَرَ الكوب؟

_____ ١ هل كَسَّرَتْ نادية الكوب؟

_____ ٢ لا، إنّ الأولاد كَسَّروا الكوب.

_____ ٣ هل تُحَسِّن الحُكومة الطريق إلى المدينة؟

_____ ٤ لا، لا تُحَسِّنهُ إطلاقاً.

_____ ٥ ماذا تُدَرِّسينَ يا أميرة؟

_____ ٦ أُدَرِّس اللُّغة الإنجليزيّة في البَحرين.

_____ ٧ هل كَسَّرَ الضُّيوف أطباقهُم في الفَرَح اليونانيّ؟

_____ ٨ هل دَرَّسْتُمْ اللُّغة العَرَبيّة في الجامعة؟

_____ ٩ هل حَسَّنْتُمْ مَهارات الفَريق هذا العام؟

_____ ١٠ لا، ولكنّنا سوف نُحَسِّنها العام القادِم.

Common form II verbs

Here are some common form II verbs in the past and the present tenses. There are many verbs in circulation using this form. In general you can see that the meanings are causative (or occasionally intensive) and clear connections can be made to the original root. However, sometimes the meaning has strayed from the original root, and the connection is less obvious.

to load, to download (file, etc.)	حَمَّل/يُحَمِّل	to prepare	جَهَّز/يُجَهِّز
to improve (something)	حَسَّن/يُحَسِّن	to move (something)	حَرَّك/يُحَرِّك
to train, to coach	دَرَّب/يُدَرِّب	to smoke	دَخَّن/يُدَخِّن
to remind	ذَكَّر/يُذَكِّر	to teach	دَرَّس/يُدَرِّس
to welcome	رَحَّب/يُرَحِّب (ب)	to organize	رَتَّب/يُرَتِّب
to believe	صَدَّق/يُصَدِّق	to heat	سَخَّن/يُسَخِّن
to repair	صَلَّح/يُصَلِّح	to exchange	صَرَّف/يُصَرِّف
to instruct	عَلَّم/يُعَلِّم	to adjust	عَدَّل/يُعَدِّل
to prefer	فَضَّل/يُفَضِّل	to inspect	فَتَّش/يُفَتِّش
to chop, to cut (something) up	قَطَّع/يُقَطِّع	to think	فَكَّر/يُفَكِّر
to present	قَدَّم/يُقَدِّم	to estimate, to appreciate	قَدَّر/يُقَدِّر
to cost, assign	كَلَّف/يُكَلِّف	to smash	كَسَّر/يُكَسِّر
to organize	نَظَّم/يُنَظِّم	to clean	نَظَّف/يُنَظِّف

EXERCISE 15·3

Write the correct Arabic verb to match the English. Remember that the Arabic present tense can be used for both the simple present (e.g., he smokes) and the present continuous (e.g., he is smoking) tenses.

EXAMPLE   أُنَظِّم I am organizing

1 we welcomed _____

2 I adjust _____

3 you (masc.) are cleaning _____

4 you (fem.) reminded _____

5 they (masc.) are teaching _____

6 she prepares _____

7 they (fem.) chopped _____

8 you (masc. pl.) will inspect _____

9 I downloaded _____

10 they (masc.) prefer _____

11 we coach _____

12 he smokes _____

EXERCISE 15·4

Choose one of the answers from Exercise 15.3 to fill in the gaps in the sentences and questions.

EXAMPLE   أُنَظِّم الحَفل لِعيد ميلاد ابني.

١ _____ عَشرة أفلام من الإنترنت أمس!

٢ هل _____ على المَدرَسة غداً؟

٣ إنّ النِساء _____ الكَعكة الكبيرة للضُيوف الصِغار في الحَفل.

٤ _____ بالضُيوف عند الباب.

٥ إنهُم _____ اللُغة العربيّة للإنجليز.

٦ _____ زَوجي سَجائِر كثيرة يَوميّاً.

٧ هل الشَباب _____ كُرة القَدَم أم كُرة السَلّة؟

٨ _____ فَريق كُرة القَدَم يوم السَّبت صَباحاً.

٩ لِماذا لا _____ السيّارة يا أحمد؟

١٠ سَـ _____ المَوائِد (the tables) قبل الحَفلة.

١١ يا نادية، هل _____ سميرة بِمَوعِد الامتِحان؟

١٢ كلّ يوم _____ أمّي الغداء للعائِلة.

Mr. Lutfi, the owner of a small restaurant, is expecting a special customer. He's very excited and is briefing his assistant, Ahmed, about what preparations they should make. Read the passage and answer the following questions. The additional vocabulary will help you.

torn	مَقطوع	customer	زَبون
you buy	تَشتَري	royal palace	قَصر مَلَكيّ
it doesn't matter to me	لا يُهِمّني	it is necessary that	يَجِب أن
bodyguards	حَرَس	greeting	تَحية
		vases	زُهريّات

يا أحمد! اليوم سوف نُجهِّز المَطعَم لِزَبون خاصّ جدّاً.

المُوَظَّفون في القَصر المَلَكيّ يَوَدّون أن أُنَظِّم لَهُم حَفل عيد ميلاد الأمير الصَّغير غداً هنا في مطعمي!

يَجِب أن تُنَظَّف الأرض جيِّداً. سَيَزورنا شَخص مُهِمّ من القَصر لِيُفَتِّش على النَّظافة ولِيُدَرِّبكُم على تَحية الأمير ولِيُعَلِّمكُم ما تَفعَلون وهو هنا.

أنا سَأُعَدِّل المَوائِد، وسأُرَتِّب لَهُم مائِدة كبيرة بِجانِب الشُّبّاك.

كيف نُحَسِّن المَنظَر من الشُّبّاك يا أحمد؟ هل أُحَرِّك بَعض هذه الزُّهريّات؟

أحمد، يجب أن تُصَلِّح هذه السِّتارة المَقطوعة.

أنا سَأُذَكِّرك غداً أن تَشتَري أجمَل زُهور في المدينة. لا يُهِمّني كَم تُكَلِّفني.

أنا سَأُرَحِّب بالأمير عند الباب، وسَأُقَدِّم لَهُ كَعكة عيد الميلاد، وهو سَيُقَطِّعها لِضُيوفه الصِّغار.

وأنت يجب أن تُسَخِّن الشاي لِلحَرَس.

هل نَسَينا شيئاً يا أحمد؟ هل فَكَّرنا في كلّ كبيرة وصغيرة؟

أنا لا أُصَدِّق أن الأمير يُفَضِّل مطعمي!

1. Who is coming to the restaurant tomorrow?

_____

2. What is the occasion?

_____

3. Who will inspect the restaurant before the visit?

_____

4. What are the reasons for the inspection?

_____

5. What preparations will Mr. Lutfi carry out himself?

_____

6. What does he want Ahmed to do before the visit?

_____

7. What will Mr. Lutfi present to the prince when he welcomes him at the door?

_____

8. What does he want Ahmed to do for the bodyguards?

_____

EXERCISE
15·6

*There are twenty form II verbs in the passage in Exercise 15.5. Can you find them all,
including any attached pronouns, and say what they mean?*

EXAMPLE   *we will prepare* سوف نُـجَهِّز

_____   _____

_____   _____

_____   _____

_____   _____

_____   _____

_____   _____

_____   _____

_____   _____

_____   _____

Form III يُفاعِل

Form III is formed by adding an *alif* after the middle root letter, and often has the meaning of carrying out an action *with* someone else.

Form I: to do/to work	عَمِل/يَعمَل
Form III: to treat/to deal with someone	عامَل/يُعامِل
Form I: to sit	جَلَس/يَجلِس
Form III: to sit with someone	جالَس/يُجالِس

Form III can also carry the meaning of *trying* to do something.

Form I: to be in front/to precede	سَبَق/يَسبِق
Form II: to try to be in front, (i.e., to race against)	سابَق/يُسابِق

Form III verbs have similar voweling to form II, the doubled middle root being replaced by *alif*:

I raced my brother to the park.	سابَقْتُ أخي إلى الحديقة.
They sat with the patient in the hospital.	جالَسوا المَريض في المُستَشفى.
The manager treats us with respect.	يُعامِلنا المدير بالاحتِرام.
We are racing the wind (i.e., We are racing against time.)	نُسابِق الريح.

The following table shows the conjugations for past and present tenses of the form III verb سابَق/يُسابِق (*to race*):

		PAST TENSE	PRESENT TENSE
SINGULAR			
I	أنا	سابَقْتُ	أُسابِق
you (masc.)	أنتَ	سابَقْتَ	تُسابِق
you (fem.)	أنتِ	سابَقْتِ	تُسابِقينَ
he/it (masc.)	هُوَ	سابَقَ	يُسابِق
she/it (fem.)	هِيَ	سابَقَتْ	تُسابِق
PLURAL			
we	نَحنُ	سابَقْنا	نُسابِق
you (masc. pl.)	أنتُم	سابَقْتُمْ	تُسابِقون
you (fem. pl.)	أنتُنَّ	سابَقْتُنَّ	تُسابِقنَ
they (masc.)	هُم	سابَقوا	يُسابِقونَ
they (fem.)	هُنَّ	سابَقْنَ	يُسابِقنَ

Common form III verbs

Here are some form III verbs in the past and present tenses. As usual, the meaning patterns are more obvious in some verbs than others.

to sit with	جالَس/يُجالِس	to argue with	جادَل/يُجادِل
to study (e.g., for an exam)	ذاكَر/يُذاكِر	to talk	حادَث/يُحادِث
to help	ساعَد/يُساعِد	to race	سابَق/يُسابِق
to review	راجَع/يُراجِع	to travel	سافَر/يُسافِر
to view, to watch	شاهَد/يُشاهِد	to participate	شارَك/يُشارِك
to leave	غادَر/يُغادِر	to deal with, to treat	عامَل/يُعامِل
to discuss	ناقَش/يُناقِش	to fight	قاتَل/يُقاتِل
		to emigrate	هاجَر/يُهاجِر

EXERCISE

15·7

Put these sentences and questions into the past tense.

EXAMPLE   أُغادِر البَلَد بالمَركَب. <u>غادَرْتُ البَلَد بالمَركَب.</u>

١ نُشاهِد التليفزيون. _____

٢ يُسافِر المَلِك بطائِرة خاصّة. _____

٣ أُساعِد اِبنَتي في دُروسها. _____

٤ هل تُسابِقونَ البَنات؟ _____

٥ أبي وأمّي يُحادِثان المدرِّس. _____

٦ تُذاكِر سميرة للاِمتِحان. _____

٧ لِماذا تُجادِلني؟ _____

٨ تُشارِك الوَزيرة في هذا الاِجتِماع. _____

٩ هل تُراجِعينَ الدُّروس يا نادية؟ _____

١٠ نُقاتِل من أجل الحُرِّية (for freedom). _____

١١ إنّ النِساء يُهاجِرنَ إلى أمريكا. _____

١٢ مَتَى يُغادِر القِطار؟ _____

Form III verbs such as حادَث/يُحادِث already carry the meaning of doing the action *with* someone else, and so they do not need an equivalent of the English preposition "to" or "with":

حادَثَتْني المُدَرِّسة عَن الامتِحانات.

The teacher talked to me about the exams.

أُجادِل أبي ثَلاث أو أرْبَع مَرّات في اليَوم.

I argue with my father two or three times a day.

يُعامِلون المُوَظَّفين كأنَّهُم أطفال.

They deal with/treat the employees as if they are children.

EXERCISE

15·8

Translate these sentences and questions into Arabic using a form III verb from the earlier list.

EXAMPLE جادَلْنا المدير في مَوضوع الخِدمة. We argued with the manager about the service.

I argued with my father about the exams. ١

_____

He treats me as if I am a child. ٢

_____

We discussed this with him yesterday. ٣

_____

Our ancestors (أجدادنا) fought for freedom. ٤

_____

I talk to them (dual هُما) every day about their son. ٥

_____

You (masc. pl.) are always arguing with the manager. ٦

_____

When will you (fem. pl.) talk to the (female) manager about the service? ٧

_____

We sat with her yesterday. ٨

_____

Read Walid's blog and fill in the verbs to match the English translation.

I am racing the wind! My friends and I want to travel (we travel) to the capital to watch (we watch) the big concert on Saturday. My father wants me to review (I review) my school work because the exams are in a week. He talks to me and I argue with him and discuss with him about studying approximately three or four times a week. I fight to explain to my father my point of view in life, and my mother doesn't participate in this argument and never helps me. He treats me as if I'm a child in spite of the fact that I'm fourteen. I sometimes think about leaving the house, but I change my mind at the last moment. For sure I will emigrate from this whole country when I become sixteen or eighteen. Nobody here understands me!

EXAMPLE   I am racing the wind! أنا أُسابِق الريح!

أنا _____ الريح! أنا وأصدِقائي نَوَدّ أن _____ إلى العاصِمة لِـ _____

الحفل الموسيقيّ الكبير يوم السبت. أبي طَلَبَ مِنّي أن _____ دُروسي لأن الامتِحانات بعد أُسبوع.

هو _____ وأنا _____ و _____ في مَوضوع المُذاكَرة ثلاث أو أربع مَرّات

في الأسبوع تَقريباً. _____ لأشرَح لأبي وَجهة نَظَري في الحَياة، وأمّي لا _____ في

هذا الجِدال ولا _____ أبداً. إنّه _____ كأنّني طِفل رَغم أنّني في الرابِعة عشرة.

أنا أحياناً أُفَكِّر في أن _____ البيت ولكنّي دائِماً أُغَيِّر رَأيي في آخِر لَحظة.

أكيد _____ من هذا البَلَد كلّه حينَ أصبَح في السادِسة عشرة أو الثامِنة عشرة. لا أحد هنا يَفهَمني!

Form IV يُفْعِل

Form IV is characterized by a *sukūn* (˚) over the first root letter. The meaning pattern is causative and similar to form II. Form IV verbs have similar voweling to forms II and III, the difference being an additional *alif* on the front of the past tense, and *sukūn* over the first root letter:

Form IV: to repair/to reform	أَصْلَح/يُصْلِح
Form IV: to announce	أَعْلَن/يُعْلِن
The spokesman announced that the president was ill yesterday.	أَعْلَنَ المُتَحَدِّث أن الرَّئيس كان مريضاً أمس.
I will announce the news tomorrow.	سوف أُعْلِن الخَبَر غَداً.
The government has reformed the system of education.	أَصْلَحَت الحُكومة نِظام التَّعليم.

Put the root letters given into the pattern for a form IV verb. The meaning of the resulting verb is given in English.

EXAMPLE   ع/ل/ن أَعْلَن/يُعْلِن to announce

_____ to hurry ع/د/س ١

_____ to do well ن/س/ح ٢

_____ to send ل/س/ر ٣

_____ to tell/to inform ر/ب/خ ٤

_____ to remove/to take out ج/د/خ ٥

_____ to take off ع/ل/ق ٦

_____ to revive/to refresh ش/ع/ن ٧

_____ to become ح/ب/ص ٨

_____ to rescue ذ/ق/ن ٩

The following table shows the conjugations for past and present tenses of the form IV verb أَرْسَل/يُرْسِل (*to send*):

	PAST TENSE	PRESENT TENSE
SINGULAR		
I أَنا	أَرْسَلْتُ	أُرْسِل
you (masc.) أَنتَ	أَرْسَلْتَ	تُرْسِل
you (fem.) أَنتِ	أَرْسَلْتِ	تُرْسِلينَ
he/it (masc.) هُوَ	أَرْسَلَ	يُرْسِل
she/it (fem.) هِيَ	أَرْسَلَتْ	تُرْسِل
PLURAL		
we نَحنُ	أَرْسَلْنا	نُرْسِل
you (masc. pl.) أَنتُم	أَرْسَلْتُم	تُرْسِلونَ
you (fem. pl.) أَنتَنَّ	أَرْسَلْتُنَّ	تُرْسِلْنَ
they (masc.) هُم	أَرْسَلوا	يُرْسِلونَ
they (fem.) هُنَّ	أَرْسَلْنَ	يُرْسِلْنَ

Three friends are talking together, but they can't seem to agree on anything. Complete their exchanges using the prompts.

EXAMPLE   أحمد أَصْلَحَ الدرّاجة. Ahmed repaired the bicycle.

لا، سميرة <u>أَصْلَحَت الدرّاجة.</u>

لا، الأولاد <u>أَصْلَحوا الدرّاجة.</u>

١ سَمير أَحْسَنَ في الإمتِحانات. Samir did well in the exams.

لا، نادية _____.

لا، أَنا _____.

٢ الناظر سَيُرْسِل النَّتائِج غَداً. The principal will send the results tomorrow.

لا، المُدَرِّسة _____.

لا، كلّ المُدَرِّسون _____.

٣ أَنْقَذْتُ الطفل من النَّهر. I rescued the child from the river.

لا، نَحنُ _____.

لا، أبي _____.

٤ سَوفَ تُصبِح قائِد الفَريق. You will become the captain of the team.

لا، أحمد _____.

لا، أنا _____.

٥ نادية أَخْبَرَت الناظِر عَن الحَفلة. Nadia informed the principal about the party.

لا، الأولاد _____.

لا، أنتِ _____.

٦ أبوها سَيُصلِح الكمبيوتر. Her father is going to repair the computer.

لا، أمّها _____.

لا، المُهَندِسات _____.

EXERCISE
15·12

*Change the subject of the sentences and questions to match the new subject in parentheses,
adjusting the verbs as necessary.*

EXAMPLE   أَرْسَلَ لي رِسالة. (هي) أَرْسَلَتْ لي رِسالة.

١ لِماذا يُخرِج الكمبيوتر مِن الغُرفة؟ (أنتَ) _____

٢ أَسْرَعوا إلى المُستَشفَى. (أنا) _____

٣ هل سَتُنْقِذ زَميلهُ (his colleague) أيضاً؟ (أنتِ) _____

٤ سوف يُنْعِشون الاقتِصاد (the economy). (نحن) _____

٥ أَقْلَعْنا دون (without) أن نُخبِر القائِد. (هو) _____

٦ هل سَتُحْسِن في الامتِحان؟ (أنتُم) _____

٧ أَنْقَذتُ أخي مِن السِّجن (prison). (هم) _____

٨ أَصبَحْنا فَقيرات بعد الحَرب (the war). (هنّ) _____

EXERCISE
15·13

*Read the story about a daring mission to rescue a prisoner (أسير) and choose the correct
answer to the questions.*

في الحَرب، عَلِمْتُ أن أخي كان أسيراً في أَحَد سُجون العَدو لأنّه أَرسَلَ لي رسالة من هناك. أَقلَعتُ مع زَميلي بِطائِرة صغيرة من المَطار الحَربيّ دون أن نُخبِر القائِد وأَسرَعنا بِها إلى بِلاد العَدو. كُنتُ أَوَدّ أن أُطلِق أخي من السِّجن. قَفَزْتُ من الطائِرة بِالمَظَلّة في الظَّلام وأَنقَذتُهُ من السِّجن. وبعد أن عُدنا قالَ القائِد إنّني أَحسَنتُ لأنّني أَنقَذتُ أخي، ولكن أَخذ طائِرة بدون إذن جَريمة ووَضَعَني في السجن. الآن أنا أَصبَحتُ سَجيناً ولكن أخي يَقضي عُطلة طَويلة على الشاطِئ!

EXAMPLE   مَتَى حَدَثَ هذا؟ في الحَرب/في العُطلة/أمس

١ مَن كان أسيراً في بِلاد العَدو؟ القائِد/زَميل الكاتِب/أخو الكاتِب

٢ أين كان أسيراً؟ في بِلاد العَدو/في الطائِرة/في المَطار

٣ كَيفَ عَلِمَ الكاتِب؟ من الانترنت/من رسالة/من زميله

٤ من أينَ أقلع؟ مَطار العَدو/المَطار الحربيّ/مَطار القاهِرة

٥ مَتَى نَزِلَ بِالمَظَلّة؟ في النَّهار/في اللَّيل/في الفَجر

٦ لِماذا وَضَعَهُ القائِد في السِّجن؟ لأنّهُ أَخَذَ الطائِرة بدون إذن/لأنّهُ أَنقَذَ أخاهُ.

٧ أين الكاتِب الآن؟ في السجن/على الشاطِئ/في الطائِرة

٨ وأين أخو الكاتِب الآن؟ في السجن/على الشاطِئ/في الطائِرة

Forms V and VI

·16·

Forms V and VI are both characterized by the addition of the syllable تَـ (*ta-*) in front of the root. They are two of the simplest derived forms to master because:

- They are closely related to forms II and III
- They are voweled in both tenses using only *fatha (a)*.

Form V يَتَفَعَّل

Form V is formed by adding تَـ (*ta-*) in front of form II, and voweling the present tense with *fatha* as well as the past tense. Whereas form II is usually transitive or causative (the subject is carrying out the action on something else), form V is usually intransitive or reflexive (the subject is itself carrying out the action).

Form II: to move something else	حَرَّك/يُحَرِّك
Form V: to move yourself/itself	تَـحَرَّك/يَتَـحَرَّك
Form II: to remind someone	ذَكَّر/يُذَكِّر
Form V: to remind yourself, or to remember	تَذَكَّر/يَتَذَكَّر

The following table shows the conjugations for past and present tenses of the form V verb تَذَكَّر/يَتَذَكَّر (*to remember*). Notice that the prefixes for the present tense produce the staccato opening syllables characteristic of forms V and VI (*tata-, yata-, nata-*)

	PAST TENSE	PRESENT TENSE
SINGULAR		
أنا I	تَذَكَّرْتُ	أَتَذَكَّر
أنتَ you (masc.)	تَذَكَّرْتَ	تَتَذَكَّر
أنتِ you (fem.)	تَذَكَّرْتِ	تَتَذَكَّرِينَ
هُوَ he/it (masc.)	تَذَكَّرَ	يَتَذَكَّر
هِيَ she/it (fem.)	تَذَكَّرْتْ	تَتَذَكَّر

	PAST TENSE	PRESENT TENSE
PLURAL		
we نَحنُ	تَذَكَّرْنا	نَتَذَكَّر
you (masc. pl.) أنتُم	تَذَكَّرْتُـمْ	تَتَذَكَّرونَ
you (fem. pl.) أنتُنَّ	تَذَكَّرْتُـنَّ	تَتَذَكَّرْنَ
they (masc.) هُم	تَذَكَّروا	يَتَذَكَّرونَ
they (fem.) هُنَّ	تَذَكَّرْنَ	يَتَذَكَّرْنَ

The negative لا يَتَذَكَّر can be used to mean both "do not remember" and "cannot remember."

EXERCISE 16·1

Translate the English into Arabic.

EXAMPLE   I can't remember his name. لا أَتَذَكَّر اسمهُ.

١. She can't remember my name. _____

٢. I will remember this day. _____

٣. Did you (masc.) remember your bag? _____

٤. Yes, I remembered it. _____

٥. You (masc. pl.) never remember my birthday. _____

٦. We remembered it last year. _____

٧. Do you (fem.) remember the war? _____

٨. I remember it (fem.) a little. _____

Common form V verbs

Some widely-used verbs are form V, for example the verb "to remember" that was previously practiced, and the most common verbs for "to talk," "to speak," "to learn," and "to move."

The verbs تَكَلَّم/يَتَكَلَّم and تَـحَدَّث/يَتَـحَدَّث are often used interchangeably for "to speak" or "to talk," for example when referring to languages spoken:

I speak Arabic a little.	أَتَـحَدَّث العَرَبيّة قليلاً
My father speaks French fluently.	يَتَكَلَّم أبي الفَرَنسيّة بِطَلاقة.
Do you (fem.) speak English?	هل تَتَكَلَّمينَ الإنجليزيّة؟

Amira's classmates come from different backgrounds and speak a variety of languages. Between them they can claim knowledge of the following:

Japanese اليابانيّة	Arabic العَرَبيّة
Greek اليونانيّة	English الإنجليزيّة
Chinese الصينيّة	French الفَرَنسيّة
Persian/Farsi الفارسيّة	German الألمانيّة

Amira is describing which languages they speak. Use the prompts to complete the descriptions.

EXAMPLE   Samya: fluent Arabic and English

<u>تتحدَّث/تتكلَّم سامية العربيّة والإنجليزيّة بطَلاقة</u>

Girgis (جرجِس): fluent Arabic and Greek ١

_____

Jacques (جاك): fluent French/a little Arabic ٢

_____

Fatima: fluent Persian/a little French ٣

_____

Ahmed: fluent Persian and Arabic/a little English ٤

_____

Lucy (لوسي): fluent Chinese/a little Japanese ٥

_____

Sami (سامي): fluent English/a little German ٦

_____

Marie (ماري): fluent French and German/a little Greek ٧

_____

Me: fluent Arabic and English/a little French ٨

_____

Form I عَلِمَ/يَعلَم means "to learn about" as well as "to know" in the context of learning about a particular piece of news. However, the form V verb from the same root, تَعَلَّم/يَتَعَلَّم, is used in the context of learning a subject or skill, such as a language.

I learned that my brother was a prisoner.	عَلِمْتُ أَن أَخي كان أَسيراً.
I learned French from my mother.	تَعَلَّمْتُ الفرنسيّة من أمّي.

Choose the correct verb for each sentence or question.

EXAMPLE   عَلِمْتُ/تَعَلَّمْتُ أَنَّ أَخي كان يَعيش في لُندُن.

١ نَعلَم/نَتَعَلَّم العربيّة في الجامِعة.

٢ كَيفَ تَعلَم/تَتَعَلَّم أَنَّ الخَبَر صَحيح؟

٣ أين عَلِمَ/تَعَلَّمَ هذ الوَلد الفَرَنسيّة؟

٤ عَلِمنا/تَعَلَّمنا أَنَّ الطائرة سوف تُقلِع بعد ساعة.

٥ إنَّ الطَلَبة يَعلَمون/يَتَعَلَّمون التَّاريخ الإسلاميّ في المدرسة.

٦ هل البَنات عَلِمْنَ/تَعَلَّمْنَ أَنَّ عِندَهُنَّ مُدرِّسة جديدة؟

٧ هل تَعلَمون/تَتَعَلَّمون اليابانيّة من أُمّكم؟

٨ عَلِمتُ/تَعَلَّمتُ بالسَرقة من الشُّرطة.

Other common form V verbs include:

to improve	تَحَسَّن/يَتَحَسَّن
to move	تَحَرَّك/يَتَحَرَّك
to climb	تَسَلَّق/يَتَسَلَّق
to act/to behave	تَصَرَّف/يَتَصَرَّف
to disperse	تَفَرَّق/يَتَفَرَّق

Fill the gaps with the correct part of the verb to match the English translation.

EXAMPLE   I climbed ten mountains in Scotland. تَسَلَّقْتُ عشرة جِبال في إِسكتلَندا.

١ سيّارَتي لا _____ من هذا المَكان. My car doesn't move from this place.

٢ _____ صِحّتها بعد أن نَقَلوها إلى أَسوان. Her health improved after they moved her to Aswan.

٣ سوف _____ في هذا الأَمر بعد الظُّهر. I will act on this matter this afternoon.

٤ هذه النَّباتات _____ الحائِط في الصَّيف. These plants climb the wall in summer.

٥ كلّ عَضَلات الجِسم _____ أثناء السِّباحة. All the muscles of the body move during swimming.

٦ سوف _____ من أخطائهم. They will learn from their mistakes.

٧ هل _____ اللِّصّ هذا السور؟ Did the thief climb this fence?

٨ ــــــــــــــ منه الإتقان في العَمَل. We learned perfectionism in work from him.

٩ هل ــــــــــــــ عُطلَتنا الرائِعة في اليونان؟ Do you (fem.) remember our great holiday in Greece?

١٠ ــــــــــــــ المُتظاهِرات حين نَزَلَ المطَر.

The (female) demonstrators dispersed when the rain came down.

١١ يَجِب أن ــــــــــــــ بِسُرعة. It is necessary that we act quickly.

١٢ ماذا ــــــــــــــ من هذه الرِّحلة يا أَبنائي؟ What did you (masc. pl.) learn from this trip, my sons?

Form VI يَتَفاعَل

Form VI is not a common form but there are some verbs in general circulation. It is formed by adding تَ *ta-* in front of form III, and like form V is voweled with *fatḥa* throughout. Whereas form III often implies doing something with someone else, form VI usually carries the meaning of doing something together as a group.

Form III: to talk with someone	حادَث/يُحادِث
Form VI: to converse, to talk to each other	تَحادَث/يَتَحادَث
Form III: to discuss with someone	ناقَش/يُناقِش
Form VI: to discuss with each other/to debate	تَناقَش/يَتَناقَش
Form III: to fight with someone	قاتَل/يُقاتِل
Form VI: to fight each other	تَقاتَل/يَتَقاتَل

Form VI can sometimes also carry the meaning of being in a particular state.

to be/become lazy	تكاسَل/يَتَكاسَل
(from the root ك/س/ل connected with laziness)	

EXERCISE 16·5

Rewrite the sentences to match the new subject.

EXAMPLE   كُلّنا نَتَحادَث في هذا الأمر. We are all talking to each other about this matter.

كُلّهُم يَتَحادَثون في هذا الأمر.

١ إنهم يَتَحادَثون بلُغة ويلز. They are conversing in the Welsh language.

إنّنا ـــ.

٢ إنّ الجُيوش تَقاتَلَت في هذا الوادي. The armies fought each other in this valley.

إنّ الرجال ـــ.

٣ الأُسود تَتَكاسَل وتَنام بعد أن تَأكُل. Lions become lazy and sleep after they eat.

كَلبي ـــ.

٤ هذه الأسماك تَتَقاتَل على قِطعة الخُبز. These fish are fighting over the piece of bread.

هؤُلاء الأطفال _____.

٥ الأخان يَتَقاتَلان من أَجل المال. The two brothers are fighting each other for the sake of money.

الأُختان _____.

٦ الأُمم المُتَّحِدة تتناقش الآن في هذه المشكلة. The United Nations is debating this problem now.

المَجلِس _____.

٧ يا شَباب، هل تَحادَثْتُم في هذا المَشروع؟ Guys, did you talk to each other about this project?

يا شابّات _____.

٨ إنّ الناس يَتَكاسَلون في الحَرارة. People become lazy in the heat.

إنّني _____.

 **Forms VII, VIII, and X**

The three forms VII, VIII, and X are all characterized by an additional *kasra* carried by *alif* (اِ, *i-*) on the front of the past tense, and similar voweling patterns on both tenses. Form IX also shares some of these characteristics but is used rarely in modern Arabic.

Form VII يَنْفَعِل

Form VII has an additional *nūn* (ن) before the root, resulting in the past tense starting with the sound *in-*, and the present tense with *yan-* (*tan-*, *nan-*, etc.). In the majority of cases, the meaning is passive.

to be broken, to break	اِنْكَسَر/يَنْكَسِر
to be divided	اِنْقَسَم/يَنْقَسِم

The first vowel of the past tense and the final vowel of the present tense is *kasra*, but otherwise both tenses are voweled with *fatḥa*. The additional *nūn* (ن) carries a *sukūn*.

The branch of the tree was broken (off) in the storm.	اِنْكَسَر فَرع الشَّجَرة في العاصِفة.
The state is divided into northern and southern provinces.	تَنْقَسِم الدَّولة إلى مُحافَظات شَماليّة وجَنوبيّة.

The following table shows the conjugations for past and present tenses of the form VII verb اِنْكَسَر/يَنْكَسِر (*to be broken*).

	PAST TENSE	PRESENT TENSE
SINGULAR		
I أنا	اِنْكَسَرْتُ	أَنْكَسِر
you (masc.) أنتَ	اِنْكَسَرْتَ	تَنْكَسِر
you (fem.) أنتِ	اِنْكَسَرْتِ	تَنْكَسِرينَ
he/it (masc.) هُوَ	اِنْكَسَرَ	يَنْكَسِر
she/it (fem.) هِيَ	اِنْكَسَرْت	تَنْكَسِر

156

	PAST TENSE	PRESENT TENSE

PLURAL

	PAST TENSE	PRESENT TENSE
نَحنُ we	اِنْكَسَرْنا	نَنْكَسِر
أنتُم (masc. pl.)	اِنْكَسَرْتُـمْ	تَنْكَسِرونَ
أنتُنَّ (fem. pl.)	اِنْكَسَرْتُـنَّ	تَنْكَسِرْنَ
هُـم (they (masc.))	اِنْكَسَروا	يَنْكَسِرونَ
هُنَّ (they (fem.))	اِنْكَسَرْنَ	يَنْكَسِرْنَ

Some other verbs that fit into this passive category are:

to be reflected	اِنْعَكَس/يَنْعَكِس
to be turned over, to overturn	اِنْقَلَب/يَنْقَلِب
to be pulled out, to withdraw	اِنْسَحَب/يَنْسَحِب

EXERCISE

17·1

Choose one of the following verbs to fit in the gaps in the sentences.

اِنْسَحَبَ	تَنْكَسِر	يَنْقَسِمونَ	اِنْعَكَسَ	تَنْقَسِم
اِنْقَلَبَت	تَنْعَكِس	اِنْقَلَبَ		سَوف تَنْسَحِب

EXAMPLE تَنْعَكِس أشِعة الشَّمس على البُحَيرة

١ _____ المَركَب في العاصِفة.

٢ إنَّ الأولاد _____ إلى فَريقَين.

٣ _____ المُلاكِم بِسَبَب الجُرح.

٤ _____ ضَوء الفلاش في المِرآة.

٥ _____ الجُيوش من وَسَط المدينة غداً.

٦ _____ الشاحِنة في الطَّريق أمس.

٧ _____ الجَزيرة إلى دَولَتَين.

٨ _____ الأطباق في الحَفلات اليونانيّة.

A few form VII verbs are not so obviously passive, for example the verb:

to depart, to leave	اِنْصَرَف/يَنْصَرِف

Majid held a party to celebrate his graduation. The party went on until late, and his friend wants to know what time everyone left. Play the role of Majid and give your friend the information using the prompts. Remember to use the dual endings when referring to two people.

EXAMPLE جِدّي/8 :30 مساءً جِدّي اِنصَرَفَ الساعة الثامنة والنِصف مساءً.

١ جِدّتي/9 مساءً _____

٢ خالي مَمدوح/10:30 مساءً _____

٣ عَمّتي سارة/11 مساءً _____

٤ أبي وأمّي/11:30 مساءً _____

٥ أبناء سارة/1 صباحاً _____

٦ بَنات مَمدوح/1:30 صباحاً _____

٧ صَديقي يونِس/2 صباحاً _____

٨ صَديقتي مَها/2:30 صباحاً _____

٩ وَليد وماري/3 صباحاً _____

١٠ أنا/4 صباحاً! _____

Form VIII يَفْتَعِل

Form VIII is an important and common derived form. It is usually, but not always, intransitive but there is no consistent meaning pattern connected with it. Form VIII is formed by adding *ta'* (ت) *between* the second and third root letters. The voweling patterns are identical to form VII.

اِحْتَفَل/يَحْتَفِل (*to celebrate*) from the root ح/ف/ل

اِرْتَفَع/يَرْتَفِع (*to rise*) from the root ر/ف/ع

Can you identify the roots of these form VIII verbs and write them out with the voweling?

EXAMPLE احتفل/يحتفل to celebrate ح/ف/ل اِحْتَفَل/يَحْتَفِل

١ ابتسم/يبتسم to smile _____

٢ اجتمع/يجتمع to meet _____

٣ اجتهد/يجتهد work hard _____

٤ احترم/يحترم to respect _____

ه اقترب/يقترب to approach _____

٦ استمع/يستمع to listen _____

٧ اعتقد/يعتقد to believe/think _____

٨ انتظر/ينتظر to wait for _____

EXERCISE 17·4

Fill in the correct Arabic verb to match the English translation.

EXAMPLE   We approached the town before dark. اِقتَرَبْنا من المَدينة قَبلَ الظَّلام.

١ _____ أبي إلى الراديو. My father is listening to the radio.

٢ _____ المَبيعات في الشَّهر الماضي. Sales rose last month.

٣ هل _____ بعيد ميلادك غداً؟ Will you (masc.) celebrate your birthday tomorrow?

٤ المُوَظَّفون _____ المُفتِّش لِمُدّة ثلاث ساعات.
The employees waited for the inspector for three hours.

٥ _____ لِنَتَحَدَّث عن تَحسين الإنتاج. We met to talk about improving production.

٦ _____ زُمَلائي عَمَلي. My colleagues respect my work.

٧ _____ في شَرِكَتنا. We work hard in our company.

٨ هل _____ إلى اِقتراحاتي؟ Are you (fem. pl.) listening to my suggestions?

٩ _____ المدير حين _____ مِنهُ. The manager smiled when I approached.

١٠ _____ أنّها _____ ابنها. I think that she is waiting for her son.

EXERCISE 17·5

The manager of a factory has gathered all the employees together and is making a speech. Read the speech and then find the expressions that follow the speech.

اِبتَسَمَ المدير وقال للمُوَظَّفين:

"أعتقد أنكم تَتَساءَلون عَن سَبَب هذا الاِجتِماع. نحن نَجتَمِع اليوم يا زُمَلائي لِنَحتَفِل معاً بِنَجاح الشَّرِكة. ارتَفَعَت المَبيعات في العام الماضي، وتَرتَفِع هذا العام أيضاً. يَحتَرِم كلّ الوُكَلاء شَرِكَتنا، والتُّجّار في السوق يَنتَظِرون بَضائِعنا، وهذا يا زملائي لأنّكم تَجتَهِدون في عَمَلكم هنا. أنا أودّ أن يَزيد هذا النَّجاح، ولذلك أودّ أن أستَمِع إلى اِقتراحاتكُم لِتَحسين الإنتاج."

ابْتَسَمَ المدير the manager smiled

all the agents respect our company ١

_____

I want to listen to your suggestions ٢

_____

we are meeting today, colleagues, to celebrate ٣

_____

sales rose last year ٤

_____

the traders in the market are waiting for our goods ٥

_____

I want this success to increase ٦

_____

to improve production ٧

_____

and that, colleagues, is because you work hard ٨

_____

I think you are wondering ٩

_____

they are rising this year also ١٠

_____

Form X يَسْتَفْعِل

Form X is the last of the main derived forms. This form has two additional consonants before the root, *sīn* (س) and *tā'* (ت), resulting in the past tense starting with the sound *ista-*, and the present tense with *yasta-* (*tasta-*, *nasta-*, etc.). Form X often has the meaning of asking for or seeking something:

Form I: to know	عَلِمَ/ يَعْلَم
Form X: to seek to know, or to inquire	اِسْتَعْلَمَ/ يَسْتَعْلِم

It can also carry the meaning of considering something to have a certain attribute.

Form I: to be good	حَسُنَ/ يَحْسُن
Form X: to consider to be good, or to admire	اِسْتَحْسَنَ/ يَسْتَحْسِن

As with forms VII and VIII, the first vowel of the past tense and the final vowel of the present tense is *kasra*, but otherwise both tenses are voweled with *fatḥa*. The additional *sīn* (س) and the first root letter both carry a *sukūn*.

I admired the statue in the park.	اِسْتَحْسَنْتُ التِّمْثال في الحَديقة.
We will inquire about the times of the trains to Luxor.	سوف نَسْتَعْلِم عن مَواعيد القِطارات إلى الأقصُر.

The following table shows the conjugations for past and present tenses of the form X verb اِسْتَعْلَم/يَسْتَعْلِم (*to inquire*).

	PAST TENSE	PRESENT TENSE
SINGULAR		
I أنا	اِسْتَعْلَمْتُ	أَسْتَعْلِم
you (masc.) أنتَ	اِسْتَعْلَمْتَ	تَسْتَعْلِم
you (fem.) أنتِ	اِسْتَعْلَمْتِ	تَسْتَعْلِمين
he/it (masc.) هُوَ	اِسْتَعْلَمَ	يَسْتَعْلِم
she/it (fem.) هِيَ	اِسْتَعْلَمَتْ	تَسْتَعْلِم
PLURAL		
we نَحنُ	اِسْتَعْلَمْنا	نَسْتَعْلِم
you (masc. pl.) أنتُم	اِسْتَعْلَمْتُم	تَسْتَعْلِمونَ
you (fem. pl.) أنتُنَّ	اِسْتَعْلَمْتُـنَّ	تَسْتَعْلِمْنَ
they (masc.) هُم	اِسْتَعْلَموا	يَسْتَعْلِمونَ
they (fem.) هُنَّ	اِسْتَعْلَمْنَ	يَسْتَعْلِمْنَ

Common form X verbs

Common form X verbs include:

to receive (guests, etc.)	اِسْتَقْبَل/يَسْتَقْبِل
to admire	اِسْتَحْسَن/يَسْتَحْسِن
to use	اِسْتَخْدَم/يَسْتَخْدِم
to inquire	اِسْتَعْلَم/يَسْتَعْلِم
to enjoy	اِسْتَمْتَع/يَسْتَمْتِع
to extract	اِسْتَخْرَج/يَسْتَخْرِج
to be arrogant/proud	اِسْتَكْبَر/يَسْتَكْبِر

EXERCISE
17·6

Write the correct Arabic verb to match the English.

EXAMPLE   أَسْتَخْدِم I am using

_____ we enjoyed ١

_____ it (fem.) used ٢

_____ he inquired ٣

_____ you (fem.) admire ٤

_____ they (masc.) are extracting ٥

_____ she was arrogant ٦

_____ it (masc.) receives ٧

_____ you (masc. pl.) are inquiring ٨

_____ I admired ٩

_____ they (fem.) enjoy ١٠

_____ we received ١١

_____ they (masc.) are arrogant ١٢

The verb اِسْتَمْتَع/يَسْتَمْتِع (*to enjoy*) is followed by the preposition بِ, and the verb اِسْتَكْبَر/يَسْتَكْبِر (*to be arrogant/proud*) by the preposition على:

We enjoyed the visit to the palace.   اِستَمتَعنا بِزيارة القَصر.

He has been arrogant toward us since   إنّه يَستَكبِر عَلَينا مُنذُ أن أَصبَحَ قائِد الفَريق.
he became captain of the team.

EXERCISE
17·7

Change the subject of the sentence or question to that in parentheses.

EXAMPLE   اِستَقبَلَ السُّلطان الوَزير في قَصره أمس. (السلطانة) اِستَقبَلَت السلطانة الوَزير في قصرها أمس.

١ الطَّبّاخ في مَطْعَمنا يَستَخدِم زَيت الزَّيتون. (الطبّاخون)

_____

٢ سوف أَستَقبِل الضُّيوف عند الباب. (هي)

_____

٣ اِستَقبَل هذا المَطار ثلاثة مَلايين راكِب في العام الماضي. (هذه المَحَطّة)

_____

٤ هل اِستَخدَمتَ هذا البَرنامَج في عَمَلك؟ (أنتُم)

_____

٥ اِستَمتَعنا بزيارة البُرج والمَتحَف. (أنا)

_____

٦ إنّه يَستَكبِر عَلَينا مُنذُ أن رَبِحَ جائِزة المِليون دولار. (أنتَ)

_____

٧ اِنّهُم يَستَخرِجون البَترول والغاز الطَّبيعيّ من هذه الآبار (wells). (نحن)

_____

٨ اِستَعلَمَت المَرأة عن مَواعيد القِطارات. (الرَجُل)

_____

٩ إنّ الضيوف استَحسَنوا فُستان العَروس. (النِساء)

_____

١٠ هل تَستَخدِم الإنترنت في المَدرَسة؟ (أنتِ)

_____

Irregular verbs in the derived forms

Irregular (doubled, weak, or *hamzated*) roots also appear in the derived forms. The behavior of an irregular root in a derived form is largely a question of the voweling for that form, combined with the general rules that apply to the type of irregularity. For a particular irregularity in a particular form there may exist only a handful of verbs, and sometimes none at all in common circulation. Rather than list every single derived form for every irregularity this unit will concentrate on the general principles of how the irregularities behave and practice some of the most common irregular derived verbs.

Doubled verbs in the derived forms

Doubled verbs in the derived forms will follow essentially the same rules as the basic form:

- ◆ If the pattern for regular verbs requires a *sukūn* over the third root letter, the doubled root letters are written separately.
- ◆ If the pattern for regular verbs requires a *vowel* over the third root letter, the doubled root letters are written together.

Note: Look back at Chapters 5 and 11 for a fuller explanation of the general rule.

أَحَبّ/يُحِبّ (to like/to love)

One of the most common derived verbs with a doubled root is the form IV verb أَحَبّ/يُحِبّ (*to like/to love*). Compare this verb with the regular form IV verb أَرْسَل/يُرْسِل (*to send*):

he sent	أَرْسَلَ
he liked	أَحَبَّ
I sent	أَرْسَلْتُ
I liked	أَحْبَبْتُ
they (masc.) sent	أَرْسَلوا
they (masc.) liked	أَحَبّوا

she sends		تُرْسِل
she likes		تُحِبّ
they (fem.) send		يُرْسِلْنَ
they (fem.) like		يُحْبِبْنَ

The following table shows the full conjugations for past and present tenses of أَحَبّ/يُحِبّ (to like/to love). Notice only the feminine plurals of the present tense do *not* have a *shadda* over the doubled root, since they are the only parts of this tense that have a *sukūn* over the third root letter in the regular pattern.

	PAST TENSE	PRESENT TENSE
SINGULAR		
أنا I	أَحْبَبْتُ	أُحِبّ
you (masc.) أنتَ	أَحْبَبْتَ	تُحِبّ
you (fem.) أنتِ	أَحْبَبْتِ	تُحِبّـين
he/it (masc.) هُوَ	أَحَبّ	يُحِبّ
she/it (fem.) هِيَ	أَحَبَّتْ	تُحِبّ
PLURAL		
we نَحنُ	أَحْبَبْنا	نُحِبّ
you (masc. pl.) أنتُم	أَحْبَبْتُمْ	تُحِبّون
you (fem. pl.) أنتُنَّ	أَحْبَبْتُنَّ	تُحْبِبْنَ
they (masc.) هُم	أَحَبّوا	يُحِبّون
they (fem.) هُنَّ	أَحْبَبْنَ	يُحْبِبْنَ

EXERCISE 18·1

Amira's mother is organizing the food for a family party. She's worried about what the various guests like and dislike and is asking Amira for her opinion. What does Amira say about their food preferences? Follow the prompts.

EXAMPLE

سامي: الدجاج ✓ / الأرانِب ✗   أَعتَقِد أن سامي يُحِبّ الدجاج ولكنّه لا يُحِبّ الأرانِب.

(I believe that Sami likes chicken but he doesn't like rabbit.)

١ فاطمة: الأرانِب ✓ / البَطّ ✗

_____

٢ زوج فاطمة: الدَّجاج والبَطّ ✓ / السَّمَك ✗

_____

٣ مُنير: الأرُزّ ✓ / الكُسكُس ✗

_____

٤ زَوجة منير: البَطاطِس ✓ / الجَزَر ✗

_____

٥ أطفال فاطمة: البيتزا ✓ / الفَلافِل ✗

_____

٦ بنات منير: عَصير التُفاح ✓ / عَصير البُرتُقال ✗

_____

The party was a success and everyone liked something. Amira is telling her mother which dishes people liked the most. Follow the prompts and write what Amira is saying.

EXAMPLE سامي: الدَّجاج بالبَطاطِس <u>سامي أَحَبَّ الدَّجاج بالبطاطس.</u>

(Sami liked the chicken with potatoes.)

١ فاطمة: الأرانِب بالجَزَر

_____

٢ زَوج فاطمة: البَطّ بالكُسكُس

_____

٣ مُنير: السمك بالأرُزّ

_____

٤ زَوجة منير: الدجاج بالبطاطس

_____

٥ أطفال فاطمة: البيتزا وعَصير البرتقال

_____

٦ بنات منير: الفلافل وعَصير التُفاح

_____

٧ أنا: كُلّ المَأكولات!

_____

Other derived doubled verbs

Doubled verbs are regular in forms II and V, as the *shadda* required by these forms on the second root letter serves to separate it from the identical third root.

Form I: to reply	رَدّ/يَرُدّ
Form II: to repeat	رَدَّد/يُرَدِّد
Form V: to hesitate	تَرَدَّد/يَتَرَدَّد

Doubled verbs in the other derived forms follow the pattern for form IV (see the full conjugations for past and present tenses of أَحَبّ/يُحِبّ earlier in this chapter). The voweling will change depending on the particular form, but the principle of whether to write the doubled root together or separately remains the same:

Form X: to continue	اِسْتَمَرّ/يَسْتَمِرّ
he continued	اِسْتَمَرَّ
I continued	اِسْتَمْرَرْتُ
Form VIII: to occupy (land, etc.)	اِحْتَلّ/يَحْتَلّ
they occupied	اِحْتَلّوا
we occupied	اِحْتَلَلْنا

As with أَحَبّ/يُحِبّ, in the present tense the doubled root is written together, with the exception of the feminine plurals [see the section "أَحَبّ/يُحِبّ (*to like/to love*)" earlier in this chapter].

Common derived verbs with doubled roots include:

to prepare	أَعَدّ/يُعِدّ
to repeat	رَدَّد/يُرَدِّد
to cause	سَبَّب/يُسَبِّب
to decide	قَرَّر/يُقَرِّر
to hesitate	تَرَدَّد/يَتَرَدَّد
to occupy	اِحْتَلّ/يَحْتَلّ
to deserve	اِسْتَحَقّ/يَسْتَحِقّ
to continue	اِسْتَمَرّ/يَسْتَمِرّ
to extend	اِمْتَدّ/يَمْتَدّ

For each of the verbs listed, decide which derived form they represent and then write the past tense and present tense parts of the verb for "I."

EXAMPLE   أَحَبّ/يُحِبّ Form IV أُحِبّ (I like) أَحْبَبْتُ (I liked)

١ رَدَّد/يُرَدِّد _____

٢ اِحْتَلّ/يَحْتَلّ _____

٣ اِسْتَحَقّ/يَسْتَحِقّ _____

٤ سَبَّب/يُسَبِّب _____

٥ اِمْتَدّ/يَمْتَدّ _____

٦ أَعَدّ/يُعِدّ _____

٧ اِسْتَمَرّ/يَسْتَمِرّ _____

٨ تَرَدَّد/يَتَرَدَّد _____

٩ قَرَّر/يُقَرِّر _____

Ahmed and his wife, Nadia, can't agree on their favorite dishes. They are having an argument about it in the kitchen. Read their conversation and answer the following questions. The additional vocabulary will help you.

stubbornness عِناد	in danger في خَطَر
telephone receiver سَمّاعة الهاتِف	delicious شَهِيّ
beneficial مُفيد	great, fantastic رائِع

(أحمد يُحِبّ السمك، ولكن نادية زَوجَته تُحِبّ الدجاج. تُعِدّ نادية وَجبة دجاج وأحمد يَدخُل المَطبَخ.)

أحمد: إنّ زَواجنا في خَطَر. أنتِ تُعِدِّين أطباق الدجاج الشَّهِيّة كلّ يوم ولكنّك لا تَطبُخين السمك أبداً!

نادية: الحَقيقة هي أنّك لا تَستَحِقّ زوجة رائِعة مِثلي.

أحمد: من اليوم، أنا سَأَحتَلّ المطبخ وسَنَأكُل سمكاً كلّ يوم.

نادية: آسِفة. الزوجة تُقَرِّر ما يَحدُث في مطبخها. وأنا قَرَّرْتُ أنّنا سنأكل الدجاج.

أحمد: سمك.

نادية: أحمد، إن عِنادك سَيُسَبِّب لَك مَشاكِل كثيرة.

أحمد: سمك. سمك. سمك.

نادية: أحمد، لِماذا رَدَّدْتَ كلمة "سمك" ثلاث مَرّات؟ أنا قُلتُ دجاج!

أحمد: سمك.

(تَمتَدّ يَد نادية نحو سَمّاعة الهاتِف. أحمد يَتَرَدَّد قليلاً.)

أحمد: مَن سَتَطلُبين؟

نادية: سأطلب من أمّي أن تُساعِدنا في حَلّ هذه المشكلة.

أحمد: عُموماً، الدجاج لَذيذ ومُفيد. ألَيسَ كذلك يا حَبيبتي؟

(نادية تُرجِع سمّاعة الهاتف وتَبتَسِم لأحمد اِبتِسامة جَميلة.)

نادية: نعم يا حَبيبي. الدجاج لذيذ ومُفيد.

1. Who prefers chicken?

_____

2. Who prefers fish?

_____

3. What does Ahmed threaten to do?

_____

4. Who does Nadia think should be responsible for what happens in the kitchen?

_____

5. Why does Nadia's hand reach for the telephone receiver?

_____

6. What does Ahmed say about chicken in the end?

_____

7. How does Nadia react to Ahmed's endorsement of chicken?

_____

8. Who wins the argument?

_____

Weak verbs in the derived forms

Weak verbs (with و or ي as one of the root letters) behave in different ways in the derived forms depending on a combination of the particular weak letter and the pattern for the derived form. In certain derived forms, some types of weak verbs behave regularly, but in others the weak letter will change into a long or short vowel, as it tends to in the basic verb (form I). We will look at each type of weak verb in turn and at the basic principles that can be applied.

Assimilated verbs

Assimilated verbs are regular in the majority of the derived forms, with the weak initial root و or ي retaining its full consonantal sound throughout. For example:

Form II

to employ	وَظَّف/يُوَظِّف
to distribute	وَزَّع/يُوَزِّع
to save	وَفَّر/يُوَفِّر
to sign	وَقَّع/يُوَقِّع
to facilitate	يَسَّر/يُيَسِّر

Form III

to agree	وافَق/يُوافِق

Form V

to stop/to desist	تَوَقَّف/يَتَوَقَّف
to expect	تَوَقَّع/يَتَوَقَّع

Form VI

to agree together/to match	تَوافَق/يَتَوافَق

Form X

to import	اِسْتَوْرَد/يَسْتَوْرِد
to wake up	اِسْتَيْقَظ/يَسْتَيْقِظ

We woke up (from sleep) at nine o'clock.	اِسْتَيْقَظْنا من النوم الساعة التاسِعة.
The manager will sign the check after lunch.	سوف يُوَقِّع المدير الشيك بعد الغَداء.
I expect to win in the elections.	أَتَوَقَّع أن أفوز في الانتِخابات.
Did your mother agree to (agree on) your request?	هل وافَقَتْ أمّك عَلى طَلَبك؟
They walked to the cinema and saved the cost of the bus.	مَشوا إلى السينما وَوَفَّروا ثَمَن الباص.

Choose a verb from the list to complete the sentences.

وَقَّع	سَيُوَظَّف	تُوَزَّع	تَتَوافَق
تَتَوَقَّف	وافَقَ	أُوَفِّر	يَسَّرَ
	يَسْتَوْرِدون	نَتَوَقَّع	نَسْتَيْقِظ

EXAMPLE   بعد حِوار طويل، وافَقَ المدير على طلبي.

١ لا _____ من النوم يوم السبت قبل الساعة العاشرة.

٢ _____ السُّلطان الشيك بِنَفسه.

٣ _____ البَترول من السَّعوديّة والكُويت.

٤ يَجِب عليها أن _____ تَماماً عن التدخين.

٥ عِندهُم ثلاث شاحِنات _____ الصَّناديق على التُّجَار.

٦ _____ المَصنَع الجديد تسعة من شَباب القَرية.

٧ سأَذهَب بالدرّاجة إلى النادي و _____ تَكاليف السيّارة.

٨ الجسر الجديد _____ الوصول إلى الشاطئ الغربي.

٩ _____ أن نفوز في الانتخابات القادمة.

١٠ سأَلبَس قُبَّعة مُختَلِفة لأن هذه الألوان لا _____ .

Assimilated verbs in forms IV and VIII

The exceptions to this regularity are forms IV and VIII. In form IV, assimilated verbs behave regularly in the past tense, but display a long *ū* at the beginning of the present tense. In form VIII, the weak و or ي drops out altogether in both tenses, being replaced by a doubling of the additional *tā'*. Here is the root و/ص/ل in forms I, IV, and VIII:

Form I: to arrive	وَصَل/يَصِل
Form IV: to deliver/to connect	أَوْصَل/يُوصِل
Form VIII: to contact/communicate	اِتَّصَل/يَتَّصِل

The verb اِتَّصَل/يَتَّصِل is followed by بِ (with):

I contact my sister in Egypt over the Internet.	أَتَّصِل بأُختي في مِصر على الإنترنت.
Have you contacted the manager?	هل اِتَّصَلْتَ بالمُدير؟

Three more common assimilated verbs in forms IV and VIII are:

Form IV: to wake (someone) up	أَيْقَظ/يوقِظ
Form IV: to deposit	أَوْدَع/يودِع
Form VIII: to agree	اِتَّفَق/يَتَّفِق

Did you deposit the checks in my account?	هل أَوْدعْتِ الشيكات في حسابي؟
I agreed to the meeting in the school.	اِتَّفَقْتُ على الاجتِماع في المدرسة.
Every day we wake Ahmed up at seven o'clock.	كلّ يوم نوقِظ أحمد الساعة السابعة.

EXERCISE 18·6

Change these sentences and questions to refer to the future.

EXAMPLE   أَيْقَظنا نادية قبل الساعة السادِسة. سَنوقِظ نادية قبل الساعة السادِسة.

١ اِتَّفَقْنا على الاجتِماع في البنك. _____

٢ أَوْصَلَ المُهَندِسون أنابيب الماء إلى البُيوت. _____

٣ أَوْدَعَتْ نادية الشيكات في حِسابها. _____

٤ أَيْقَظْتَ أُسرَتي كلّها بِتِليفونك! _____

٥ اِتَّصَلْتُ بِمدير البنك في مَكتَبه. _____

٦ إنّ الأطفال أَوْصَلوا الكَلِمات والصُوَر. _____

٧ هل اِتَّفَقْتم على الحَفلة؟ _____

٨ إنّ النِساء اِتَّصَلْنَ بالمدرِّسة يوم الخميس. _____

Hollow verbs

Hollow verbs with و or ي as the middle root letter behave regularly in several of the derived forms. This is because the pattern for some derived forms (e.g., doubling the middle root or adding a long vowel after it) protects the consonantal value of the و or ي. Other derived forms display a long vowel in place of the middle root as for basic hollow verbs.

Hollow roots in forms II, III, V, and VI

Hollow verbs are regular in the forms II, III, V, and VI, with the weak middle root و or ي retaining its full consonantal sound throughout. For example:

Form II: to change/to alter	غَيَّر/يُغَيِّر
Form III: to try	حاوَل/يُحاوِل
Form V: to shop/to go shopping	تَسَوَّق/يَتَسَوَّق
Form VI: to get annoyed	تَضايَق/يَتَضايَق

They are changing the menu for the summer season.	إنّهم يُغَيِّرون قائِمة الطعام لِفَصل الصَّيف.
Nadia tried to answer all the questions.	حاوَلَتْ نادية أن تَرُدّ على كُلّ الأَسئِلة.
We shop together every Thursday.	نَتَسَوَّق معاً كلّ يوم خَميس.
I got a little annoyed with (from) my brother.	تَضايَقْتُ من أَخي قليلاً.

Translate the English sentences into Arabic.

EXAMPLE   أُحاوِل أَن أَرُدّ على الأَسئِلة. I am trying to answer the questions.

_____	Ahmed got annoyed with his sister a little. ١
_____	We changed the menu for the winter season. ٢
_____	When do you (masc. pl.) shop together? ٣
_____	Why did you (fem.) change the menu? ٤
_____	You (masc.) are not trying to answer the questions. ٥
_____	They (fem.) shopped together last Thursday. ٦
_____	I got annoyed with this music. ٧
_____	We (masc.) tried to answer these questions yesterday. ٨

Hollow roots in forms IV, VII, VIII, and X

Hollow verbs in forms IV, VII, VIII, and X follow the same general rules as in the basic form I (see "Hollow verbs" in Chapters 6 and 12).

- If the pattern for regular verbs requires a *vowel* over the third root letter, a long vowel appears instead of the middle root letter
- If the pattern for regular verbs requires a *sukūn* (˚) over the third root letter, the middle root letter changes to a short vowel

The voweling for form I hollow verbs depends on whether the middle root letter is و or ي. However, in the derived forms, the voweling depends on the pattern for the form itself and not on the middle root letter.

Forms IV and X are voweled with *fatḥa* over the middle root in the past tense, but *kasra* over the middle root in the present tense. A hollow verb in these forms will display *ā/a* in place of the middle root in the past tense, and *ī/i* in the present tense, no matter whether the original middle root was و or ي.

Form IV: to want/would like	أَراد/يُريد
Form X: to be able to/can	اِسْتَطاعَ/يَسْتَطيع
We wanted the fish but they wanted the chicken.	أَرَدْنا السَّمَك ولكنّهُم أَرادوا الدَّجاج.
I could visit my mother yesterday but I can't visit her today.	اِسْتَطَعْتُ زيارة أمّي أمس ولكنّي لا أسْتَطيع زيارتها اليوم.

The following table shows the full conjugations for past and present tenses of the form IV hollow verb أَراد/يُريد (*to want/would like*), showing how the vowel changes from long to short. This pattern will also work with form X.

	PAST TENSE	PRESENT TENSE
SINGULAR		
I أَنا	أَرَدْتُ	أُريد
you (masc.) أَنتَ	أَرَدْتَ	تُريد
you (fem.) أَنتِ	أَرَدْتِ	تُريدينَ
he/it (masc.) هُوَ	أَرادَ	يُريد
she/it (fem.) هِيَ	أَرادَتْ	تُريد
PLURAL		
we نَحنُ	أَرَدْنا	نُريد
you (masc. pl.) أَنتُم	أَرَدْتُـمْ	تُريدونَ
you (fem. pl.) أَنتُنَّ	أَرَدْتُـنَّ	تُرِدْنَ
they (masc.) هُـم	أَرادوا	يُريدونَ
they (fem.) هُنَّ	أَرَدْنَ	يُرِدْنَ

Amira is going to Paris. Her family members have asked her to bring back things for them.
Follow the prompts and write what everyone wants.

EXAMPLE أبو أَميرة: قَميص من الحرير (a silk shirt)

<u>أَبو أَميرة يُريد قَميصاً من الحَرير.</u> (Amira's father wants a silk shirt.)

١ أَمّ أَميرة: زُجاجة عِطر (a bottle of perfume) _____

٢ مُنير: حِزام من الجلد (a leather belt) _____

٣ زَوجة منير: قَلادة فَضِّيّة (a silver necklace) _____

٤ أطفال فاطمة: كُتُب فَرَنْسِيّة (French books) _____

٥ بنات منير: شكولاتة (chocolate) _____

٦ نادية وزَوجها: مَفْرَش من القُطن (a cotton tablecloth) _____

Hollow verbs in forms VII and VIII are similar to IV and X except that the past tense *and* the present tense displays *ā/a* in place of the middle root.

The following table shows the full conjugations for past and present tenses of the form VIII hollow verb اِحْتاج/يَحْتاج (*to need*).

	PAST TENSE	PRESENT TENSE
SINGULAR		
I أنا	اِحْتَجْتُ	أَحْتاج
you (masc.) أنتَ	اِحْتَجْتَ	تَحْتاج
you (fem.) أنتِ	اِحْتَجْتِ	تَحْتاجينَ
he/it (masc.) هُوَ	اِحْتاج	يَحْتاج
she/it (fem.) هِيَ	اِحْتاجَتْ	تَحْتاج
PLURAL		
we نَحنُ	اِحْتَجْنا	نَحْتاج
you (masc. pl.) أنتُم	اِحْتَجْتُمْ	تَحْتاجونَ
you (fem. pl.) أنتُنَّ	اِحْتَجْتُـنَّ	تَـحْتَجْنَ
they (masc.) هُم	اِحْتاجوا	يَحْتاجونَ
they (fem.) هُنَّ	اِحْتَجْنَ	يَحْتَجْنَ

The verb اِحْتاج/يَحْتاج is followed by the preposition إلى:

I needed the book yesterday.	اِحْتَجْتُ إلى الكِتاب أمس.
We don't need this problem.	لا نَحتاج إلى هذه المُشكِلة.

EXERCISE
18·9

Amira's friend, Maha, is looking at the list of Paris presents. Maha doesn't think that the recipients need all these items. Look back at Exercise 18.8 and give all of Maha's objections.

EXAMPLE   أبوكِ لا يَحتاج إلى قَميص من الحَرير! (Your father doesn't need a silk shirt!)

_____ ١

_____ ٢

_____ ٣

_____ ٤

_____ ٥

_____ ٦

EXERCISE
18·10

Put the hollow roots given into the pattern for the derived form shown. The meaning of the resulting verb is given in English.

EXAMPLE   ر/و/د form IV   to want   أَراد/يُريد

_____	to reply/respond	form IV	١ ج/و/ب
_____	to develop	form V	٢ ط/و/ر
_____	to frighten	form II	٣ خ/و/ف
_____	to choose	form VIII	٤ خ/ي/ر
_____	to imagine	form V	٥ ص/و/ر
_____	to hand over	form III	٦ ن/و/ل
_____	to add	form IV	٧ ض/ي/ف
_____	to rest	form X	٨ ر/و/ح

_____	to vote	form II	٩ ص/و/ت
_____	to marry	form V	١٠ ز/و/ج
_____	to manage/run	form IV	١١ د/و/ر
_____	to pollute/to contaminate	form II	١٢ ل/و/ث
_____	to be polluted/soiled	form V	١٣ ل/و/ث
_____	to help	form III	١٤ ع/و/ن
_____	to cooperate/help each other	form VI	١٥ ع/و/ن

EXERCISE

18·11

Fill in the correct Arabic verb to match the English translation, using one of the verbs in Exercise 18.10 in the proper place.

EXAMPLE

لا يُعاوِن سمير في البيت أبداً. Samir never helps in the house.

١ الأستاذ منير _____ المطعم وأنا أعمل فيه.

Mr. Munir manages the restaurant and I work in it.

٢ سـ _____ ابني بعد شَهرَين تَقريباً.

My son will marry after about 2 months.

٣ _____ الأحداث بِسُرعة.

Events developed quickly.

٤ _____ في لَيلة الامتِحان.

We rested on the night of the exam.

٥ _____ أنّها أحسن مُدرِّسة في العالَم.

She imagines that she is the best teacher in the world.

٦ _____ جميعاً في حَلّ هذه المُشكِلة.

We all cooperated in solving this problem.

٧ إنّ كل سُكّان القَريَة _____ لي في الانتِخابات.

All the residents of the village voted for me in the elections.

٨ كَلبك الكبير سـ _____ الأطفال.

Your large dog will frighten the children.

٩ لا _____ مِنه أن _____.

I don't want him to help (that he helps) me.

١٠ نُفايات هذه المَصانِع _____ البُحَيرة.

The waste from these factories has polluted the lake.

١١ سـ _____ البُحَيرة لِمُدّة طويلة.

The lake will be polluted for a long time.

١٢ _____ المَسامير وهو واقِف على الكُرسيّ.

I handed him the nails while he was standing on the chair.

١٣ هل _____ على كلّ الأَسئِلة؟

Did you (fem.) respond to all the questions?

١٤ لا، _____ أَسهَل الأسئِلة.

No, I chose the easiest questions.

١٥ _____ أن _____ الدجاج إلى السَلاطة.

We can add some chicken to the salad.

Defective verbs

Defective verbs, with و or ي as their final root letter, fall into three different categories in the basic form I (see "Defective verbs" in Chapters 6 and 12). However, all three types behave similarly in the derived forms.

Defective verbs in the derived forms are largely characterized by a final ى (alif maqsūra) in the past tense, and a final ي (ī) in the present tense.

Form IV: to give	أَعْطى/يُعْطي
Form VIII: to buy	اِشْتَرَى/يَشْتَري

They behave like the form I defective verb مَشَى/يَمْشِي (to walk) when the subject endings are added (see the table under "Defective verbs: Model 2" in Chapter 6).

I bought a white hat in the market.	اِشْتَرَيْتُ قُبّعة بَيضاء في السوق.
They (masc.) always buy a fresh cake.	يَشْتَرونَ دائماً كَعكة طازِجة.
We gave the manager the door key.	أَعطَيْنا المُدير مِفتاح الباب.
Will you (fem.) give the ticket to your mother?	هل سَتُعْطينَ التَذكِرة لأُمّك؟

EXERCISE 18·12

Decide which form the following defective verbs belong to.

EXAMPLE   *Form II* to sing غَنَّى/يُغَنِّي

١ لاقى/يُلاقي to meet _____

٢ اِنْتَهى/يَنْتَهي to finish/to be completed _____

٣ صَلّى/يُصَلّي to pray _____

٤ أَعْطَى/يُعْطي to give _____

٥ اِسْتَثْنى/يَسْتَثْني to exclude _____

٦ نادى/يُنادي to call out _____

٧ اِنْحَنى/يَنْحَني to bow/to bend _____

٨ سَمّى/يُسَمّي to name _____

٩ اِرْتَدى/يَرْتَدي to wear _____

١٠ أَنْهى/يُنْهي to finish (something)/to complete _____

EXERCISE 18·13

Write the correct Arabic verb to match the English.

EXAMPLE   تُغَنِّي she sings

١ I am meeting _____

٢ we named _____

٣ you (masc. pl.) bought _____

٤ you (fem.) are wearing _____

٥ they (masc.) are praying _____

٦ she excluded _____

٧ you (masc.) sang _____

٨ it (fem.) will finish/will be completed _____

٩ I will give _____

١٠ it (masc.) bends _____

١١ he finished/completed (something) _____

١٢ they (fem.) are calling (out) _____

Irregular verbs in the derived forms   **179**

Defective verbs behave slightly differently in forms V and VI in that *both* tenses are characterized by a final *alif maqsūra*. In the present tense, they behave like the defective verb نَسِيَ/يَنْسَى (*to forget*)—see "Defective verbs: Model 3" in Chapters 6 and 12.

Form V: to amuse yourself/be amused	تَسَلَّى/يَتَسَلَّى
Form V: to have lunch	تَغَدَّى/يَتَغَدَّى
Form V: to have dinner	تَعَشَّى/يَتَعَشَّى
Form V: to wish/to hope	تَمَنَّى/يَتَمَنَّى
Form VI: to meet up	تَلاقَى/يَتَلاقَى

She amused herself by eating popcorn.	تَسَلَّتْ بِأَكل الفِشار.
They never have lunch before one o'clock.	لا يَتَغَدَّوْنَ أَبداً قبل الساعة الواحدة.
We wish/hope to visit them soon.	نَتَمَنَّى أن نزورهُم قَريباً.
The friends met up at the club.	إنّ الأصدقاء تلاقَوْا في النادي.

Remember that when an attached pronoun is added to a final *alif maqsūra* (ى), it changes to a regular *alif* (ا):

He gave me the book.	أَعْطَاني الكتاب.
He bought it yesterday.	اِشتَراهُ أمس.

EXERCISE 18·14

What do these sentences mean?

EXAMPLE   كلّ يوم نَتَعَشَّى الساعة الثامِنة. *Every day we have dinner at 8 o'clock.*

١ عادَ زوجي من عَمَله وتَغَدَّى ثُمَّ نامَ.

_____

٢ يا خَليل، أَبوك يُنادي عَلَيك!

_____

٣ سَنُسَمِّي اِبنَتنا داليا لأنّه اِسم جَدَّتي.

_____

٤ أَعْطاني صَندوقاً صغيراً لِأمّي.

_____

٥ أَنْهَيْنا الاِمتِحانات وذَهَبنا إلى النادي.

_____

٦ يُصَلِّي أَنوَر في الجامِع الجديد.

_____

٧ إِنّها تُغَنّي وتَعزِف على العود والبيانو.

_____

٨ سَنُلاقي أصدقاءَنا أمام السينما.

_____

٩ تَسَلَّينا بِأَكل الفِشار ومُشاهَدة الأفلام.

_____

١٠ الأصدقاء تَعَشَّوْا معاً في مطعم السمك.

_____

١١ أَتَمَنَّى أن أزورَكُم في العام القادِم.

_____

١٢ يَتَلاقَى العُمّال في هذه الكافيتريا كلّ صباح.

_____

١٣ هل سَتَرتَدَيْنَ الفُستان الأصفَر الجديد؟

_____

١٤ سَأَشتَري قُبَّعة سَوداء من هذا المَحَلّ.

_____

١٥ اِنتَهَتْ سارة من كِتابة الرِّواية في ديسمبر.

_____

Hamzated verbs in the derived forms

As with basic form I, verbs with *hamza* (ء) as one of the root letters behave largely regularly in the derived forms, the main consideration being how to write the *hamza*. The general rules for writing *hamza* are given in Chapter 7.

The voweling for a particular derived form will determine how the *hamza* is written. For example, the vowel before the *first* root letter of form II present tense is *ḍamma* and so, in the case of a verb with initial root *hamza*, this will be written on *wāw* (ؤ):

he rents out   يُؤَجِّر

However, the vowel before the *third* root letter of form II present tense is *kasra*, and so, in the case of a verb with final root *hamza*, this will be written on *yā'* (ئ):

he congratulates   يُهَنِّئ

Verbs with *hamza* as the first root letter start with *madda* (آ) in the past tense of both forms III and IV. This is because the initial *hamza* combines with the *alif* before it in the case of form IV, and the *alif* after it in the case of form III:

Form III: he blamed	آخَذَ
Form IV: he believed in	آمَنَ

Common *hamzated* verbs in the derived forms

Derived *hamzated* verbs with *hamza* as a root letter include:

Form II: to influence	أَثَّر/يُؤَثِّر
Form II: to found/establish	أَسَّس/يُؤَسِّس
Form II: to confirm	أَكَّد/يُؤَكِّد
Form II: to congratulate	هَنَّأ/يُهَنِّئ
Form III: to blame	آخَذ/يُؤَاخِذ
Form III: to reward	كافَأ/يُكافِئ
Form IV: to believe in	آمَن/يُؤْمِن
Form IV: to hurt	آلَم/يُؤلِم
Form IV: to construct/establish	أنشَأ/يُنشِئ
Form V: to be influenced	تَأَثَّر/يَتَأَثَّر
Form V: to be late	تَأَخَّر/يَتَأَخَّر
Form VI: to wonder	تَساءَل/يَتَساءَل
Form VIII: to begin	إبتَدَأ/يَبتَدِئ
Form X: to rent	اِستَأجَر/يَستَأجِر

EXERCISE
18·15

Complete the English translation to match the Arabic.

EXAMPLE   I will _rent_ a car _tomorrow_. سَأَستَأجِر سيّارة غداً.

١ أكَّدتُ الحجز مع مُوَظَّفة الاِستِقبال في الصباح.

I _____ the reservation with the receptionist in the _____.

٢ لِماذا دائِماً تَتَأخَّرونَ؟

Why are you always _____?

٣ إنّ النِّساء تَأَثَّرنَ بِرِوايات نَجيب مَحفوظ في كِتاباتهنَّ.

The women were _____ by the novels of Naguib Mahfouz in their _____.

٤ اِبتَدَأَ الحَفل حين وَصَلَت العَروس.

The party _____ when the bride _____.

٥ وَقَفَ الضُّيوف في صَفّ وهَنَّأوا العَروس والعَريس.

The guests _____ in a row and _____ the bride and bridegroom.

٦ آخَذَني أبي لأنّي نَسِيتُ المِفتاح.

My father _____ me because I _____ the key.

٧ بَعضَ الناس يُؤمِنون أن المال يَجلِب السَّعادة.

Some people _____ that money brings _____.

٨ اِستَأجَرْنا شَقّة صغيرة تُطِلّ على البَحر.

We _____ a small apartment overlooking the _____.

٩ كافَأَني المَلِك وأعطاني هذا الوِسام.

The king _____ me and _____ me this sash.

١٠ هل تُؤلِمك رَقَبَتكِ حين تَجلِسين أمام الكومبيوتر؟

Does your neck _____ when you _____ in front of the computer?

١١ حاولَتْ أن تُؤَثِّر على القاضي في هذه القَضِية.

She tried to _____ the judge in _____ case.

١٢ أسَّسَ جَدّي الشَرِكة وأبي وأعمامي وَرَثوها عَنه.

My grandfather _____ the company and my father and uncles _____ it from him.

١٣ الفَراعِنة أنشَأوا الأهرامات مُنذُ آلاف السِّنين.

The Pharaohs _____ the pyramids _____ of years ago.

١٤ تَساءَلَتْ نادية عن سِرّ الزُّهور التي تَصِل كلّ يوم.

Nadia _____ about the secret of the flowers that _____ every day.

Use the vocabulary in Exercise 18.15 to translate the sentences and questions into Arabic.

EXAMPLE اِستَأجَروا سيّارة أمس. They (masc.) rented a car yesterday.

My neck is hurting me. ١

_____

My sister congratulated the bride and the groom. ٢

_____

The party will begin when my mother arrives. ٣

_____

Why did you (masc.) try to influence the judge? ٤

_____

We rewarded our son and gave him a bicycle. ٥

_____

My grandmother founded the company, and I inherited it from her. ٦

_____

I will rent a large apartment overlooking the park. ٧

_____

They (fem.) wondered about the secret of the pyramids. ٨

_____

The pharaohs believed in the power (قُدرة) of the stars. ٩

_____

The king will construct his new palace here. ١٠

_____

I blamed her because she forgot the book. ١١

_____

Ahmed was late and so we didn't go to the cinema. ١٢

_____

Have you (fem.) confirmed the reservation? ١٣

_____

Were you (masc. pl.) influenced by his wealth? ١٤

_____

MOODS OF THE VERB AND VERBAL NOUNS

Variations can occur to the present tense verb in certain situations. Grammarians often call these variations "moods of the verb." The two moods you need to know in Arabic are the *subjunctive* (المُضارِع المَنصوب) and the *jussive* (المُضارِع المَجزوم)—on which the *imperative* used for commands and instructions is also based. Only in a minority of cases do these moods affect the way a verb is written or generally pronounced. However, you do need to know the whole story; otherwise you cannot understand or work out the changes that occur in this significant minority.

In addition, this part looks at how to form and use verbal nouns (*swimming, conversation, teaching,* etc.). Arabic verbal nouns are very important and are used more frequently than their English equivalents.

The subjunctive

19

The *subjunctive* (المُضارِع المَنصوب) is the first of the two important Arabic variations or "moods" of the present tense. It is often used for a second verb whose meaning has been modified in some way. The subjunctive has some important differences from the standard present tense.

Formation of the subjunctive

For regular verbs, the subjunctive is very similar to the standard present tense. This is also true of the derived forms.

The most significant change is that when the standard present tense ends in ن (*nūn*), this is dropped in the subjunctive. This affects the masculine plural ending ونَ (-*ūna*), the feminine ينَ (-*īna*) used for أَنتِ, and the dual ending انِ (-*āni*). Only the feminine plural ending نَ (-*na*) remains unaffected.

Less significantly, the final (often unpronounced) *ḍamma* that ends many parts of the standard present tense (see "Present tense formation" in Chapter 9) changes to a *fatḥa* in the subjunctive. In other words يَجلِسُ (*yajlisu*) becomes يَجلِسَ (*yajlisa*). As both these alternatives are usually written without vowels and pronounced يَجلِس (*yajlis*), you would not normally notice the change.

Irregular verbs do not stray much from the rules for regular verbs in the subjunctive. There are some minor differences in defective verbs—those that end in ي ـ (*ī*) or و ـ (*ū*) in the standard present tense, will end in يَ ـ (*iya*) or وَ ـ (*uwa*) in the subjunctive (if fully pronounced). Defective verbs that end in ى (*ā*) do not change.

The following table shows the subjunctive for the regular verb يَجلِس *yajlis* (*sits*), including the dual parts:

	PREFIX/ SUFFIX	EXAMPLE
SINGULAR		
I أَنا	أَ ـ	أَجْلِس*
you (masc.) أَنتَ	تَ ـ	تَجْلِس*
you (fem.) أَنتِ	تَ ـ/ي	تَجْلِسي
he/it (masc.) هُوَ	يَ ـ	يَجْلِس*
she/it (fem.) هِيَ	تَ ـ	تَجْلِس*

(continued)

	PREFIX/SUFFIX	EXAMPLE
DUAL		
you (dual) أنتُما	تَـ/ا	تَـجْلِسا
they (masc. dual) هُما	يَـ/ا	يَجْلِسا
they (fem. dual) هُما	تَـ/ا	تَـجْلِسا
PLURAL		
we نَحنُ	نَـ	نَـجْلِس*
you (masc. pl.) أنتُم	تَـ/وا	تَـجْلِسوا†
you (fem. pl.) أنتُنَّ	تَـ/نَ	تَـجْلِسْنَ
they (masc.) هُم	يَـ/وا	يَجْلِسوا†
they (fem.) هُنَّ	يَـ/نَ	يَجْلِسْنَ

*These parts of the present verb include a final *fatḥa* (أَجْلِسَ *ajlisa*, I sit; يَشْرَبَ *yashraba*, he drinks, etc.). However, this final vowel is only pronounced in more formal Modern Standard Arabic.

†The masculine plurals have an extra *alif* in the subjunctive. As with the past tense, this *alif* is silent (see "Past tense formation and uses" in Chapter 4).

EXERCISE 19·1

Write out all the parts of the subjunctive for the verb يَسْكُن *(yaskun, lives), following the example in the preceding table. Include the more formal final vowels.*

EXAMPLE   أَسْكُنَ أنا /

Singular ١

_____

_____

_____

_____

_____

Dual ٢

_____

_____

_____

_____

_____

_____

_____

_____

Uses of the subjunctive

The subjunctive is used when verbs follow particular words (or *particles*, as they are sometimes called).

أن + subjunctive

The most common particle requiring the subjunctive is probably أن *an* (*to*). The structure أن + *subjunctive* is used frequently in Arabic to add a second verb after an initial modifying verb, where in English we would use the infinitive (e.g., *can't go* or *want to vote*), for example after verbs such as:

to be able	إستَطاع/يَستَطيع
to want	أراد/يُريد، وَدَّ/يَوَدّ
to hope	أمَل/يَأمَل
to order, command	أمَرَ/يَأمُر
to request	رَجا/يَرجو
to wish	تَـمَنّى/يَتَمَنّى

The structure أن + *subjunctive* is also used after expressions such as:

it is necessary	يَجِب
it appears	يَبدو
it is possible	من المُمكِن

I live in an apartment near my mother's house.	أسكُن في شقّة قَريبة من بيت أمّي.
I'd like to live (that I live) in an apartment near my mother's house.	أريد أنْ أسكُن في شقّة قَريبة من بيت أمّي.
They go to the cinema every week.	يَذهَبونَ إلى السينما كلّ أُسبوع.
They can't go (that they go) today.	لا يَستَطيعون أنْ يَذهَبوا اليوم.

Are you (fem.) leaving now?	هل تُغادِرين الآن؟
Do you have to leave (that you leave) now?	هل يَجِب أَن تُغادِري الآن؟
You (masc. pl.) are listening to him.	تَستَمِعون إلَيه
The singer is requesting you to listen (that you listen) to him.	يَرجو المُغَنّي مِنكم أن تَستَمِعوا إلَيه.

Rewrite the sentences and questions with the opening expressions.

EXAMPLE

يَسكُنونَ في شقّة قَريبة من المدرسة.

يُجبّرون أن <u>يسكنوا في شقّة قريبة من المدرسة.</u>

١ أَلعَب التنس كلّ يوم.

لا أَستَطيع أن ــ.

٢ تَترُكونَ الحَقائِب عَند الباب.

يَجِب أن ــ.

٣ نَزور أمّنا قبل السَفَر.

أَمَلنا أن ــ.

٤ هل تَركَبين دَرّاجَتكِ في الحَديقة؟

هل تَوَدّينَ أن ــ؟

٥ أزورهُم قَريباً.

أَتَمَنّى أن ــ.

٦ يَرجَع إلى البيت للغداء.

يَجِب أن ــ.

٧ يَحضُران اِجتِماعاً يوم الخَميس.

يَجِب أن ــ.

٨ يَنامونَ الساعة التاسعة.

طَلَبتُ مِنهم أن ــ.

٩ يَجلِسنَ على الأرض.

رَجَوْنا مِنهُنَّ أن ــ.

١٠ يُنَظِّمون لَها حَفلة.

يَوَدّون أن ــ.

١١ نَتَّصِل بِمدير البنك.

يَجِب أن ــ.

١٢ مَتى تَتَزَوَّجان؟

مَتى تُريدان أن ــ.

When أَنْ is followed by a negative verb with لا, the combination becomes أَلّا:

We'd like not to go to the market today.	نُريد أَلّا نَذهَب إلى السوق اليوم.
They hope not to change the menu.	يأمَلونَ أَلّا يُغَيِّروا قائمة الطعام.
I tried not to get annoyed with my brother.	حاوَلتُ أَلّا أَتَضايَق من أَخي.
Is it possible that you (masc. pl.) don't study math?	هل من المُمكِن أَلّا تَدرُسوا الرِّياضيّات؟

EXERCISE
19·3

Rewrite the following sentences, making the verb after أَنْ negative.

EXAMPLE آمَل أَنْ أذهب إلى السوق. <u>آمَل أَلّا أذهب إلى السوق.</u>

١ يَجِب أن تُغادِري الآن، يا نادية. ــ

٢ أَمَرَتْني أمّي أن أُساعِد أَخي. ــ

٣ يأمَلونَ أن يناموا بَعد الظُّهر. ــ

٤ حاوَلوا أن يَتَضايَقوا من أُختهم. ــ

٥ هل من المُمكِن أن أشتَري السيّارة؟ ــ

٦ نرجو منكُما أن تَستَمِعا إلى الراديو. ــ

٧ طَلَبتُ منه أن يَجلِس على الأرض. ــ

٨ أتمَنّى أن تجدوا الكَنز المَدفون. ــ

"in order to"/"so that"

Other common particles that are followed by the subjunctive include:

to/in order to	لِ
in order to	لِكَيْ
so that	حَتّى*

―――――――

*Also means "until." The subjunctive is only used when حَتّى means "so that."

We went to the market to buy vegetables.	ذَهَبنا إلى السوق لِنَشتَري خُضاراً.
They (masc.) waited for two hours in order to enter the club.	اِنتَظَروا لِمُدّة ساعتَين لِكَيْ يَدخُلوا النادي.
Are you (fem.) working now so that you (can) go out in the evening?	هل تَعمِلينَ الان حتّى تَخرُجي في المَساء؟

Fill in the gaps with the correct part of the subjunctive verb to match the English translation.

EXAMPLE

ذَهَبتُ إلى المَطار لِأَستَقبِل أُمّي.

I went to the airport to meet my mother.

١ تَرَكَ نادِر دُروسه لِ _____ كُرة القَدَم في النادي.

Nadir left his studies to play soccer in the club.

٢ هل تَرجِعينَ لِ _____ اِبنَتك؟

Are you (fem.) returning to help your daughter?

٣ سَأَحتاج إلى سُلَّم وَحَبل لكي _____ الشَّجَرة.

I will need a ladder and a rope in order to climb the tree.

٤ عادوا إلى نَفس المَحَلّ لكي _____ واحِدة أُخرى.

They (masc.) returned to the same shop in order to buy one more.

٥ سَأَخذك مَعي إلى الشاطِئ حتّي _____ السِّباحة.

I will take you to the beach so that you learn (how) to swim.

٦ سَنَنتَظِر بِجوار الباب حتّي _____ مَن سَيَدخُل.

We will wait near the door so that we observe who will come in.

٧ هل فَتَحتُنَّ الصَّندوق لِ _____ ما بِداخِله؟

Did you (fem. pl.) open the box in order to know what is inside it?

٨ تَرَكتُها على نار هادِئة حتّي لا _____ .

I left it on a low flame so that it doesn't burn.

٩ كَتَبوا خِطاباً لِ _____ الوَزير على اِهتِمامه.

They (masc.) wrote a letter to thank the minister for his concern.

١٠ خَلَعْنا أَحذِيَتنا حتّي لا _____ ـنا أُمّي.

We took off our shoes so that my mother doesn't hear us.

١١ هل عُدْتُم إلى هُنا لكي ــــــــــــــــــــــــ ني مَعكُم؟

Did you (masc. pl.) return here in order to take me with you?

١٢ نادية وابراهيم ذَهَبا إلى المَطار لِـ ــــــــــــــــــــــــ أحمد.

Nadia and Ibrahim went to the airport to meet Ahmed.

Future tense negative with لَنْ

The future tense is indicated in Arabic by adding سَ or سَوفَ to a present tense verb (see Chapter 10). However, the future tense negative is formed using the structure لَنْ + *subjunctive*.

I will write a letter to the manager.	سَوفَ أَكتُب خِطاباً للمُدير.
I won't write a letter to the manager.	لَنْ أَكتُب خِطاباً للمُدير.
They will travel by private plane.	سَيُسافرون بِطائرة خاصّة.
They won't travel by private plane.	لَنْ يُسافِروا بِطائرة خاصّة.
You (fem.) will find the ring.	سَتَجِدينَ الخاتِم.
You (fem.) will never find the ring.	لَنْ تَجِدي الخاتِم أبداً.

EXERCISE
19·5

Make these sentences negative.

EXAMPLE سَوفَ يَخرُجونَ اليوم. لَنْ يَخرُجوا اليوم.

١ سَأَدرُس الهَندَسة في الجامِعة. ــ

٢ سَيَزورون المَزرَعة. ــ

٣ سوف أَقُصّ شَعري. ــ

٤ سَتَدفَعينَ أكثر من خمسة، يا سميرة. ــ

٥ سَتَسمَع أُختي نَصيحَتي. ــ

٦ سَتذهبونَ إلى الشاطِئ غداً. ــ

٧ سَنبدأ قبل الساعة الخامسة. ــ

٨ سَيملأون حمّام السباحة بالماء. ــ

٩ سَيُخَوِّف كَلبك الأطفال. ــ

١٠ سَيُوَقِّع المَلِك هذه الرِّسالة. ــ

١١ سَتُعِدّينَ العَقد قَبلَ يَوم الخَميس. ــ

١٢ سوف تَكونونَ أصدِقاء بَعدَ اليوم. _____

١٣ سَتَحتَفل بعيد ميلادك غداً. _____

١٤ أبي وأمّي سوف يَستَقبِلان الضُيوف عند الباب. _____

١٥ ستَعود ماري إلى زَوجها. _____

١٦ سوف يَبيعونَ السَّمَك هنا. _____

١٧ سَتُعِدّينَ الدجاج. _____

١٨ سَيُسَبِّب لَك مَشاكِل. _____

١٩ سوف يُفَتِّشونَ المَطعَم المَوجود بِجانِب النَّهر. _____

٢٠ أنتُما سوف تكونان مُهِمَّين في حَياتنا. _____

The jussive

20

The second variation or "mood" of the present tense is the *jussive*. The jussive mood has some important uses and its formation has a greater impact on the spelling of verbs than the subjunctive.

Formation of the jussive: Regular verbs

As with the subjunctive, the final ن (*nūn*) of the endings ونَ (-*ūna*), ينَ (-*īna*), and انِ (-*āni*) is dropped in the jussive. Only the feminine plural ending نَ (-*na*) remains unaffected.

Importantly, the final (often unpronounced) *ḍamma* of the present tense (see "Present tense formation" in Chapter 9) that changes to *fatḥa* in the subjunctive, in turn changes to *sukūn* (ْ) in the jussive. So يَجْلِسُ (*yajlisu*) becomes يَجْلِسْ (*yajlis*). However, in the case of regular verbs, whether basic form I or derived, there is no difference in the basic spelling, and the change is not normally noticeable. *Hamzated* and assimilated verbs also generally behave regularly in the jussive.

The following table shows the jussive for the regular verb يَجْلِس (*yajlis*), sits, including the dual parts:

	PREFIX/SUFFIX	EXAMPLE
SINGULAR		
I أنا	أَ	أَجْلِسْ
you (masc.) أنتَ	تَـ	تَجْلِسْ
you (fem.) أنتِ	تَـ/ي	تَجْلِسي
he/it (masc.) هُوَ	يَـ	يَجْلِسْ
she/it (fem.) هِيَ	تَـ	تَجْلِسْ
DUAL		
you (dual) أنتُما	تَـ/ا	تَجْلِسا
they (masc. dual) هُما	يَـ/ا	يَجْلِسا
they (fem. dual) هُما	تَـ/ا	تَجْلِسا

(continued)

195

	PREFIX/ SUFFIX	EXAMPLE
PLURAL		
نَحنُ we	نَـ	نَجْلِسْ
أنتُم (.you (masc. pl	تَـ/وا	تَـجْلِسوا
أنتنَّ (.you (fem. pl	تَـ/نَ	تَـجْلِسْنَ
هُم (.they (masc	يَـ/وا	يَجْلِسوا
هُنَّ (.they (fem	يَـ/نَ	يَجْلِسْنَ

EXERCISE
20·1

Write out all the parts of the jussive for the verb يَستَمِع *(listens), following the example in the preceding table. Include any final* sukūn.

EXAMPLE   أَسْتَمِعْ أَنا /

Singular ١

_____

_____

_____

_____

_____

Dual ٢

_____

_____

_____

Plural ٣

_____

_____

_____

_____

_____

Uses of the jussive

The jussive has three main uses in modern Arabic. Two of the uses are covered in this chapter. The third use (to form imperatives) is covered separately in Chapter 21.

فَلْ + jussive

The jussive can be used after the particle فَلْ (or less commonly لَـ) to mean "(so) let's." Notice that فَلْ is joined to the verb that follows it:

Let's start!	فَلْنَبْدَأْ!
The weather is sunny, so let's go to the park.	الطَّقس مُشمِس فَلْنَذهَبْ إلى الحَديقة.

EXERCISE
20·2

Ibrahim is out for the day with his family. He's in a good mood and making lots of suggestions about what they could do. Make suggestions following the prompts.

EXAMPLE الطَّقس مُشمِس/يَذهَب إلى حَديقة الحَيَوانات

الطَّقس مُشمِس فَلْنَذهَبْ إلى حَديقة الحَيَوانات.

١ الطَّقس حارّ/يأكُل آيس كريم

_____

٢ الحَديقة واسِعة/يلعَب كُرة القَدَم

_____

٣ المَنظَر جَميل/يأخُذ صورة

_____

٤ النَّهر هادِئ/يركَب قارِباً

_____

٥ هذه السَّندَويتشات لَذيذة/يَرجَع هُنا للغداء

_____

٦ هذه الحَقائِب رَخيصة/يدخل المَحَلّ

_____

٧ السينما قريبة/يُشاهِد الفيلم الجديد

_____

٨ لا أعرِف الطَّريق إلى السينما/يسأَل الشُّرطيّ

_____

Past tense negative with لَمْ

There are two ways to form the past tense negative in Arabic. The simplest way is to add ما in front of a past tense verb (see "Forming the past tense negative with ما" in Chapter 4). This is common in classical texts and spoken Arabic, but modern standard Arabic tends to use the structure لَمْ + *jussive*:

He didn't drink the milk.	لَمْ يَشرَبْ الحَلِيب. (= ما شَرِبَ الحَلِيب.)
They (masc.) didn't go to the market yesterday.	لَمْ يَذهَبوا إلى السوق أمس. (= ما ذَهَبوا إلى السوق أمس.)
I didn't see that program.	لَمْ أُشاهِدْ ذلك البَرنامَج. (= ما شاهَدْتُ ذلك البَرنامَج.)
You didn't (fem.) celebrate your birthday.	لَمْ تَـحتَفِلي بـعيد ميلادك. (= ما احتَفَلْتِ بـعيد ميلادك.)

EXERCISE 20·3

Twins Shukri and Nadia have completely different memories of a childhood family outing to the seaside. Play the part of Shukri and contradict Nadia's memories, using لَمْ + jussive and the prompts in parentheses.

EXAMPLE سافَرْنا بالسّيارة. (بالباص) لم نُسافِرْ بالسيّارة، سافَرْنا بالباص.

١ ذَهَبْنا إلى البَحر الأحمَر. (البَحر المُتَوَسِّط)

_____

٢ ذَهَبَتْ جِدَّتنا معنا. (خالَتنا)

_____

٣ تَسَلَّقَ أبونا جَبَلاً. (بُرجاً)

_____

٤ انْكَسَرَتْ آلة التَّصوير. (مَظَلّة الشَّمس sun umbrella)

_____

٥ غادَرْنا بعد الغَداء. (العَشاء)

_____

٦ رَكِبْتُ جَمَلاً. (حِماراً)

_____

٧ لَعِبْتَ كُرة القَدَم. (الكُرة الطائِرة volleyball)

_____

٨ أبونا وأمّنا طَبَخا سَمَكاً على الشاطئ. (دَجاجاً)

_____

EXERCISE 20·4

Rewrite the sentences using لَمْ *+ jussive.*

EXAMPLE ما طَلَبْنا هذه المَشروبات. لم نَطلُبْ هذه المَشروبات.

١ ما خَرَجَ المُدير من المَكتَب. _____

٢ ما سَكَنَتْ سَميرة في هذا الشارِع. _____

٣ ما عَرَفوا سَبَب هذا الإجتِماع. _____

٤ ما نَظَّفْتُم الأرض جَيِّداً. _____

٥ ما تَعَلَّمْتِ من أخطائِك. _____

٦ ما رَكِبْتُ سيّارة بهذه السُّرعة في حَياتي. _____

٧ ما تَحَدَّثْنا في هذا المَوضوع أمام الأولاد. _____

٨ ما تَذَكَّرْتِ عيد ميلادي! _____

٩ ما ضَحِكَ المُشاهِدون كَثيراً. _____

١٠ ما صَلَّحْتَ هذه المائِدة المَكسورة. _____

١١ لِماذا ما طَبَخْتُنَّ السمكة؟ _____

١٢ البَنات ما اِستَمتَعْنَ بِزيارة القَصر القَديم. _____

١٣ أَكَل الرِّجال وما دَفَعوا الحِساب. _____

١٤ ما شَكَرتُ صَديقي على الهَدِية. _____

١٥ ما اِنصَرفوا لكنّني ما طَلَبْتُ الشُّرطة. _____

١٦ وَردة وأحمد ما تَحادَثا معي في مَوضوع زَواجِهما. _____

Irregular verbs in the jussive

The final *sukūn* of the jussive can fundamentally affect irregular verbs, since the formation of some types is governed by whether there is a *sukūn* over the final root letter. *Hamzated*, doubled, and assimilated verbs generally behave as regular verbs in the jussive, but hollow and defective verbs need special attention.

Doubled verbs

The rule affecting whether the identical root letters are written separately or together in a doubled verb is generally connected with the vowel over the third root letter in a regular verb:

- *Sukūn* over third root letter of regular verb = second and third root letters written *separately* in doubled verb
- Vowel over third root letter of regular verb = second and third root letters written *together* in doubled verb

Therefore, strictly speaking, the *sukūn* that characterizes much of the jussive means that the second and third root letters should be written separately in most parts of the jussive with يَشُكّ (*yashukk*), "he doubts," becoming يَشْكُكْ (*yashkuk*) in the jussive. However, in modern Arabic this rarely happens and the jussive of a doubled verb is normally written in the same way as the standard present tense.

The following table shows the jussive for the doubled verb يَشُكّ (*yashukk*), "doubts," including the dual parts.

	PREFIX/ SUFFIX	EXAMPLE
SINGULAR		
أنا I	أَ	أَشُكّ
أنتَ you (masc.)	تَـ	تَشُكّ
أنتِ you (fem.)	تَـ/ي	تَشُكّي
هُوَ he/it (masc.)	يَـ	يَشُكّ
هِيَ she/it (fem.)	تَـ	تَشُكّ
DUAL		
أنتُما you (dual)	تَـ/ا	تَشُكّا
هُما they (masc. dual)	يَـ/ا	يَشُكّا
هُما they (fem. dual)	تَـ/ا	تَشُكّا
PLURAL		
نَحنُ we	نَـ	نَشُكّ
أنتُم you (masc. pl.)	تَـ/وا	تَشُكّوا
أنتُنَّ you (fem. pl.)	تَـ/نَ	تَشْكُكْنَ
هُم they (masc.)	يَـ/وا	يَشُكّوا
هُنَّ they (fem.)	يَـ/نَ	يَشْكُكْنَ

EXERCISE
20·5

Write out all the parts of the jussive for the doubled verb يَرُدّ (answers, replies), following the example in the preceding table.

EXAMPLE   أَرُدّ أنا /

Singular ١

_____

_____

_____

_____

_____

Dual ٢

_____

_____

_____

Plural ٣

_____

_____

_____

_____

EXERCISE
20·6

Translate these questions and sentences into Arabic using the jussive.

EXAMPLE   لَمْ أَرُدّ على الهاتِف I didn't answer the telephone.

Why didn't you (masc.) answer the telephone? ١

_____

The boy didn't answer his mother. ٢

_____

Let's answer the letter. ٣

_____

Why didn't you (fem.) answer yesterday? ٤

_____

Let's reply to the invitation. ٥

_____

I asked the girls but they didn't answer. ٦

_____

Let's answer the telephone. ٧

_____

They (masc.) didn't answer because they were in the garden. ٨

_____

Rewrite the sentences and questions using لَمْ + jussive. (Refer to "Common basic doubled verbs" in Chapter 5 and "Doubled verbs in the derived forms" in Chapter 18 for meanings.)

EXAMPLE   ما أَحَبَّ أحمد السمك. <u>لم يُحِبّ أحمد السمك.</u>

١ ما مَرَّت الطائرة فوق أسبانيا. _____

٢ ما بَثَّت المَحَطّة هذا الخَبَر أمس. _____

٣ ما أَحَبَّتْ سميرة الفَلافِل. _____

٤ ما عَدَدْنا الضُّيوف عند الباب. _____

٥ لِماذا ما قَصَصْتِ شَعرك؟ _____

٦ ما غَيَّرْنا قائمة الطَّعام. _____

٧ ما ضَمَّني المُدَرِّب للفَريق. _____

٨ ما اِستَحَقّوا كلّ تلكَ المَشاكِل. _____

٩ أبي وأمّي ما أَعَدّا الحَقيبة للسَّفَر. _____

١٠ لِماذا ما رَدَدْتَ؟ _____

Hollow verbs

Hollow verbs (with و or ي as the second root letter) change significantly in the jussive. These changes affect both the pronunciation and the spelling. The basic rules for hollow verbs are:

- *Sukūn* over third root letter = short vowel in the middle of hollow verb
- Vowel over third root letter = long vowel in the middle of hollow verb

A hollow verb in the standard present tense or in the subjunctive usually has a long vowel in the middle since, except for the relatively uncommon feminine plurals, the third root letter has a vowel over it (even if this is not generally pronounced), for example: يَزورُ *yazūr(u)*, "he visits" (or يَزورَ *yazūr[a]* in the subjunctive). In the jussive, however, the third root letter has a *sukūn* over it, so the vowel in the middle becomes shortened to *ḍamma*: يَزُرْ *yazur*. The following table shows the complete jussive for this hollow verb, including the dual parts.

	PREFIX/SUFFIX	EXAMPLE
SINGULAR		
I أنا	أ	أَزُرْ
you (masc.) أنتَ	تَ	تَزُرْ
you (fem.) أنتِ	تَ/ي	تَزوري
he/it (masc.) هُوَ	يَ	يَزُرْ
she/it (fem.) هِيَ	تَ	تَزُرْ

	PREFIX/SUFFIX	EXAMPLE
DUAL		
you (dual) أنتُما	تَـ/ا	تَزورا
they (masc. dual) هُما	يَـ/ا	يَزورا
they (fem. dual) هُما	تَـ/ا	تَزورا
PLURAL		
we نَحنُ	نَـ	نَزُرْ
you (masc. pl.) أنتُم	تَـ/وا	تَزوروا
you (fem. pl.) أنتُنَّ	تَـ/نَ	تَزُرْنَ
they (masc.) هُم	يَـ/وا	يَزوروا
they (fem.) هُنَّ	يَـ/نَ	يَزُرْنَ

You can apply the same principle to all hollow verbs, whether basic and derived, except that a long *ā* in the standard present tense becomes *fatḥa* in the jussive and a long *ī* becomes *kasra*:

Form I (to fly)
standard present tense   يَطير

jussive   يَطِرْ

Form I (to sleep)
standard present tense   يَنام

jussive   يَنَمْ

Form VIII (to need)
standard present tense   يَحتاج

jussive   يَحتَجْ

Form X (to be able)
standard present tense   يَستَطيع

jussive   يَستَطِعْ

EXERCISE

20·8

Write out all the parts of the jussive for the hollow verbs يَطير (flies) and يَحتاج (needs), following the example in the preceding table. Include the any final sukūn.

EXAMPLE ١ أَحتَجْ أَطِرْ

Singular ١

_____ _____

_____ _____

_____ _____

_____ _____

Dual ٢

_____ _____

_____ _____

_____ _____

Plural ٣

_____ _____

_____ _____

_____ _____

_____ _____

EXERCISE

20·9

Fill in the gaps with the correct part of the jussive to match the English translation. (Refer to "Common hollow verbs in the present tense" in Chapter 12, and "Hollow verbs in the derived forms" in Chapter 18 to remind yourself of the meanings.)

EXAMPLE I didn't add salt to the food. لَمْ أُضِفْ المِلح للطّعام.

١ لَمْ _____ الطائرة فوق الجبال.

The plane didn't fly above the mountains.

٢ الطقس حارّ فَـ _____ في الخَيمة اللَّيلة.

It's hot, so let's sleep in the tent tonight.

٣ لَمْ _____ إلى هذه المَشاكِل.

They (masc.) didn't need these problems.

٤ صَديقنا مَريض فَلـ _____ في المُستَشفى.

Our friend is sick, so let's visit him in hospital.

٥ لَمْ _____ الأسعار هذا العام.

Prices didn't increase this year.

٦ لَمْ _____ أحمد أن يُعِدّ الغَداء.

Ahmed wasn't able to prepare lunch.

٧ الأُرُزّ مَطبوخ فَلـ _____ الصَّلصة الآن.

The rice is cooked so let's add the sauce now.

٨ لَمْ _____ في شَهر رَمَضان لأنّني كُنتُ مَريضاً.

I didn't fast in Ramadan because I was sick.

٩ الطالِبات لَمْ _____ حينَ دَخَلَت المُدَرِّسة.

The (female) students didn't stand up when the teacher came in.

١٠ خَرَجَ الوالِدان قَبلَ الإفطار ولكنّهُما لَمْ _____ .

The parents went out before breakfast but they haven't returned.

١١ لِماذا لَمْ _____ القَميص الأبيض يا إبراهيم؟

Why didn't you choose the white shirt, Ibrahim?

١٢ لا نَحتاج إلى سيّارتَين فَلـ _____ القَديمة.

We don't need two cars, so let's sell the old one.

١٣ ألَمْ _____ لسَميرة إنّك حامل يا نادية؟

Didn't you tell Samira that you're pregnant, Nadia?

١٤ لِماذا لَمْ _____ في لَيلة الامتِحان.

Why didn't you (masc. pl.) rest on the night of the exam?

Defective verbs

Defective verbs (with و or ي as the third root letter) also change significantly in the jussive. These verbs often have a long vowel at the end of the standard present tense (see "Defective verbs" in Chapter 12); this changes to a short vowel in the jussive. For example, in the case of the standard present tense يَمْشي *yamshī* (*he walks*), the final vowel is shortened to *kasra* in the jussive: يَمْشِ *yamshi*. In effect, form I defective verbs in the jussive can look as if they only have two root letters, especially if shown without vowels. The following table shows the complete jussive for يَمْشي *yamshī*, including the dual parts.

	PREFIX/ SUFFIX	EXAMPLE
SINGULAR		
I أنا	أَ	أَمْشِ
you (masc.) أنتَ	تَـ	تَـمْشِ
you (fem.) أنتِ	تَـ/ي	تَـمْشي
he/it (masc.) هُوَ	يَـ	يَـمْشِ
she/it (fem.) هِيَ	تَـ	تَـمْشِ
DUAL		
you (dual) أنتُما	تَـ/ا	تَـمْشيا
they (masc. dual) هُما	يَـ/ا	يَـمْشيا
they (fem. dual) هُما	تَـ/ا	تَـمْشيا
PLURAL		
we نَحنُ	نَـ	نَمْشِ
you (masc. pl.) أنتُم	تَـ/وا	تَـمْشوا
you (fem. pl.) أنتُنَّ	تَـ/نَ	تَـمْشينَ
they (masc.) هُم	يَـ/وا	يَـمْشوا
they (fem.) هُنَّ	يَـ/نَ	يَمشينَ

Translate the following into Arabic using the verbs يَمْشي yamshī (walks), يَرْمي yarmī (throws), or يَجْري yajrī (runs).

EXAMPLE الطَّقس مُشمِس فَلْنَمْشِ إلى الحديقة. It's sunny so let's walk to the park.

I didn't throw the book on the floor. ١

_____

Why didn't you (masc.) walk to my house? ٢

_____

They (masc.) didn't run to (the) school. ٣

_____

We're late (مُتَأَخِّرون) so let's run. ٤

_____

Samira didn't throw the ball. ٥

_____

Why didn't you (fem.) throw the ball? ٦

_____

The girls walked but didn't run. ٧

_____

Let's throw the stick (العَصا) for the dog. ٨

_____

Didn't you (masc. dual) walk to the park? ٩

_____

We have a lot of time so let's walk to the museum. ١٠

_____

As with hollow verbs, the short vowel in the jussive of defective verbs depends on the original long vowel, with a long *ā* in the standard present tense becoming *fatḥa* in the jussive and a long *ū* becoming *ḍamma*:

Form I (to forget)

standard present tense   يَنْسَى

jussive   يَنسَ

Form I (to complain)

standard present tense   يَشْكو

jussive   يَشْكُ

Form V (to wish)

standard present tense   يَتَمَنَّى

jussive   يَتَمَنَّ

Form VIII (to buy)

standard present tense   يَشْتَري

jussive   يَشْتَرِ

Make these sentences negative using لَمْ *+ jussive. (Refer to "Defective verbs" in Chapters 12 and 18 if you need to remind yourself of the meanings.)*

EXAMPLE   بَكَيْتُ في المدرسة. لَمْ أَبْكِ في المدرسة.

١ لِماذا أَعْطَيْتِ التَذكِرة لأمّكِ؟ _____

٢ لاقَيْنا سارة في الحَديقة. _____

٣ جَرَتْ نادية في سِباق الأُمَّهات. _____

٤ اِشْتَرَيْتُ قُبّعة في السوق. _____

٥ دَعَوْنا صَديقنا على العَشاء. _____

٦ أَعْطَاني أحمد الكتاب. _____

٧ مَشوا في الصَّحراء لِمُدّة طويلة. _____

٨ اِنتَهَتْ سارة من كِتابة الرِّواية. _____

٩ شكا المُوَظَّفون من حَرارة المَكتَب. _____

١٠ إنّ الصَديقين تَلاقَيا في النادي. _____

١١ جَرَى الأولاد وَراء السيّارة ورَموا الزُّهور. _____

١٢ اِرتَدَيْتِ الفُستان الجديد في الحفل. _____

١٣ رَضينا عَن الخِدمة في المَطعَم. _____

١٤ أَعْطانا المُدير مِفتاح الباب. _____

١٥ رَجَوْتُ منكُم الامتِناع من التَدخين. _____

The imperative

21

The *imperative* is the grammatical term given to verbs used as an order or as an instruction (*Run!*, *Look!*, etc.). In Arabic, the imperative is based on the jussive mood of the verb (see Chapter 20) and varies depending on how many people are being addressed and their gender.

Formation of the imperative

The majority of Arabic verbs can be turned into instructions, or imperatives, by following a few straightforward steps:

1. Take the appropriate part of the jussive verb (see Chapter 20) depending on who is being addressed (e.g., one male, one female, group, etc.).

you (masc. sing.) drink	تَشْرَبْ
you (fem. sing.) look	تَنْظُري
you (masc. sing.) say	تَقُلْ
you (fem. sing.) sleep	تَنامي
you (masc. sing.) eat	تَأْكُلْ
you (fem. sing.) reply	تَرُدّي
you (masc. pl.) try	تُحاوِلوا
you (fem. pl.) move	تَتَحَرَّكْنَ
you (masc. pl.) run	تَجْروا
you (dual) wait	تَنْتَظِرا

2. Remove the initial prefix تَ (*ta*) or تُ (*tu*) and any initial *hamza*.

you (masc. sing.) drink	شْرَبْ
you (fem. sing.) look	نْظُري
you (masc. sing.) say	قُلْ
you (fem. sing.) sleep	نامي
you (masc. sing.) eat	كُلْ
you (fem. sing.) reply	رُدّي

you (masc. pl.) try	حاوِلوا
you (fem. pl.) move	تَحَرَّكْنَ
you (masc. pl.) run	جْروا
you (dual) wait	انْتَظِرا

3. If the result doesn't begin with a *sukūn*, the imperative is complete.

Say! (talking to a single male)	قُلْ!
Sleep! (talking to a single female)	نامي!
Eat! (talking to a single male)	كُلْ!
Reply! (talking to a single female)	رُدّي!
Try! (talking to a mixed or male group)	حاوِلوا!
Move! (talking to a female group)	تَحَرَّكْنَ!

4. If the result begins with a *sukūn*, an initial vowel is needed. This vowel is generally ٱ (*i*), but changes to ٱ (*u*) if the present tense verb has *ḍamma* as its middle vowel.

Drink! (talking to a single male)	اِشْرَبْ!
Look! (talking to a single female)	اُنْظُري!
Run! (talking to a mixed or male group)	اِجروا!
Wait! (talking to two people)	انتَظِرا!

Form IV imperatives are something of an exception as they always have an initial *fatḥa*.

Hurry!	أَسرِعْ!
Answer!	أَجِبْ!

Use the following list of verbs to form an imperative. Remember to start with the appropriate jussive part of the verb (see Chapter 20 for details).

decides يُقَرِّر	removes يُخْرِج	puts يَضَع
gives يُعْطي	tidies يَرَتِّب	gathers/collects يَجْمَع
sits يَجْلِس	leaves يَتْرُك	flies يَطير
finds يَجِد	listens يَسْتَمِع	reads يَقْرَأ
looks يَنْظُر	forgets يَنْسَى	changes يُغَيِّر
smiles يَبْتَسِم	wakes up يَسْتَيْقِظ	takes يَأْخُذ
walks يَمْشي	advances/goes forward يَتَقَدَّم	concentrates يُرَكِّز

EXAMPLE   اِمْشِ! Walk! (to a single male)

_____ Look! (to a single male) ١

_____ Leave! (to a single female) ٢

_____ Read! (to a mixed or male group) ٣

_____ Collect/gather! (to a single male) ٤

_____ Take! (to a single female) ٥

_____ Give! (to a single male) ٦

_____ Remove! (to a mixed or male group) ٧

_____ Smile! (to a single female) ٨

_____ Sit! (to a group of females) ٩

_____ Fly! (to a single male) ١٠

_____ Tidy! (to two people) ١١

_____ Advance! (to a mixed or male group) ١٢

_____ Put! (to a single female) ١٣

_____ Forget! (to a single male) ١٤

_____ Decide! (to a group of females) ١٥

_____ Find! (to a mixed or male group) ١٦

_____ Change! (to a single male) ١٧

_____ Listen! (to two people) ١٨

_____ Wake up! (to a single female) ١٩

_____ Concentrate! (to a mixed or male group) ٢٠

Nadir's mother goes to his room to wake him up at midday and is appalled at the state of his bedroom. She wants him to tidy it up and is giving him instructions on what he needs to do. Put the instructions in the order Nadir's mother says them, as in the example.

يا نادر، غُرفَتك قَذِرة! اِجْمَعْ زُجاجات الكولا الفارِغة كلّها، وضَعها في هذا الصَّندوق. غَيِّر المِلايات ورَتِّب السَّرير. اُنظُر تحت السَّرير! أَعْطِني عُلَب البيتزا الفارِغة هذه! أَخرِج هذا الجَورب من عُلبة البيتزا يا نادر وضَعه في سَلّة الغَسيل! اِفتَح الشُّباك. خُذ هذه الأطباق والأكواب إلى المَطبَخ واتُرُكها بِجوار الحَوض. اِرم بَقايا هذا السندَويتش القَديم في الزِّبالة. متى سَتَتَعَلَّم يا نادر! اِستَيقِظ!

_____ Take these plates and glasses to the kitchen.

_____ Remove this sock from the pizza box.

__1__ Collect all the empty cola bottles.

_____ Change the sheets.

_____ Look under the bed.

_____ Open the window.

_____ Leave them next to the sink.

_____ Put them in this box.

_____ Put it in the laundry basket.

_____ Wake up!

_____ Throw the remains of this old sandwich in the trash.

_____ Give me these empty pizza boxes.

_____ Tidy the bed.

Imagine that the instructions in Exercise 21.2 are directed at Nadia instead of Nadir. Rewrite the passage changing all the imperatives to the feminine.

EXAMPLE   يا نادية غُرفَتك قَذِرة! اِجْمَعي زُجاجات الكولا الفارِغة كلّها

_____

_____

_____

_____

_____

_____

Negative commands

Negative imperatives are formed by لا + *jussive* (with prefix) to mean "don't" as an order or instruction.

Don't smoke! (talking to a single male)	لا تُدَخِّنْ!
Don't drive the car! (talking to a single female)	لا تَقودي السيّارة!
Don't despair! (talking to a mixed or male group)	لا تَيْأَسوا!
Don't doubt that you are the best team! (talking to group of females)	ولا تَشْكُكْنَ في أنّكُنَّ الفَريق الأفضَل!
Don't wait! (talking to two people)	لا تَنتَظِرا!

EXERCISE
21·4

Change the instructions in Exercise 21.1 into negative commands.

EXAMPLE   لا تَمْشِ! Don't walk! (to a single male)

_____ ١

_____ ٢

_____ ٣

_____ ٤

_____ ٥

_____ ٦

_____ ٧

_____ ٨

_____ ٩

_____ ١٠

_____ ١١

_____ ١٢

_____ ١٣

_____ ١٤

_____ ١٥

_____ ١٦

_____ ١٧

_____ ١٨

_____ ١٩

_____ ٢٠

EXERCISE 21·5

A soccer coach is giving a half-time talk, after the first half (الشوط الأوّل) in which his team let in six goals (سِتّة أهداف). Underline all the instructions, positive or negative, in the coach's team talk.

EXAMPLE   لا تَيْأَسوا يا شَباب!

لا تَيْأَسوا يا شَباب! ولا تَشُكّوا أبداً في أنّكم الفَريق الأَفضل.

لا تَنظُروا إلى النَّتيجة الآن، ولا تَدعوا الأهداف السِتّة تُؤَثِّر على عَزيمتكم.

في الشوط الثاني لا تَتَركوا "كاكي" و"مِشمِش" يَلمِسان الكُرة.

يا إبراهيم، لا تَدَع "ميمو" يَهرِب مِنك في وَسَط المَلعَب.

يا أحمد، رَكِّز على "فرفور" حَتّي لا يَغيب عن عَينك لِثانية واحدة.

لا تَتَقَّدموا كلّكم معاً. لا تَمنَحوهُم مَساحات خالية في المَلعَب. لا تُعطوهم الوقت لِلتَّفكير.

لا تَنسوا تَعليماتي، وأكيد لَن يَستطيعوا أن يُسَجِّلوا سِتّة أهداف أُخرى في الشوط الثاني.

EXERCISE 21·6

Write the coach's instructions to the team in Exercise 21.5 next to the equivalent English.

EXAMPLE   لا تَـمنَحوهُم مَساحات خالية don't allow them free spaces

don't forget my instructions ١

_____

concentrate on Farfur ٢

_____

don't go forward all together ٣

_____

don't despair, boys ٤

_____

214   Moods of the verb and verbal nouns

don't look at the result now ٥

---

don't let Mimo get away from you ٦

---

never doubt that you are the better team ٧

---

don't give them time to think ٨

---

don't let Kaki and Mishmish touch the ball ٩

---

don't let the six goals affect your determination ١٠

The verbal noun

Verbal nouns are formed in English by adding endings such as "-tion," "-ment," or "-ing" (e.g., information, treatment, swimming, etc.). In Arabic the root letters are put into different patterns to make verbal nouns, known as المَصدَر.

Forming verbal nouns: Basic verbs

Basic (form I) verbs have a number of different patterns for forming verbal nouns that need to be learned individually. The majority of form I verbal nouns fit into one of the five common patterns:

PATTERN	EXAMPLE	VERB
فَعْل	ضَرْب hit(ting)	ضَرَب/يَضْرِب
فُعول	دُخُول entering	دَخَل/يَدْخُل
فَعال	ذَهاب going	ذَهَب/يَذْهَب
فِعالة	سِباحة swimming	سَبَح/يَسْبَح
فَعَل	عَمَل work(ing)	عَمِل/يَعْمَل

But some verbal nouns have more unusual patterns, for example مَعرِفة (knowing/knowledge) from the verb عَرَف/يَعرِف (to know).

EXERCISE

22·1

Decide from which form I verb each noun is derived, and then give its meaning.

EXAMPLE   "search(ing)" from the verb بَحْث بَحَث/يَبْحَث

١ رَقْص _____

٢ جُلوس _____

٣ كِتابة _____

٤ رُجوع _____

216

٥ نَظَر _____

٦ رُكوب _____

٧ فَهْم _____

٨ زِراعة _____

٩ خُروج _____

١٠ قَوْل _____

١١ فَتْح _____

١٢ مُرور _____

١٣ أَكْل _____

١٤ رَدّ _____

١٥ وَصْف _____

١٦ قِراءة _____

١٧ صِياح _____

١٨ كَوْن _____

١٩ نِسيان _____

٢٠ نَوْم _____

Forming verbal nouns: Derived verbs

Verbal nouns from derived forms are largely predictable. Only form III has a widely-used alternative.

FORM	PATTERN	EXAMPLE	VERB
II	تَفْعيل	تَدْريس (teaching)	دَرَّس/يُدَرِّس
III	فِعال	جِدال (argument)	جادَل/يُجادِل
	مُفاعَلة	مُغادَرة (leaving)	غادَر/يُغادِر
IV	إفْعال	إعلام (information)	أَعْلَم/يُعْلِم
V	تَفَعُّل	تَزَوُّج (marriage)	تَزَوَّج/يَتَزَوَّج
VI	تَفاعُل	تَناقُش (debating)	تَناقَش/يَتَناقَش
VII	انْفِعال	انْقِسام (division)	انْقَسَم/يَنْقَسِم
VIII	افْتِعال	اسْتِماع (listening)	اسْتَمَع/يَسْتَمِع
X	اسْتِفْعال	اسْتِخْدام (usage)	اسْتَخْدَم/يَسْتَخْدِم

Form the verbal noun from these derived verbs. (Form III verbs are all formed with the مُفاعَلة *pattern.)*

EXAMPLE   حَسَّن/يُحَسِّن to improve تَحْسين <u>*improvement*</u>

١ اِسْتَقْبَل/يَسْتَقْبِل (to receive guests, etc.)

_____

٢ نَظَّف/يُنَظِّف to clean

_____

٣ تَحَدَّث/يَتَحَدَّث to speak

_____

٤ ساعَد/يُساعِد to help

_____

٥ تَسَلَّق/يَتَسَلَّق to climb

_____

٦ اِنْسَحَب/يَنْسَحِب to withdraw

_____

٧ أَصْلَح/يُصْلِح to reform

_____

٨ اِحْتَفَل/يَحْتَفِل to celebrate

_____

٩ اِسْتَعْلَم/يَسْتَعْلِم to inquire

_____

١٠ دَخَّن/يُدَخِّن to smoke

_____

١١ اِبْتَسَم/يَبْتَسِم to smile

_____

١٢ أَرْسَل/يُرْسِل to send

_____

١٣ شاهَد/يُشاهِد to view/to watch

_____

١٤ تَكاسَل/يَتكاسل to be lazy

_____

١٥ اِحْتَرَم/يَحْتَرِم to respect

_____

١٦ تَصَرَّف/يَتَصَرَّف to act/to behave

_____

١٧ راجَع/يُراجِع to review

_____

١٨ رَتَّب/يُرَتِّب to organize/tidy

_____

١٩ عَدَّل/يُعَدِّل to adjust

_____

٢٠ اِسْتَخْرَج/يَسْتَخْرِج to extract

_____

Uses of verbal nouns

Verbal nouns are found extensively in Arabic. They are used not only for generalizations, as they are in English, but also to replace or qualify verbs. In addition, many verbal nouns have also acquired a specific meaning making it important to be comfortable with the various patterns.

Generalization

Verbal nouns are used for generalizing, much as they are in English. Note that generalizations are definite in Arabic (by including *al-* or by putting in an *iḍāfa* construction).

Smoking is prohibited.	مَـمنوع التَدْخين.
Reform of the system will take a long time.	إصلاح النِّظام سَيستَغرِق مُدّة طَويلة.

Many verbal nouns have also acquired a specific meaning in general circulation. For example, the verbal noun from خاطَب/يُخاطِب (*to talk formally/speak in public*) is خِطاب and this is also the word in general circulation for "a letter"; the verbal noun from سَوَّق/يُسَوِّق (*to sell, to take to market*) is تَسويق which is used for "marketing."

You are running a summer vacation camp for teenagers from the Arab world and have been asked to write a list of rules in Arabic showing what is prohibited. Look at the prohibited activity and write the Arabic rule.

EXAMPLE   مَـمنوع رُكوب الدرّاجات. riding bicycles

smoking in the garden ١

_____

writing on the desks ٢

_____

talking to the bus driver (سائِق الباص) ٣

_____

going out of the school ٤

_____

climbing the fence (السور) ٥

_____

swimming in the river ٦

_____

watching television after 9 o'clock ٧

_____

using the computer before lunch ٨

_____

shouting in the corridor ٩

_____

behaving without respect ١٠

_____

Verbal nouns in place of a second verb

Arabic does not have the equivalent of the English infinitive "to walk," "to see," and so on. Chapter 19 shows how the subjunctive can be used in Arabic for a second verb where English would use an infinitive. Another common alternative is to use the verbal noun. Look at these pairs of sentences with the same meaning. The first uses the subjunctive and the second a verbal noun:

We'd like to tidy the room.

نُريد أَنْ نُرَتِّب الغُرفة.

نُريد تَرْتيب الغُرفة.

They can't go to the cinema.

لا يَستَطيعون أَنْ يَذهَبوا إلى السينما.

لا يَستَطيعون الذَّهاب إلى السينما.

I asked you to help your mother.

طَلَبتُ مِنكَ أَنْ تُساعِد أُمَّك.

طَلَبتُ مِنكَ مُساعَدة أُمَّك.

It is considered good style to use verbal nouns in this way, and it is often less clumsy than the subjunctive.

EXERCISE
22·4

Rephrase these sentences and questions using a verbal noun.

EXAMPLE

لا أَستَطيع أَن أَرجِع إلى البيت. <u>لا أَستَطيع الرُّجوع إلى البيت.</u>

١ يُحِبّ أَبي أَن يُشاهِد كُرة السَّلّة. _____

٢ أُريد أَن أَكتُب رواية. _____

٣ يَوَدّ الولد أَن يَتَسَلَّق الشَّجَرة. _____

٤ يَأمَلونَ أَن يزوروا أوروبا. _____

٥ هل تُحِبّ أَن تَقْرأ؟ _____

٦ رَجَوْنا مِنهُنَّ أَن يَجلِسنَ على الأرض. _____

٧ طَلَبتُ مِنكُم أَن تَترُكوا الحَقائِب عَند الباب. _____

٨ طَلَبَت مِنّي أُمّي أَن أَحتَرِم المُدَرِّسين. _____

٩ هل تَستَطيعينَ أَن تَستَقبِلي خالَتِك في المَطار؟ _____

١٠ يَأمَلونَ أَن يُغَيِّروا قائِمة الطعام قبل بِداية الصَّيف. _____

١١ أرادَتْ نادية أَن تَزور صديقتها يَوم الجُمعة. _____

١٢ يَوَدّ أَن يَحضُر الاِجتِماع يوم الخَميس. _____

١٣ نَرجو مِنكُما أَن تَستَمِعا إلى الراديو. _____

١٤ يَتَمَنَّى أحمد أَن يَستَخدِم الكمبيوتر. _____

١٥ حاوَلوا أَن يَحِلّوا مَشاكِلهُم. _____

To qualify a verb

A verbal noun can be used together with the equivalent verb to qualify, or add information about, the action:

I visited my mother for a short time (lit: "a short visit").	زرْتُ أُمِّي زِيارة قَصيرة.
He hit me hard (lit: "a hard hit").	ضَرَبَني ضَرباً شَديداً.
They cooperated with us fruitfully (lit: "a fruitful cooperation").	تَعاوَنوا مَعَنا تَعاوُناً مُثْمِراً.

EXERCISE
22·5

Match the English sentences with the Arabic ones.

a. The scientists made an astonishing discovery. ـــــــ

b. We treated them successfully. ـــــــ

c. She sang angelically yesterday. ـــــــ

d. They paid me a long visit. ـــــــ

e. He made us a definite promise. ـــــــ

f. I was completely refreshed. ـــــــ

g. The runner set off like a rocket. ـــــــ

h. My fiancée smiled charmingly. ـــــــ

١ زارونا زِيارة طويلة.

٢ عالَجْناهُم عِلاجاً ناجِحاً.

٣ انتَعَشْتُ انتِعاشاً كامِلاً.

٤ انطَلَقَ العَدّاء انطِلاقة صاروخيّة.

٥ ابتَكَرَ العُلَماء ابتِكاراً مُذهِلاً.

٦ ابتَسَمَتْ خَطيبَتي ابتِسامة ساحِرة.

٧ وَعَدَني وَعداً أكيداً.

٨ غَنَّتْ أمس غِناءً ملائكيّاً.

OTHER ASPECTS OF VERBS

Part VI gathers together information and practice material on important aspects of Arabic verbs not covered in the previous parts. This includes unusual or very irregular verbs, verbs with four roots (*quadriliterals*), compound tenses, conditional sentences, and passive verbs.

Unusual verbs

◆23◆

Doubly weak verbs

Doubly weak verbs are those that have more than one weak root letter. The term "doubly weak" usually includes verbs with *hamza* as one of the two "weak" roots, as well as و or ي. Such verbs are not very common but they do include a few high-frequency ones.

In general, doubly weak verbs follow the rules for both irregularities. For example, the verb وَعَى/يَعِي (*to pay attention, to watch out*) has the root letters و/ع/ي and so follows the rules for both assimilated verbs (with و or ي as the first root letter) and defective verbs (with و or ي as the final root letter).

In the past tense the verb وَعَى/يَعِي retains the و, behaving like the defective verb مَشَى/يَمْشِي (*to walk*):

he paid attention	وَعَى
I paid attention	وَعَيْتُ

In the present tense the verb also loses the و, behaving like the assimilated verb وَصَلَ/يَصِل (*to arrive*):

he pays attention	يَعِي
I pay attention	أَعِي

In the jussive any final ي changes to *kasra*:

he didn't pay attention	لَمْ يَعِ
I didn't pay attention	لَمْ أَعِ

And, theoretically at least, the imperative is reduced to a single consonant with *kasra*:

Pay attention!	عِ!

In reality, however, writers will generally find a way to avoid this kind of grammatical extreme.

Two other doubly weak verbs that follow the same pattern as وَعَى/يَعِي are وَقَى/يَقِي (*to protect, to guard*) and وَفَى/يَفِي (*to fulfill*, e.g., a promise).

Write out these verbs in Arabic following the preceding pattern.

EXAMPLE   وَقَى he guarded

١ وَقَى/يَقِي

_____ he guarded

_____ I guarded

_____ he guards

_____ I guard

_____ he didn't guard

_____ I didn't guard

٢ وَفَى/يَفِي

_____ he fulfilled

_____ I fulfilled

_____ he fulfills

_____ I fulfill

_____ he didn't fulfill

_____ I didn't fulfill

Doubly weak verbs with و as the second root letter and ي as the third root letter, for example
رَوَى/يَرْوِي (*to relate*, e.g., a story, etc.) will behave as other defective verbs with the و retaining its
consonantal sound (*w*) throughout.

he related	رَوَى
I related	رَوَيْتُ
he relates	يَرْوِي
I relate	أَرْوِي
he didn't relate	لَمْ يَرْوِ
I didn't relate	لَمْ أَرْوِ

Another verb that follows the same pattern is نَوَى/يَنوِي (*to intend*).

Translate the English sentences and questions into Arabic.

EXAMPLE   رَوَى القِصّة لأُمّه. He related the story to his mother.

أَنوي أَن أَخرُج بَعدَ الغَداء. I intend to go out after lunch.

I related the story to the children. ١

_____

We intend to go to the market tomorrow. ٢

_____

The (fem.) teacher related the story of Ali Baba. ٣

_____

Are you (masc.) intending to cook this fish? ٤

_____

We didn't relate to her the details of our story. ٥

_____

We will relate the whole story to you (masc. pl.). ٦

_____

Nadia is not intending to celebrate her birthday. ٧

_____

I didn't intend to travel this morning. ٨

_____

Will you (fem.) relate everything to your mother? ٩

_____

We are not intending to relate the details here. ١٠

_____

أَتى/يَأتي and جاءَ/يجيء (to come)

The two verbs commonly used to mean "to come" are both doubly weak.

جاءَ/يجيء (to come)

The verb جاءَ/يجيء has the root letters ج/ي/ء and so follows the rules for both hollow verbs such as طار/يَطير (to fly) and *hamzated* verbs such as بَدَأَ/يَبْدَأ (to begin).

The following table shows the full conjugations for past and present tenses of the verb جاءَ/يجيءُ:

	PAST TENSE	PRESENT TENSE
SINGULAR		
أنا I	جِئْتُ	أَجيءُ
أنتَ (.you (masc	جِئْتَ	تَجيءُ
أنتِ (.you (fem	جِئْتِ	تَجيئينَ
هُوَ (.he/it (masc	جاءَ	يَجيءُ
هِيَ (.she/it (fem	جاءَتْ	تَجيءُ
DUAL		
أنتُما (you (dual	جِئْتُما	تَجيئانِ
هُما (they (masc. dual	جاءَا	يَجيئانِ
هُما (they (fem. dual	جاءَتا	تَجيئانِ
PLURAL		
نَحنُ we	جِئْنا	نَجيءُ
أنتُم (.you (masc. pl	جِئْتُمْ	تَجيئونَ
أنتُنَّ (.you (fem. pl	جِئْتُنَّ	تَجِئْنَ
هُم (.they (masc	جاءوا	يَجيئونَ
هُنَّ (.they (fem	جِئْنَ	يَجِئْنَ

The long middle vowel of the present tense changes to a *kasra* in the jussive (see "Hollow verbs" in Chapter 20):

Let's come tomorrow.	فَلْنَجِئْ غداً.
My son didn't come from the club.	لَمْ يَجِئْ ابني من النادي.

EXERCISE 23·3

Choose the correct part of the verb from the parentheses to complete the sentence.

EXAMPLE   جاءَتْ (جاءَتْ/جاءَ/جِئْتُ) أُمّي ومَعَها كَعك.

١ ــــــــــــــــــ (جاءَتْ/جاءَ/جِئْتُ) أحمد ومَعَهُ دَجاجة مَشوية.

٢ متى ــــــــــــــــــ (نَجيء/تَجيء/يَجيء) بابا؟ أنا جَوعان!

٣ أنتَ ــــــــــــــــــ (جِئْتِ/جِئْتَ/جِئْتُمْ) في الوَقت المُناسِب.

٤ أنا ــــــــــــــــــ (جِئْتَ/جاءَتْ/جِئْتُ) من المَطار إلى هنا مُباشِرةً.

٥ _____ (جِئْنَ/جاءَ/جِئْنا) لِنَحتَفِل بعيد ميلادك.

٦ لَم _____ (يجِئ/يجيءَ/جاءَ) نادِر من المدرسة.

٧ الرِّجال _____ (سَيَجيئونَ/سَيَجيئى/سَيَجِئْنَ) إلى قَريَتِنا غَداً.

٨ المُدَرِّسات _____ (جاءواً/جِئْنَ/جاءَتْ) بِأفكار جَديدة.

٩ لا _____ (تَجيء/جِئْنَ/تَجيئ) مَعَنا هذه المَرّة، يا أحمد.

١٠ أنا لَم _____ (جِئْتُ/أَجيء/أَجِئْ) إليكُم إلا لِعَمَل الخَير.

١١ _____ (سَيَجيئونَ/سَتَجيئونَ/سَتَجيء) أنتم إلى بَيتِنا في المَرّة القادِمة.

١٢ هل _____ (جاءَتْ/جاءَ/جاءوا) رسائِل من شُكري؟

أتى/يأتي (to come)

The doubly weak verb أتى/يأتي is also used commonly to mean "to come." The root letters are ء/ت/ي and so the verb follows the rules for both defective verbs such as مَشَى/يَمشي (to walk) and *hamzated* verbs such as أَكَل/يَأكُل (to eat).

The following table shows the full conjugations for past and present tenses of the verb أتى/يأتي:

		PAST TENSE	PRESENT TENSE
SINGULAR			
I أنا		أَتَيتُ	آتي
you (masc.) أنتَ		أَتَيتَ	تَأتي
you (fem.) أنتِ		أَتَيتِ	تَأتينَ
he/it (masc.) هُوَ		أَتى	يَأتي
she/it (fem.) هِيَ		أَتَتْ	تَأتي
DUAL			
you (dual) أنتُما		أَتَيتُما	تَأتيانِ
they (masc. dual) هُما		أَتَيا	يَأتيانِ
they (fem. dual) هُما		أَتَتا	تَأتيانِ
PLURAL			
we نَحنُ		أَتَينا	نَأتي
you (masc. pl.) أنتُم		أَتَيتُم	تَأتونَ
you (fem. pl.) أنتُنَّ		أَتَيتُنَّ	تَأتينَ
they (masc.) هُم		أَتَوا	يَأتونَ
they (fem.) هُنَّ		أَتَينَ	يَأتينَ

In the case of أَتَى/يَأْتِي the final long vowel of the present tense changes to a *kasra* in the jussive (see "Defective verbs" in Chapter 20):

فَلْنَأْتِ غَداً.   Let's come tomorrow.

لَمْ يَأْتِ ابني من النادي.   My son didn't come from the club.

EXERCISE
23·4

Fill in the gaps with the correct part of the verb أَتَى/يَأْتِي *to match the English translation.*

EXAMPLE

أَتَيْتُ إلى المُستَشفى حين سَمِعْتُ عن الحادِثة.

I came to the hospital when I heard about the accident.

١ أنا ــــــــــــــــــــــــــــ الآن من عند الحَلّاق.

I am coming now from the barber's.

٢ يا إبراهيم، هل ــــــــــــــــــــــــــــ لَنا بِأَخبار جَديدة؟

Ibrahim, did you come to us with (any) new news?

٣ حين ــــــــــــــــــــــــــــ أبوكم سَأَروي لَهُ كلّ شيء.

When your father comes, I will relate everything to him.

٤ ــــــــــــــــــــــــــــ إلى النادي بَعدَ الغداء.

We will come to the club after lunch.

٥ لا نَعرَف من أَينَ ــــــــــــــــــــــــــــ ولا إلى أَينَ ذَهَبَتْ.

We don't know from where she came nor where she went.

٦ إنّهُم ــــــــــــــــــــــــــــ دائماً إلى بيتنا دون دَعوة.

They always come to our house without an invitation.

٧ هل ــــــــــــــــــــــــــــ من غُرفة الجِراحة؟

Have you (fem. pl.) come from the operating theater?

٨ لا ــــــــــــــــــــــــــــ إلى هنا يا نادِر! أنا ــــــــــــــــــــــــــــ إلى البيت حالاً.

Don't come here, Nadir. I will come to the house immediately.

٩ ــــــــــــــــــــــــــــ ماما بَعدَ قليل وتَفتَح لَنا الباب.

Mom will come in a little while and open the door for us.

١٠ لَم ــــــــــــــــــــــــــــ مَعَكم لأنّ الطَّقس كان بارِداً.

We didn't come with you because the weather was cold.

١١ هل ــــــــــــــــــــــــــــ إلى هنا أمس؟

Did you two come here yesterday?

رَأَى/يَرَى (to see)

The verb رَأَى/يَرَى (*to see*) has the root letters ر/ء/ي. It is unusual even amongst doubly weak verbs since the *hamza* drops out altogether in the present tense:

We saw the king and queen.	رَأَيْنا المَلِك والمَلِكة.
We (can) see a river in the picture.	نَرَى نَهراً في الصورة.

The following table shows the full conjugations for past and present tenses of the verb رَأَى/يَرَى:

	PAST TENSE	PRESENT TENSE
SINGULAR		
I أنا	رَأَيْتُ	أَرَى
you (masc.) أنتَ	رَأَيْتَ	تَرَى
you (fem.) أنتِ	رَأَيْتِ	تَرَيْنَ
he/it (masc.) هُوَ	رَأَى	يَرَى
she/it (fem.) هِيَ	رَأَتْ	تَرَى
DUAL		
you (dual) أنتُما	رَأَيْتُما	تَرَيان
they (masc. dual) هُما	رَأَيا	يَرَيان
they (fem. dual) هُما	رَأَتا	تَرَيان
PLURAL		
we نَحنُ	رَأَيْنا	نَرَى
you (masc. pl.) أنتُم	رَأَيْتُمْ	تَرَوْنَ
you (fem. pl.) أنتُنَّ	رَأَيْتُـنَّ	تَرَيْنَ
they (masc.) هُم	رَأَوْا	يَرَوْنَ
they (fem.) هُنَّ	رَأَيْنَ	يَرَيْنَ

The verb رَأَى/يَرَى can also carry the meaning of "to think" or "to believe":

I think that she is stubborn.	أرى أنّها عَنيدة.
Some people believe that bananas are good for (your) health.	يَرى بَعض الناس أن المَوز مُفيد للصِحّة.

Translate the English sentences and questions into Arabic using the verb رَأَى/يَرَى.

EXAMPLE   هلْ رَأَيْتَ المَلِك؟ Did you (masc.) see the king?

I saw the king. ١

_____

We (can) see a horse in the picture. ٢

_____

I want to see my mother. ٣

_____

Where did you (fem. pl.) see the queen? ٤

_____

We saw her on the balcony (في الشُّرفة) with the king. ٥

_____

Ahmed's mother thinks that he is stubborn. ٦

_____

I don't think that he is stubborn. ٧

_____

They (masc.) saw a boat on the river. ٨

_____

My brother and sister are there, and they (can) see the boat also. ٩

_____

Some people believe that apricots are good for health. ١٠

_____

Fatima went to the center of the capital yesterday to see the prince's wedding. She arrived early and got a good place to view the proceedings. Fatima posted on her social network page about what she saw. She mentions nine separate things. Describe what she saw in English.

ذَهَبْتُ أمس إلى وَسَط العاصِمة لأَرى حَفل زَفاف الأمير. وَصَلْتُ قبل الحَفل بثلاث ساعات ووَجَدْتُ مَكاناً جَيِّداً بِجانِب باب القَصر. رَأَيْتُ كلّ شيء:

رأَيْتُ وُصول الضُّيوف كلّهم.

رأَيْتُ رئيس الوُزَراء وزَوجَته.

رأَيْتُ المُمَثِّلة المَشهورة "كراملّة كريم".

رأَيْتُ لاعِب الكُرة المَشهور "فَرفور".

رأيتُ الأمير في المَركَبة الذَهَبيّة.

رأيتُ العَروس وفُستانها الجَميل.

رأيتُ المَلِك والمَلِكة في المَركَبة المَلَكيّة.

رأيتُ الخُيول البَيضاء.

رأيتُ العائِلة المَلَكيّة في شُرفة القَصر.

EXAMPLE   *She saw the arrival of all the guests.*

1. _____

2. _____

3. _____

4. _____

5. _____

6. _____

7. _____

8. _____

EXERCISE 23·7

Fatima is talking to her mother on her cell phone as she watches the wedding. She is telling her what she can see. Using the information in Exercise 23.6, write down what Fatima is saying. (For more of a challenge, you can try writing the sentences from memory.)

EXAMPLE   أَرَى وُصول الضُّيوف كلّهُم. (I [can] see the arrival of all the guests.)

_____ ١

_____ ٢

_____ ٣

_____ ٤

_____ ٥

_____ ٦

_____ ٧

_____ ٨

The final long vowel of the present tense يَرى changes to *fatḥa* in the jussive, effectively leaving the verb with just a single consonant after the prefix:

فَلْنَرَ   Let's see.

لَمْ أَرَ المَرْكَبة المَلَكيّة.   I didn't see the royal carriage.

EXERCISE 23·8

Some of Fatima's friends and family also went to see the wedding but didn't get there early so they only saw some of the action. Describe what they saw and didn't see using the prompts.

EXAMPLE   Nadia: arrival of the guests ✓ / royal carriage ✗

رَأَتْ نادية وُصول الضُّيوف ولكنّها لَمْ تَرَ المَرْكَبة المَلَكيّة.

١ Shukri: prime minister ✓ / his wife ✗

_____

٢ Sara: prince ✓ / bride ✗

_____

٣ Shukri's wife: golden carriage ✓ / white horses ✗

_____

لَيسَ (not to be)

Arabic does not have a verb "to be" (is/are/am, etc.) in simple positive sentences (see Chapter 1). However, it does have a verb "not to be." The sentence أحمد مُدرِّس (*Ahmed is a teacher*) can be made negative by adding لَيسَ (or sometimes لَيسَ بِـ):

لَيسَ أحمد مُدرِّساً. (لَيسَ أحمد بِـمُدرِّس.)   Ahmed isn't a teacher.

The verb لَيسَ is unusual since it looks like a past tense verb but always has a present tense meaning. It is conjugated using past tense endings, with the stem varying in a similar way to a hollow verb:

he/it is not	لَيسَ
she/it is not	لَيسَتْ
they (masc.) are not	لَيسوا
I am not	لَسْتُ
you (masc.) are not	لَسْتَ
you (fem.) are not	لَسْتِ
we are not	لَسْنا
you (masc. pl.) are not	لَسْتُمْ
you (fem. pl.) are not	لَسْتُنَّ
they (fem.) are not	لَسْنَ

The verb لَيسَ will affect the predicate in the same way as كان (see "كان [*was/were*]" in Chapter 6).

My son is a doctor.	اِبني طَبيب.
My son isn't a doctor.	لَيسَ اِبني طبيباً (بِطَبيب).
Nadia is busy.	نادية مَشغولة.
Nadia isn't busy.	لَيسَتْ نادية مَشغولة.
I am in Ahmed's house.	أنا في بيت أحمد.
I am not in Ahmed's house.	لَسْتُ في بيت أحمد.
We are cooks.	نَحنُ طَبّاخون.
We are not cooks.	لَسْنا طَبّاخين.

EXERCISE
23·9

Make these sentences negative using the verb لَيسَ.

EXAMPLE   أنا في وَسَط المدينة. <u>لَسْتُ في وَسَط المَدينة.</u>

١ نَحنُ في مِصر. _____

٢ شُكري في المَكتَبة. _____

٣ سَميرة في بيتها. _____

٤ أنا أمامَ البنك. _____

٥ أنتِ مَشغولة الآن. _____

٦ هم مع المُدرّس. _____

٧ هم مهندسون في العراق. _____

٨ البُحيرة هادِئة. _____

٩ أنتَ المدير. _____

١٠ الباب مَفتوح. _____

١١ السيّارات في الشارع. _____

١٢ أنتُم مُتَأَخِّرون. _____

١٣ أَأَنتُنَّ في المدرسة؟ _____

EXERCISE
23·10

Use the verb لَيسَ *to create Arabic sentences and questions to match the English.*

EXAMPLE   We're not in the school. لَسنا في المَدرَسة.

١ I'm not in the garden.

_____

٢ Nadia isn't in America.

_____

٣ Shukri isn't stubborn.

_____

٤ My sister isn't tall.

_____

The car isn't in front of the house. ٥

_____

Isn't your son a cook? ٦

_____

We're not (male) teachers. ٧

_____

Aren't you (masc.) in the school? ٨

_____

This shirt isn't clean. ٩

_____

Aren't the books in the bag? ١٠

_____

Using لَيسَ to express "there isn't" and "don't/doesn't have"

The verb لَيسَ can be placed in front of the phrase هناك to express "there isn't/aren't":

There isn't a dog in the garden.	لَيسَ هناك كلب في الحديقة.
There isn't a mosque near the river.	لَيسَ هناك جامِع بجانب النَّهر.

EXERCISE
23·11

Fatima is telling you about the facilities at her sporting club. Complete her descriptions following the prompts.

EXAMPLE   مَلعَب تنس ✓/مَلعَب كُرة سَلّة ✗   هناك ملعب تنس ولكن لَيسَ هناك ملعب كرة سلّة.

(There's a tennis court but there isn't a basketball court.)

١ ملعب كرة القَدَم ✓/ملعب جولف ✗

_____

٢ جِمنازيوم ✓/حمّام سِباحة ✗

_____

٣ كافتيريا ✓/مَطعَم ✗

_____

٤ حديقة ✓/مَقاعِد ✗

_____

٥ ملعب أطفال ✓/ مُنزَلِق ✗ (a slide)

_____

٦ اِسطَبلات رُكوب الخَيل ✓/ مِضمار ✗ (a racetrack)

_____

The verb لَيسَ can also be placed in front of the phrases used to express "to have," producing a negative meaning:

We don't have a house in the Red Sea.	لَيسَ لَدَينا بيت في البَحر الأَحمر.
They don't have any dogs.	لَيسَ لَهُم كِلاب.
The grocer didn't have fresh figs yesterday.	لَيسَ عِندَ البَقّال تين طازِج أمس.
He doesn't have (with him) the key to the car.	مِفتاح السيّارة لَيسَ مَعَهُ.

EXERCISE
23·12

Your friend is asking questions about you and your family, but his information is completely out of date. Correct your friend, using the verb لَيسَ.

EXAMPLE هل عِندكُم شَقّة في القاهرة؟ <u>لا، لَيسَ عِندنا شقّة في القاهرة الآن.</u>

١ هل عِندكُم كِلاب؟ _____

٢ هل لَدَيكُم دَرّاجات؟ _____

٣ هل عندك ألم في رِجلك؟ _____

٤ هل عِندَ البقّال تين طازِج؟ _____

٥ هل لاِبنكُم سيّارة سريعة؟ _____

٦ هل لاِبنتكُم بَيت في البَحر الأحمَر؟ _____

٧ هل لَدَيكم شجرة طويلة في الحديقة؟ _____

٨ هل مَعَك صُوَر العائِلة اليَوم؟ _____

Quadriliteral verbs

Most Arabic words are based on roots of three consonants. A few are based on roots of *four* consonants, and these are known as *quadriliterals*. Sometimes the four root letters are a repeated sequence of two consonants (see "4-letter [quadriliteral] roots" in Chapter 1).

Verbs based on quadriliteral roots have their own specific voweling patterns. There is a basic form I and two significant derived forms.

Basic (form I) quadriliteral verbs

The voweling pattern for basic quadriliteral verbs is similar to the pattern for regular verbs in forms II–IV—*fathas* in the past tense and *ḍamma/fatha/kasra* in the present tense.

to translate	تَرْجَم/يُتَرْجِم
to crackle	طَقْطَق/يُطَقْطِق

The subject prefixes and endings remain the same as other verbs:

I translated the contract into Farsi.	تَرْجَمْتُ العَقد إلى الفارسيّة.
We will translate it into French tomorrow.	سَوفَ نُتَرْجِمهُ إلى الفَرَنسيّة غَداً.
The dry leaves crackled on the fire.	طَقْطَقَتْ أوراق الشَجَر الجافّة على النار.
They are crackling now.	إنّها تُطَقْطِق الآن.

Common quadriliteral verbs

Common quadriliteral verbs include:

to roll	دَحْرَج/يُدَحْرِج
to adorn, to decorate	زَخْرَف/يُزَخْرِف
to mutter/to recite under your breath	تَمْتَم/يُتَمْتِم
to gargle	غَرْغَر/يُغَرْغِر
to chatter	ثَرْثَر/يُثَرْثِر
to hum	دَنْدَن/يُدَنْدِن
to shake	زَلْزَل/يُزَلْزِل

EXERCISE

23·13

Write the correct part of the quadriliteral verb in the past tense and give its meaning.

EXAMPLE   تَرْجَم (نحن) تَرْجَمْنا <u>*we translated*</u>

_____ تَمْتَم (أنا) ١

_____ زَلْزَل (هي) ٢

_____ دَحْرَج (أنتَ) ٣

_____ ثَرْثَر (أنتم) ٤

_____ دَنْدَن (نحن) ٥

_____ غَرْغَر (هم) ٦

_____ زَخْرَف (هو) ٧

_____ طَقطَق (هي) ٨

Now write the correct part of the verb in the present tense and give its meaning.

EXAMPLE   it/she rolls, is rolling يُدَحْرِج (هي) تُدَحْرِج

_____ ١ يُتَرْجِم (أنتُم)

_____ ٢ يُثَرْثِر (نحن)

_____ ٣ يُطَقْطِق (هي)

_____ ٤ يُزَخْرِف (أنتِ)

_____ ٥ يُغَرْغِر (هُنَّ)

_____ ٦ يُدَنْدِن (هم)

_____ ٧ يُزَلْزِل (هو)

_____ ٨ يُتَمْتِم (أنتَ)

Write the correct Arabic verb to match the English.

EXAMPLE   يُدَنْدِن he is humming

_____ you (fem.) chatter ١

_____ we gargle ٢

_____ it (fem.) rolled ٣

_____ it (masc.) shakes ٤

_____ I muttered/recited under my breath ٥

_____ it (masc.) is crackling ٦

_____ they (masc. pl.) translated ٧

_____ you (fem. pl.) decorate ٨

Choose one of the verbs you created in Exercise 23.15 to complete the following sentences.

EXAMPLE مَنْ يُدَنْدِنِ في الحَمّام؟

١ ــــــــــــــــــــــــ الفيلم العَربيّ إلى الإنجليزيّة.

٢ هل سَـ ـــــــــــــــــــــــ الأطباق بعد أن تَخرُج من الفُرن؟

٣ ـــــــــــــــــــــــ كَلِمات الأُغنية قَبل أن أُسَجِّلها.

٤ ـــــــــــــــــــــــ بالماء والمِلح كما نَصَحَنا طَبيب الأسنان.

٥ أنتِ لا ـــــــــــــــــــــــ كَثيراً مِثل نادية وسُعاد.

٦ ـــــــــــــــــــــــ الخَشَب الرَّطِب على النار.

٧ صَوت جارَتنا وهي غاضِبة ـــــــــــــــــــــــ المَبنى كُلّه.

٨ ـــــــــــــــــــــــ الصَّخْرة من قِمّة الجَبَل نَحوَ الوادي.

Quadriliteral verbs in the derived forms

In theory there are three derived forms for quadriliteral verbs. However, in practice form III has all but died out, and forms II and IV represent no more than a handful of verbs in common circulation. The voweling patterns are:

Form II: to philosophize

تَفَلْسَف/يَتَفَلْسَف

Form IV: to shudder/to quake

اِقْشَعَرّ/يَقْشَعِرّ

To philosophize about a topic is: تَفَلْسَف/يَتَفَلْسَف في مَوضوع

I like to philosophize about life.

أُحِبّ أن أَتَفَلْسَف في الحَياة.

Ahmed and his friends like to spend their idle hours philosophizing. Their favorite subjects vary. Describe what they like to philosophize about, using the prompts.

EXAMPLE Ahmed: psychology عِلم النَّفس يُحِبّ أحمد أن يَتَفَلْسَف في عِلم النَّفس.

١ Khalid: human nature الطَّبيعة البَشَريّة

_____

٢ Samia: history التاريخ

_____

٣ نَظَرِيّة التَّطَوُّر Khalid's (male) friends: theory of evolution

_____

٤ الأدَب Samia's (female) friends: literature

_____

٥ عِلم الوَراثة Mahmoud and Nadir: genetics

_____

٦ الأخلاقيات Amira and Sara: ethics

_____

Compound tenses and conditional sentences

·24·

The verb كان (see "كان [*was/were*]" in Chapter 6) can be combined with either the past tense or the present tense to produce variations:

past perfect	كان + فَعَلَ	
past continuous	كان + يَفعَل	

Past perfect كان + فَعَلَ

The *past perfect* (sometimes also known as the *pluperfect*) is the equivalent of the English "had done," moving the action further into the past tense. It is often used with the reinforcement word قَدْ. Both كان and the following past tense verb change according to the subject:

he did it.	فَعَلَهُ.
he had (already) done it.	كانَ (قَدْ) فَعَلَهُ.
I found the keys.	وَجَدْتُ المَفاتيح.
I had (already) found the keys.	كُنْتُ (قَدْ) وَجَدْتُ المَفاتيح.

EXERCISE

24·1

Turn these past tense sentences into the past perfect and give their meaning.

EXAMPLE   رُزْتُ أمّي. كُنْتُ (قَدْ) رُزْتُ أمّي. *I had (already) visited my mother.*

١ وَجَدْتَ القَلَم. _____

٢ فَعَلْتُهُ. _____

٣ اِشتَرَينا ملابِس. _____

٤ غادَروا البيت. _____

٥ مَشَى إلى المَحَطّة. _____

٦ صَلَّحَتِ الكُرسيّ المَكسور. _____

٧ ذَهَبْنَ إلى النادي. _____

٨ شَرِبنا العَصير. _____

٩ اِستَيْقَظَتْ. _____

١٠ أَكَلوا الكَعك. _____

١١ بِعتُم السيّارة. _____

١٢ اِستَخدَمْتُ الكُمبيوتر. _____

١٣ رَدَدْتِ على الهاتِف. _____

١٤ رَأَينا المَلِك. _____

١٥ رَتَّبا غُرفَتَهُما. _____

EXERCISE
24·2

Fill in the gaps to match the English translation with the correct part of the past perfect verb in parentheses.

EXAMPLE

قَفَلْتُ الباب ولكنّ القِطّة كانَتْ (قَدْ) هَرَبَتْ. (هَرَب)

I closed the door but the cat <u>had (already) escaped.</u>

١ عادَت القِطّة إلى البيت ولكنّي _____ لِأَبحَث عَنها. (خَرَج)

The cat returned to the house but <u>I had (already) gone out</u> to search for it.

٢ وَقَفْنا أمام شُبّاك التَّذاكِر ساعتَين ولكن التَذاكِر _____ . (نَفَذ)

We stood at the ticket office for two hours but the tickets <u>had (already) run out</u>.

٣ وَصَلوا إلى المَحَطّة ولكن القِطار _____ . (غادَر)

They arrived at the station but the train <u>had (already) left it</u>.

٤ طَلَبتُ حِساب المَطعَم ولكن أصدِقائي _____ . (دَفَع)

I asked for the restaurant check but my friends <u>had already paid</u>.

٥ أَرَدتُ أن أطبُخ العَشاء ولكنّكِ _____ . (طَبَخ)

I wanted to cook dinner but you (fem.) <u>had (already) cooked it</u>.

٦ أَرَدتَ أن تُعيد الجِهاز ولكنك _____ العُلبة واستَخدَمتَهُ. (فَتَح)

You (masc.) wanted to return the appliance but <u>you had (already) opened</u> the box and used it.

٧ ذَهَبنا إلى المَدرَسة ولكن أحمد وخالد _____ إلى البيت. (عاد)

We went to the school but Ahmed and Khalid <u>had (already) returned</u> home.

٨ اِشتَرَيتُ بيتزا لدالِيا ولكنّها _____ مع أمّها. (تَعَشَّى)

I bought pizza for Dalia but she <u>had (already) had dinner</u> with her mother.

Past continuous كان + يَفعَل

The *past continuous* is the equivalent of the English "was doing" or "used to do," implying a continuous state or routine action in the past. As with the past perfect, كان and the following present tense verb both change according to the subject:

he does it	يَفعَلُهُ
he was doing it	كانَ يَفعَلُهُ
we reside in Cairo	نُقيم في القاهرة
we were residing/used to reside in Cairo	كُنّا نُقيم في القاهرة

EXERCISE
24·3

Mohammed and his family have arrived at immigration, and the officer is asking questions about their personal details. However, it seems the database is out of date and Mohammed has to correct all the information. Play the part of Mohammed and correct the information, using the prompts in parentheses.

EXAMPLE

تُقيمونَ في القاهرة. (الإسكَندَرِيّة)

لا، كُنّا نُقيم في القاهرة ولكِن الآن نُقيم في الإسكَندَرِيّة.

(No, we used to live in Cairo but now we live in Alexandria.)

١ تَعمَل أنتَ كَنَجّار. (مُهَندِس)

_____

٢ تَعمَل زَوجَتك كَمُدرِّسة. (مُفَتِّشة)

_____

٣ يَدرُس ابنك في بَيروت. (باريس)

_____

٤ تُقيم ابنِتك في الكُوَيت. (عُمان)

_____

٥ تُسافِرون إلى أمريكا كلّ صَيف. (فَرَنسا)

_____

٦ يَكتُب أبوك مَقالات لجَريدة "الأهرام". (جَريدة "الدُّستور")

_____

The subject can be placed between كان and the main verb. In the case of a plural or dual subject, كان will be singular because it comes before the subject, but the main verb after the subject will be plural *or* dual (see "Word order and singular/plural agreement" in Chapter 4 for more explanation):

The boys used to play tennis every day.   كان الأولاد يَلعَبونَ رِياضة التنس كلّ يوم.

But the girls used to play basketball.   ولكن كانَت البَنات يَلعَبْـنَ كُرة السَّـلّة.

EXERCISE

24·4

Put these sentences into the past tense using the past continuous. Place any subject between كان *and the main verb.*

EXAMPLE   يَلعَب الأطفال في الحَديقة. <u>كان الأطفال يَلعَبونَ في الحَديقة.</u>

١ تَلْعب زَينة كُرة القَدَم يوم السَّبت. _____

٢ أُقيم في دِمَشق. _____

٣ يَركَب عَمّي الخَيل. _____

٤ نَسْمَع قِصَصاً غَريبة عَن هذا البيت. _____

٥ يَصِل الأولاد إلى المَدرَسة الساعة الثامنة. _____

٦ أنتَ تَنْسَى عيد ميلادي. _____

٧ يَظُنّون أن هُناك أَمَل. _____

٨ هل تَسْتَمِعون إلى الموسيقى قَبلَ النَّوم؟ _____

٩ هل تُنَظِّفينَ الأرض؟ _____

١٠ يَتَلاقَى الأصدقاء في النادي. _____

١١ يَذهَب الصَّيّاد إلى النَّهر في الفَجر. _____

١٢ نَتَحَدَّث عن تَحسين الإنتاج. _____

١٣ تَبْتَسِم البنات كَثيراً. _____

١٤ يَطبُخ أبي وأَخي الغَداء كلّ يوم. _____

Conditional sentences

There are two main types of conditional (if) sentence:

- Possible ("if he comes, he'll repair the bicycle"/"if you see my father, give him this")
- Impossible or unlikely ("if he had come, he would have repaired the bicycle"/"if I were the prime minister, I would abolish all taxes")

Possible conditionals

Possible conditionals are formed using إذا or إِن, both meaning "if." The first verb is in the past tense—literally "if we went," "if he came"; although the meaning is "if we go," "if he comes." It is usual to introduce the second half of the sentence using فَ (*then* or *so*):

If we go to the market, (then) we'll buy apples.	إذا/إن ذَهَبنا إلى السوق فَسَنَشْتَري تُفاحاً.
If he comes, (then) he'll repair the bicycle.	إذا/إن جاءَ فَسَيُصَلِّح الدرّاجة.

EXERCISE 24·5

Join together the two sentences to make conditional sentences, taking care to change the verbs to the correct tense.

EXAMPLE   يَجيء أبي/نذهب إلى الحديقة. إذا/إن جاءَ أبي فَسَنَذهَب إلى الحَديقة.

(If my father comes, [then] we'll go to the park.)

١ أذهب إلى الحفلة./ألبس فُستاني الجديد.

_____

٢ تأخُذ هذا الطَّريق./تَصِل إلى المَطار.

_____

٣ أُعطيكُم الدولارات كلّها./تُنفِقونَهُ في أسبوع.

_____

٤ نَشتَري سَمَكة./نَشويها على الفَحم.

_____

٥ يَجيئني العَقد./أُوَقِّعهُ اليوم.

_____

٦ يَقرَأ أبي مُدَوَّنَتي./يأخُذ الكمبيوتر منّي.

_____

The second half of a possible conditional sentence can be an imperative (see Chapter 21):

If you (fem.) arrive before me, then reserve a seat for me.	إذا/إن وَصَلتِ قَبلي فاحجِزني لي مَقعَداً.
If you (masc. pl.) are not busy, then help your sister.	إذا/إن لَم تَكونوا مَشغولين فَساعِدوا أختكُم.

Samia has left her teenage son, Ibrahim, in charge of the house and his baby sister for the afternoon. She left a list of instructions, but unfortunately Ibrahim ripped the paper in half by mistake. Join the two halves of the instructions back together again, as in the example.

١ فَأَعطِها زُجاجة من حليب الأطفال.	٥ إذا رَأَيتَ البُستانيّ...
٢ فَكُلْ سَندَويتش من الثلاجة.	___ إذا أَرَدتَ أن تَجلِس في الحديقة...
٣ فَخُذْ الهاتِف معك.	___ إن أُختك اِستَيقَظَتْ...
٤ فَقُلْ لها إنّي سأَرجِع الساعة الخامسة.	___ إذا رَنَّ الجَرَس...
٥ فَأَعطِه عشرة جُنيهات.	___ إن اِتّصَلَت جَدّتك بالهاتِف...
٦ فَضَعْها على المائدة.	___ إذا شَعَرتَ بالجوع...
٧ فَلا تَفتَح الباب لأَحَد.	___ إن أَرَدتَ أن تَستَمِع إلى الموسيقى...
٨ فَأَخْفِض الصَّوت.	___ إذا وَجَدتَ مفاتيحي...

Impossible or unlikely conditionals

Impossible or unlikely conditionals are usually formed using لَوْ with the second half of the sentence introduced with لَـ. Both verbs are in the past tense, with the first verb often in the past perfect (with كان) to emphasize the fact that the possibility has gone:

If I were rich, (then) I would buy the fastest car in the world.	لَوْ كُنتُ غَنيّاً لَاشتَرَيتُ أَسرَع سيّارة في العالَم.
If we had gone to the market, we would have bought apples.	لَوْ كُنّا ذَهَبنا إلى السوق لَاشتَرَينا تُفّاحاً.
If he had come, he would have repaired the bicycle.	لَوْ كانَ جاءَ لَصَلَّحَ الدرّاجة.

Translate these sentences into Arabic.

EXAMPLE   If I had gone to the market, I would have bought a bag.

لَوْ كُنتُ ذَهَبتُ إلى السوق لَاشتَرَيتُ حقيبة.

If my father had come, we would have played tennis. ١

_____

If Ibrahim had found the keys, he would have put them on the table. ٢

_____

If Samira had arrived before me, she would have reserved a seat for me. ٣

_____

If I were rich, I would buy a large yacht. ٤

_____

If you (fem.) had heard the bell, you would have opened the door. ٥

_____

If they (masc.) had known, they would have watched the news. ٦

_____

The passive

The passive is generally used when an action and its object are being emphasized rather than the subject of the action. For example "the goods are transported (by train)" or "my son was found in the street (by a policeman)" in contrast to "a train transported the goods" or "a policeman found my son in the street."

In Arabic, the passive is formed by altering the voweling on the verb.

Past passive

The first vowel of the past passive is *ḍamma*, and the final vowel (before any subject ending) is *kasra*:

transported	نَقَل
was transported	نُقِل
found	وَجَد
was found	وُجِد
The goods were transported.	نُقِلَت البَضائِع.
My son was found in the street.	وُجِدَ اِبني في الشارِع.

A verb commonly found in the past passive is وُلِد (*was born*), from the feminine verb وَلَدَت/تَلِد (*to give birth*):

I was born in Chicago.	وُلِدْتُ في شيكاغو.
The author Naguib Mahfouz was born in the year 1911.	وُلِدَ المُؤَلِّف نَجيب مَحفوظ عام ١٩١١.

250

EXERCISE
25·1

Ibrahim has made a family tree and is telling his friend about the year and birthplace of some of his relatives. Play the part of Ibrahim and use the prompts to make sentences.

EXAMPLE   وُلِدَ أَبي في بيروت عام ١٩٥١.   أبي/بَيروت/١٩٥١

١ أُمّي/باريس/١٩٥٤ _____

٢ جَدّي/حَيفا/١٩٢٨ _____

٣ جَدّتي/القُدس/١٩٣١ _____

٤ أخي/بيروت/١٩٧٦ _____

٥ أختي/الكُويت/١٩٧٨ _____

٦ أنا/عَمّان/١٩٨٠ _____

٧ زَوجتي/إربِد/١٩٨٢ _____

٨ اِبني/عَمّان/٢٠٠٧ _____

٩ اِبنتي/جَرَش/٢٠٠٩ _____

١٠ التَّوأَم (the twins)/أمريكا/٢٠١٢ _____

Derived forms are also characterized by *ḍamma/kasra* in the passive, but may need an additional *ḍamma* in the middle:

cleaned	نَظَّف
was cleaned	نُظِّف
used	اِستَخدَم
was used	أُستُخدِم
The bathroom was cleaned.	نُظِّفَ الحَمّام.
The boxes were used for storage.	أُستُخدِمت الصَّناديق للتَّخزين.

The *kasra* of the past passive creates a long *ī* in hollow verbs:

sold	باع
was sold	بيع
add	أَضاف
was added	أُضيف
The building was sold.	بيعَ المَبنى.
The sugar was added in the factory.	أُضيفَ السُكَّر في المَصنَع.

The passive   **251**

Convert these sentences into the passive.

EXAMPLE باعوا البيت. (The house was sold.) بيعَ البيت. (They sold the house.)

١ وَجَدوا الكِتاب. _____

٢ باعوا السيّارة. _____

٣ كَتَبوا اسمي. _____

٤ سَرَقوا ساعتي. _____

٥ فَتَحوا الشُّبّاك. _____

٦ أضافوا البَصَل للَّحم. _____

٧ شَرِبوا عصير البرتقال. _____

٨ حَجَزوا الصالة للحَفل. _____

٩ قالوا إنّهُم لُصوص. _____

١٠ تَرَكوا المَفاتيح على المائِدة. _____

١١ حَمَّلوا الفيلم من الإنترنت. _____

١٢ وَرِثوا المزرَعة عن الجَدّ. _____

١٣ رَسَموا صورة جميلة للمُدرِّسة. _____

١٤ اِسْتَخْدَموا زَيت الزَيتون في هذا الطَبَق. _____

١٥ اِستَخرَجوا النواة (the stone) من المِشمِش. _____

Present passive

In the present passive, as in the past passive, the first vowel changes to a *ḍamma*, but the final vowel changes to *fatḥa*. Again this is true for all forms of the verb. Basic (form I) verbs in the present passive have only *ḍamma/fatḥa*; derived verbs retain any additional voweling in the middle:

picks	يَقطِف
is picked	يُقطَف
uses	يَستَخدِم
is used	يُستَخدَم
packages	يُعَبِّئ
is packaged	يُعَبَّأ

Oranges are picked in winter.	يُقطَف البُرتُقال في الشِّتاء.
This room is used for meetings.	تُستَخدَم هذه الغُرفة للِإجتِماعات.
The cans are packed in boxes.	تُعَبَّأ العُلَب في صَناديق.

The final *fatḥa* vowel of the present passive turns any long vowel in hollow and defective verbs into a long ā:

sells	يَبيع
is sold	يُباع
says	يَقول
is said	يُقال
adds	يُضيف
is added	يُضاف

The tomatoes are sold in the market.	تُباع الطَماطِم في السوق.
It is said that the house is haunted.	يُقال إن البيت مَسكون.
Water is added to the juice.	يُضاف الماء إلى العَصير.

EXERCISE 25·3

Translate these sentences into Arabic.

EXAMPLE   Cars are sold here. <u>تُباع السيّارات هنا.</u>

Apples are picked in October. ١

_____

The floor is cleaned every day. ٢

_____

(the) Sugar is added to the juice. ٣

_____

The clothes are sold in America. ٤

_____

The boxes are transported to the factory. ٥

_____

Every day they (masc.) are left in the park for (a period of) an hour. ٦

_____

It is said that the princess is beautiful. ٧

_____

The books are packed in boxes. ٨

_____

Olive oil is always used in this restaurant. ٩

_____

Toys are stolen from the market every day. ١٠

_____

Assimilated verbs drop the first root letter و in the active present tense, but it reappears as a long *ū* in the passive.

finds	يَجِد
is found	يوجَد
puts	يَضِع
is put	يوضَع

The passive يوجَد (*it is found*) is commonly used to mean "there is" as an alternative to هناك. Unlike هناك which remains constant, يوجَد changes to توجَد when referring to the feminine or to nonhuman plurals.

There is a mosque in the town.	يوجَد جامِع في المَدينة.
There is a school next to the mosque.	توجَد مَدرسة بجانب الجامِع.
There are some cars in the street.	توجَد سيّارات في الشارع.

EXERCISE 25·4

Rewrite the following sentences using يوجَد *(for masculine) or* توجَد *(for feminine/nonhuman plural).*

EXAMPLE   هناك زُجاجة كبيرة تحت المائدة. توجَد زُجاجة كبيرة تحت المائِدة.

١ هناك كُرسيّ في الحَديقة. _____

٢ هناك كُتُب على الكرسيّ. _____

٣ هناك مَحَطّة أُتوبيس في وَسَط المدينة. _____

٤ هناك جامِع بجانب النَّهر. _____

٥ هناك مَحَلّات كَثيرة قَريبة من بيتنا. _____

٦ هناك سيّارة للبيع. _____

٧ هناك مَلابِس في الدُّرج. _____

٨ هناك مَشاكِل كَثيرة بِهذا المَشروع. _____

٩ هناك لُصوص وراء السور. _____

١٠ هناك الزُّهور على كلّ مائِدة. _____

EXERCISE 25·5

Look at the description of the process of jam production. Complete the description by writing the correct present passive part of the verb in parentheses, as in the example. Use the additional vocabulary to help you.

أجزاء parts	أقفاص crates	ثِمار fruits	
عَبَوات jars	غَلَيان boiling	نار هادِئة gentle heat	
	تُجّار traders	شاحِنات trucks	

إنتاج المُرَبَّى

١ تُقطَف (يَقطِف picks) ثِمار الفاكِهة الناضِجة ثمّ _____ (يُعَبِّئ packages).

في أقفاص و _____ (يَنقُل transports) إلى مَصنَع المربّى.

٢ _____ (يُنَظِّف cleans) الثِمار ثمّ _____ (يَفصِل separates).

عَنها النَّواة. أحياناً _____ (يَقطَع cuts) الثِمار إلى أجزاء صغيرة.

٣ _____ (يُضيف adds) السُّكَّر ثمّ _____ (يَضَع puts) المُرَبَّى على نار هادِئة.

بعد الغليان _____ (يَضَع puts) جانِباً و _____ (يَترُك leaves) حتّى تَبْرَد.

٤ بعد ذلك _____ (يُعَبِّئ packages) المُرَبَّى في العَبَوات الزُّجاجيّة، ثمّ (يَرُصّ stacks) في صَناديق.

٥ أخيراً _____ (يُغلِق closes) الصناديق و _____ (يُحَمِّل loads) على الشاحِنات

و _____ (يَنقُل transports) إلى الأسواق لـ _____ (يُوَزِّع distributes) على التُّجّار.

Review

EXERCISE

26·1

Write out the complete past and present tenses of the four verbs, as in the example.

	خ/د/ج (TO EXIT)	ع/د/د (TO COUNT)	ز/و/ر (TO VISIT)	ج/د/ى (TO RUN)
SINGULAR				
I أنا	خَرَجْتُ/أَخْرُج	عَدَدْتُ/أَعُدّ	زُرْتُ/ أَزور	جَرَيْتُ/ أَجري
you (masc.) أنتَ	_____	_____	_____	_____
you (fem.) أنتِ	_____	_____	_____	_____
he/it (masc.) هُوَ	_____	_____	_____	_____
she/it (fem.) هِيَ	_____	_____	_____	_____
PLURAL				
we نَحنُ	_____	_____	_____	_____
you (masc. pl.) أنتُم	_____	_____	_____	_____
you (fem. pl.) أنتُنَّ	_____	_____	_____	_____
they (masc. pl.) هُمْ	_____	_____	_____	_____
they (fem.) هُنَّ	_____	_____	_____	_____
DUAL				
you (dual) أنتُما	_____	_____	_____	_____
they (masc. dual) هُما	_____	_____	_____	_____
they (fem. dual) هُما	_____	_____	_____	_____

EXERCISE 26·2

This is Samira's schedule for next week. Describe what she will do on each day.

EXAMPLE   Saturday morning: visit her friend in hospital.

يوم السَّبت صباحاً سَتزور صَديقتها في المُستشفى.

_____ Saturday evening: go to the cinema with Nadia. ١

_____ Sunday morning: take the broken watch to the shop. ٢

_____ Sunday evening: write a letter to her grandmother. ٣

_____ Monday morning: wash the clothes. ٤

_____ Monday evening: attend a meeting in the school. ٥

_____ Tuesday morning: reply to the e-mail from the bank. ٦

_____ Tuesday evening: play tennis in the club. ٧

_____ Wednesday morning: go to the market. ٨

_____ Wednesday evening: cook dinner for her mother. ٩

_____ Thursday morning: wash the car. ١٠

_____ Thursday evening: read a book. ١١

_____ Friday morning: run 3 miles. ١٢

_____ Friday evening: eat in the new restaurant. ١٣

EXERCISE 26·3

Ibrahim's mother has asked him to do some chores and is checking that he has done them. He assures her he has done everything. Play the part of Ibrahim and answer the questions.

EXAMPLE   هَلْ غَسَلْتَ الأطباق؟ نَعَم، غَسَلْتُها.

١ هَلْ طَبَخْتَ الأرُزّ؟ _____

٢ هَلْ فَتَحْتَ شُبّاك غُرفتك؟ _____

٣ هَلْ حَجَزْتَ التَذاكِر للفيلم الجديد؟ _____

٤ هَلْ وَضَعْتَ درّاجَتك في الجَراج؟ _____

٥ هَلْ أخَذْتَ الأولاد إلى الحديقة؟ _____

٦ هَلْ قَرأْتَ الرسالة من المُدَرِّب؟ _____

٧ هَلْ زُرْتَ جَدّك؟ _____

٨ هَلْ وَجَدْتَ المَفاتيح؟ _____

Choose the correct part of the verb in parentheses to complete the sentence or question.

EXAMPLE   تتحدّث (يتحدّث/تتحدّث/تتحدّثين) أمّي الفَرَنسيّة بِطَلاقة.

١ ـــــــــــــــــــــــ (أتحسّن/يتحسّن/تتحسّن) صِحّتي بعد يَومَين في المستشفى.

٢ أنا ـــــــــــــــــــــــ (سابقتُ/سابقت/سابقتِ/سابقتَ) أخي إلى الحديقة.

٣ يا لوسي، هل ـــــــــــــــــــــــ (يتذكّر/تتذكّر/تتذكّرين) عُطلَتنا في مِصر؟

٤ نادية ـــــــــــــــــــــــ (استمع/استمعوا/استمتعَتْ) بالحفلة.

٥ نحن ـــــــــــــــــــــــ (ستستقبل/سأستقبل/سنستقبل) الضُيوف عند الباب.

٦ الأصدقاء ـــــــــــــــــــــــ (يتقاتل/يتقاتلون/يتقاتلان) أحياناً من أجل المال.

٧ ـــــــــــــــــــــــ (سأعلن/سيُعلن/ستُعلن) المتحدّث الرَّسميّ الخَبَر غَداً.

٨ ـــــــــــــــــــــــ (كسّرَت/كسّرَ/كسّروا) اللصوص زُجاج الشُّبّاك.

٩ نظر الأولاد إلى الصورة و ـــــــــــــــــــــــ (ابتسموا/ابتسم/ابتسمَتْ).

١٠ لا ـــــــــــــــــــــــ (يستخدمون/استخدموا/سَيستخدمون) هذا البَرنامَج في العمل.

١١ هم ـــــــــــــــــــــــ (درّستم/درّسوا/درّس) اللُّغة العَرَبيّة في الجامعة.

١٢ أبي وأمّي لا ـــــــــــــــــــــــ (يسافر/يسافران/سيسافران) بالطائرة أبداً.

١٣ لماذا لا ـــــــــــــــــــــــ (تنظّف/تنظّفنَ/تنظّفين) السيّارة يا بنات؟

١٤ ـــــــــــــــــــــــ (تنقسم/ينقسمون/تنقسمون) الدَّولة إلى مُحافظات شَماليّة وجَنوبيّة.

Make the sentences and questions negative. Use لَن *for the future and* لَم *for the past. Check the following examples of each.*

EXAMPLE   سيَشرَب الطِّفل زُجاجة حَليب. لَنْ يَشرَب الطِّفل زُجاجة حَليب.

شاهَدوا ذلك البَرنامَج أمس. لَمْ يُشاهِدوا ذلك البَرنامَج أمس.

١ سَوفَ أكتُب خِطاباً للوَزير. ـــــــــــــــــــــــ

٢ سَيُسافِرون بِطائِرة خاصّة. ـــــــــــــــــــــــ

٣ احتَفَلنا بِعيد ميلاد زوجي. ـــــــــــــــــــــــ

٤ رَكِبْتُ جَمَلاً في مِصر. ـــــــــــــــــــــــ

٥ سوف يَبيعونَ السيّارة في العام القادِم. ـــــــــــــــــــــــ

٦ وَجَدوا الخاتِم في السيّارة. ـــــــــــــــــــــــ

٧ سَنَتَحَدَّث في هذا المَوضوع أمامَ الأولاد. _____

٨ ارتَدَيْتِ الفُستان الجديد. _____

٩ لماذا طَبَخْتُنَّ السمكة؟ _____

١٠ زادَت الأسعار هذا العام. _____

١١ سَيُسَبِّب لَك مَشاكِل. _____

١٢ لماذا قَصَصْتَ شَعرك؟ _____

١٣ سَتَجري سميرة في سِباق الأُمَّهات. _____

١٤ استَطاعَتْ نادية أن تَستَقبِل خالَتَها في المَطار. _____

١٥ لماذا رَدَدْتُم على الهاتِف؟ _____

١٦ سَيُعِدّ المُدير العَقد قَبلَ الساعة الخامِسة. _____

EXERCISE
26·6

A teacher is organizing a party for the end of the school semester. She is giving her pupils instructions on what to do. Playing the part of the teacher, follow the English prompts and write her instructions in Arabic using the following list of verbs.

opens يَفْتَح	washes يَغْسِل	draws يَرسُم
removes يُخرِج	sits يجلِس	helps يُساعِد
says يَقول	counts يَعُدّ	carries يَحمِل
hurries يُسرِع	tidies يُرَتِّب	waits يَنتَظِر
stands يَقِف	gives يُعطي	puts يَضَع
closes يَقْفِل	asks for يَطْلُب	moves يَتَحَرَّك
		goes يذهَب

EXAMPLE   Nadia, Ahmed, and Samira: sit on the floor here

نادية وأحمد وسميرة: اجلِسوا على الأرض هنا.

١ Jamila: put your bag over there _____

٢ Bakr: open the window _____

٣ Warda: wash this plate _____

٤ Anwar: draw a picture of a house _____

٥ Mona, Farida, and Nabila: remove these clothes from the room _____

٦ Sara: help Anwar please _____

_____ Hussein, Jihan, and Maha: give the principal this invitation ٧

_____ Lucy, Tom, and Karim: tidy the books ٨

_____ Fatima, Zeinah, and Noura: wait here ٩

_____ Badr: adjust these pictures ١٠

_____ Amira: carry this desk over there ١١

_____ Nadir and Zainab: request a ball from the coach ١٢

_____ Zahra, Jamal, and Hassan: count the pens ١٣

_____ Mohammed: stand next to the door ١٤

_____ Ashraf and Sharifa: close the box of toys ١٥

_____ Ibrahim: tell me, what did you do? ١٦

_____ Quickly children. Move! Hurry up! ١٧

EXERCISE
26·7

This is the process for producing apple juice from orchard to supermarket shelf. Put the passive verbs in the list in the correct gaps to complete the process.

تُنقَل	يُقطَف	يُستَخرَج
يُضاف	تُحَمَّل	توضَع
يوضَع	يُصَبّ	تُعَبَّأ

EXAMPLE   يُقطَف التفّاح في البُستان.

_____ التفّاح في الأقفاص. ١

_____ الأقفاص إلى المصنع بالقِطار. ٢

_____ العَصير في المصنع. ٣

_____ السُكَّر إلى العصير. ٤

_____ العصير في زجاجات. ٥

_____ الزجاجات في صَناديق. ٦

_____ الصَناديق على شاحِنات. ٧

_____ زجاجات العصير على رُفوف السوبرماركت. ٨

Answer key

 ROOTS, NONVERBAL SENTENCES, AND PRONOUNS

1 Word roots

1.1

to look ٤	to open ٣	to write ٢	to study ١
to go ٨	to carry ٧	to break ٦	to wear ٥
to kill ١٢	to work ١١	to drink ١٠	to hear ٩
	to understand ١٥	to wash ١٤	to do ١٣

1.2

ع/د/ف ٤	ق/ف/ل ٣	ط/ب/خ ٢	س/ك/ن ١
خ/د/ج ٨	ل/ع/ب ٧	ق/ف/ز ٦	ر/ج/ع ٥
ظ/ه/ر ١٢	ض/د/ب ١١	س/ق/ط ١٠	ر/س/م ٩
	ص/ن/ع ١٥	ط/ل/ب ١٤	ض/ح/ك ١٣

1.3

I worked ٤	I went out ٣	I sat ٢	I studied ١
I closed ٨	I drank ٧	I wore ٦	I opened ٥
		I broke ١٠	I laughed ٩

1.4

to wear س/ب/ل ٤	to learn ع/ل/م ٣	to write ك/ت/ب ٢	to study د/ر/س ١
to hear س/م/ع ٨	to carry ح/م/ل ٧	to land ه/ب/ط ٦	to search ب/ح/ث ٥
to stay ن/ز/ل ١٢	to look ن/ظ/ر ١١	to collect ج/م/ع ١٠	to draw ر/س/م ٩
	to own م/ل/ك ١٥	to do ف/ع/ل ١٤	to plant ز/ر/ع ١٣

1.5

to repeat ك/ر/ر ٤	to show/prove د/ل/ل ٣	to reply ر/د/د ٢	to cause س/ب/ب ١
to count ع/د/د ٨	to join ض/م/م ٧	to cut ق/ص/ص ٦	to turn ل/ف/ف ٥
		to doubt ش/ك/ك ١٠	to pass by م/ر/ر ٩

1.6

defective; to walk ٣	assimilated; to arrive ٢	hollow; to visit ١
hollow; to fly ٦	assimilated; to wake up ٥	hollow; to say ٤
defective; to give ٩	assimilated; to put ٨	defective; to request ٧
assimilated; to give birth ١٢	defective; to sing ١١	hollow; to shout ١٠

1.7

و/ص/ف ٤	ب/ي/ع ٣	و/ص/ل ٢	م/ش/ي ١
ل/ق/ي ٨	ن/ه/ي ٧	ج/د/ي ٦	ع/و/د ٥
ي/ق/ظ ١١	ق/و/م ١٠	ر/ج/و ٩
س/ق/ط ١٥	ش/ك/و ١٤	ش/د/ي ١٣

1.8	٤ و/ج/د to find	٣ و/ض/ع to put	٢ ش/ر/ي to buy	١ ش/ك/و to complain
	٨ و/ل/د to give birth	٧ ب/د/و to appear	٦ غ/ن/ي to sing	٥ ط/ي/ر to fly
	١٢ ج/ر/ي to run	١١ ي/ق/ن to be certain	١٠ ق/و/م to stand up	٩ د/و/ر to go round

1.9	٤ م/ل/ء	٣ ب/د/ء	٢ ق/ر/ء	١ س/ء/م
	٨ ء/خ/ذ	٧ ب/ط/ء	٦ ء/م/ر	٥ س/ء/ل
			١٠ ج/ر/ء	٩ ء/ك/ل

1.10	٤ we asked	٣ we hoped	٢ we read	١ we took
	٨ we became slow	٧ we commanded/ordered	٦ we got fed up	٥ we began
			١٠ we dared	٩ we filled

1.11	٤ to roll	٣ to crackle	٢ to mutter	١ to adorn
	٨ to translate	٧ to chatter	٦ to shake	٥ to hum

1.12	٤ يُغَرْغِر	٣ يُزَلْزِل	٢ يُتَمْتِم	١ يُتَرْجِم
	٨ يُزَخْرِف	٧ يُثَرْثِر	٦ يُطَقْطِق	٥ يُدَحْرِج

2 Nonverbal sentences and pronouns

2.1
٣ شُكري في بَيتي.
٢ نادية في أَمريكا.
١ نَحنُ في الحَديقة.
٦ أَنا في المدرسة.
٥ المَدرَسة بجانِب الجامِع.
٤ هُناكَ جامِع في المَدينة.
٩ بَيتي في أَمريكا.
٨ الكُتُب على الكُرسيّ.
٧ هُناكَ كُرسيّ في الحَديقة.
١٢ أَنا بِجانِب شكري.
١١ هُناكَ كُتُب في السيّارة.
١٠ شُكري أَمامَ السيّارة.

2.2
٣ لا، المَلابِس في السيّارة.
٢ لا، نادية في الجامِع.
١ لا، شكري في البيت.
٦ لا، هُناكَ مَلابِس تَحت الكُرسيّ.
٥ لا، هُناكَ كُتُب على الكُرسيّ.
٤ لا، الكُتُب تَحت السيّارة.
٩ لا، نحن أمامَ المدرسة.
٨ لا، نادية في الكُوَيْت.
٧ لا، أَنا في أمريكا.
١٢ لا، المَلابِس بجانِب الكُرسيّ.
١١ لا، المَلابِس تَحت الكُرسيّ.
١٠ لا، نحن بجانِب الجامِع.
١٤ لا، هُناك كُرسيّ في السيّارة.
١٣ لا، هُناك مَلابِس في الحَديقة.

2.3
٤ جَديدة new
٣ صَغيرة small
٢ مَقفولة closed
١ ثَقيلة heavy
٨ قَديمة old
٧ كَبيرة big/large
٦ غَريبة strange
٥ قَصيرة short
١٢ طَويلة long/tall
١١ جَميلة beautiful
١٠ نَظيفة clean
٩ مَفتوحة open
١٥ مَكسورة broken
١٤ بَطيئة slow
١٣ خَفيفة light

2.4
٣ هناك قَلَم قصير في الدُرج.
٢ هناك مَحفَظة خفيفة في الدُرج.
١ هناك مِفتاح صغير في الدُرج.
٦ هناك نَظّارة قديمة في الدُرج.
٥ هناك خاتِم جميل في الدُرج.
٤ هناك مِسطَرة طويلة في الدُرج.
٩ هناك قُفّاز نظيف في الدُرج.
٨ هناك ساعة مكسورة في الدُرج.
٧ هناك صورة كبيرة في الدُرج.
١٠ هناك حَشَرة غريبة في الدُرج.

2.5
٢ نادية خفيفة الوَزن .
٢ نادية سَريعة.
١ نادية نَشيطة.
٦ نادية مُهَندِسة.
٥ نادية نَكِيّة جِدّاً.
٤ نادية مَشغولة دائِماً.
٩ نادية خائِفة من الحَشَرات.
٨ نادية عَصَبيّة.
٧ نادية مُجتَهِدة في العَمَل.
١٠ نادية صَبورة مع الأطفال.

١ هُنَّ   ٢ أَنْتُـنَّ   ٣ هُمْ

٤ أَنْتُمْ   ٥ أَنْتَ   ٦ أَنا

٧ هِيَ   ٨ أَنْتِ

2.7

١ هِيَ مشغولة دائِماً.   ٢ هُمْ في البيت.   ٣ هُوَ مهندس.

٤ هي بجانب البيت.   ٥ هو في وَسَط المدينة.   ٦ هي طويلة وجميلة.

٧ نَحنُ في الحديقة.   ٨ هو طَويل.   ٩ هُنَّ في المدرسة.

١٠ هُمْ في أمريكا.

2.8

١ هي   ٢ هو   ٣ هو

٤ هي   ٥ هي   ٦ هُم

٧ هو   ٨ هي   ٩ هُم

١٠ هُنَّ

2.9

١ خاتِمان   ٢ المهندسان   ٣ المهندسان المشغولان

٤ جامعان   ٥ جامعان كبيران   ٦ مَمَرّان طويلان

٧ القلمان الجديدان   ٨ الحديقتان الجميلتان

2.10

١ هما مشغولتان.   ٢ أنتُما مُجتَهِدان.   ٣ هما طويلَتان وجميلَتان.

٤ هما خائِفان من الحَشَرات.   ٥ أنتُما بنتان ذَكيَّتان.   ٦ أنتُما وَلَدان طَويلان.

٧ هما بيتان قديمان.   ٨ هما سيّارتان سريعَتان.

2.11

١ الخَواتم جَميلة.   ٢ المُدُن مَشهورة.   ٣ هذِه السيّارات جَديدة.

٤ الحَشَرات صغيرة وسَريعة.   ٥ هذِه البُيوت قَديمة.   ٦ المفاتيح الصغيرة تحت الملابس.

٧ هذه الحَقائِب مَفتوحة.   ٨ هناك مُدُن كبيرة في الجَنوب.   ٩ هذه هي المَفاتيح.

١٠ هذه هي الحَقائِب.   ١١ هذه هي أقلام شكري.   ١٢ هذه هي ساعات أُمّي.

2.12

١ البُيوت جَميلة.   ٢ المَفاتيح ثَقيلة.   ٣ الصُوَر كَبيرة.

٤ هذه الحَقائِب خَفيفة.   ٥ هذه الساعات قَديمة.   ٦ هذه هي البُيوت.

٧ هذه هي الأقلام.   ٨ هذه هي خَواتم أُمّي.   ٩ هذه هي مَفاتيح شُكري.

١٠ المُدُن صَغيرة في الجَنوب.   ١١ السيّارات جديدة في هذا الشارع.   ١٢ هناك صُوَر جميلة في بَيتي.

١٣ هناك بُيوت قديمة في هذه المَدينة.   ١٤ هناك حَشَرات غريبة في الدُرج.

2.13

١ فَهِمَتْنا   ٢ فَهِمَتْهُم   ٣ فَهِمَتْك

٤ فَهِمَتْهُ   ٥ فَهِمَتْكُم   ٦ فَهِمَتْهُما

٧ فَهِمَتْني   ٨ فَهِمَتْهُنَّ   ٩ مِفتاحي

١٠ مِفتاحُك   ١١ مِفتاحُهُنَّ   ١٢ مِفتاحُها

١٣ مِفتاحُهُ   ١٤ مِفتاحُهُم   ١٥ مِفتاحُكم

١٦ مِفتاحُنا   ١٧ سَمِعتُهُ   ١٨ سَمِعتُك

١٩ سَمِعتُهُم   ٢٠ سَمِعتُها   ٢١ سَمِعتَكَ

٢٢ سَمِعتُهُنَّ   ٢٣ سَمِعتُكم   ٢٤ سَمِعتُكُما

٢٥ شاحناتُها   ٢٦ شاحناتُكم   ٢٧ شاحناتُهُم

٢٨ شاحناتُنا   ٢٩ شاحناتُكَ   ٣٠ شاحناتي

٣١ شاحناتُهَما   ٣٢ شاحناتُهُنَّ

٣ بَدَأَتْهُ.	٢ طَبَخْتَهُ.	١ أَكَلْناهُ.
٦ غَسَلْتُها.	٥ مَسَكْتُها.	٤ سَمِعَهُ.
٩ دَرَسْتُمُها.	٨ فَهِمتُهُم.	٧ قَفَلْنَهُ.
١٢ تَبِعناهُما.	١١ سَمِعَتْهُنَّ.	١٠ وَجَدَها.

2.14 (above)

2.15

٢ لِأُمّي (عِندَ أُمّي) خَواتِـم كثيرة في الدُرج.	١ لِنادية (عِندَ نادية) بيت جميل في المَدينة.
٤ لِلمُدَرِّسة (عِندَ المُدَرِّسة) مَكتَب صَغير في المَدرسة.	٣ لِصَديقي (عِندَ صَديقي) سيّارة سريعة في الشارع.
٦ لِلبِنت (عِندَ البِنت) مَلابِس نَظيفة في الدرج.	٥ لِابن أُختي (عِندَ ابن أُختي) شَجَرة طويلة في الحَديقة.
٨ لِلمُدير (عِندَ المُدير) صورة جميلة في المَكتَب.	٧ لِأحمَد (عِندَ أحمَد) صَديق في أمريكا.
١٠ لِلمَلِك (عِندَ المَلِك) طائرة كبيرة في المَطار.	٩ لِلرَّجُل (عِندَ الرَّجُل) نَظّارة في السيّارة.
١٢ لِهذا الوَلَد (عِندَ هذا الوَلَد) حَشَرة غريبة في الصَندوق.	١١ لِلرَّسّام (عِندَ الرَّسّام) ساعة قديمة في الصالة.

2.16

٣ عِندَكِ you (fem.) have	٢ عِندَهُم they (masc.) have	١ عِندَها she has
٦ عِندَكَ you (masc.) have	٥ عِندَكُم you (masc. pl.) have	٤ عِندَهُ he has
٩ عِندَهُما they (dual) have	٨ عِندَهُنَّ they (fem.) have	٧ عِندي I have
	١٠ عِندَكُنَّ you (fem. pl.) have	

2.17

٣ عِندَهُ	٢ عِندَهُ	١ عِندَها
٦ عِندَهُما	٥ عِندَهُ	٤ عِندَهُم
	٨ عِندَهُنَّ	٧ عِندَها

2.18

٣ لَكِ you (fem.) have	٢ لَهُم they have	١ لَها she has
٦ لَكَ you (masc.) have	٥ لَكُم you (pl.) have	٤ لَهُ he has
٩ لَهُما they (dual) have	٨ لَهُنَّ they (fem. pl.) have	٧ لي I have
	١٠ لَكُنَّ you (fem. pl.) have	

2.19

٣ لَكِ حديقة جميلة.	٢ لي أُخت في أمريكا.	١ لَهُم ثَلاثة بُيوت.
٦ لَهُ أُخت اسمها نادية.	٥ لَها أخ اسمُهُ شَكري.	٤ لَنا ساعة مَكسورة في الدُرج.
٩ لَكَ سيّارة سَريعة.	٨ لَهُما شِقّة كبيرة.	٧ لَهُم صورة غريبة في الصالة.
١٢ لَكُما ابن ذَكيّ!	١١ لَهُنَّ مَكتَب صَغير في المَدرسة.	١٠ لي سيّارة بَطيئة جِدّاً.

2.20

٣ لَدَينا مَكتَب صَغير في المَصنَع.	٢ لَدَيكُم تين طازِج اليوم.	١ مَعَكِ كِتاب نادية.
٦ مَعَهُنَّ مِفتاح الشِقّة.	٥ لَدَيكِ شَقّة جميلة في وَسَط المدينة.	٤ مَعَهُ شُموع كثيرة.
٩ لَدَيها خَواتِم جميلة.	٨ لَدَيكُما ابنة ذَكِيّة ومُجتَهِدة.	٧ مَعي ثلاث دولارات.
		١٠ مَعَكُم الأقلام والكُتُب.

3 Forming questions

3.1

٣ هَل الكُرسيّ في الحَمّام؟	٢ هَل هو في المَدرسة؟	١ هَل هي مُهَندِسة؟
٦ هَل المُدير في المَكتَب؟	٥ هَل الأقلام بِجانِب الكُتُب؟	٤ هَل لِشَريف سيّارة جديدة؟
٩ هَل وَجَدَتْ نادية المِفتاح؟	٨ هَل هُناك حَديقة جميلة في وَسَط المدينة؟	٧ هَل هي مُهَندِسة؟
١٢ هَل يَسكُن شَريف في شَقّة صغيرة؟	١١ هَل أَكَلَ شكري السَّمَك؟	١٠ هَل عِندَهُم أطفال؟

3.2	٢ هَل لَهُ (عِندَهُ) شَقّة صغيرة؟	١ هَل يَسكُن قَريب من بَيتك؟
٣ هَل الشَّقّة جديدة؟	٥ هَل لَهُ (عِندَهُ) سيّارة؟	٤ هَل لَهُ (عِندَهُ) أطفال؟
٦ هَل لَهُ (عِندَهُ) حَديقة؟	٨ هَل المكتب في وَسَط المَدينة؟	٧ هَل الشَّقّة قَريبة من المَكتَب؟
٩ هَل ابنك مُهَندِس؟	١١ هَل هو مَشغول دائماً؟	١٠ هَل هو مُجتَهِد؟
١٢ هَل مُديرُهُ صَبور؟		
3.3	٢ أهُنَّ مُمَرِّضات؟	١ أأنتَ المُهندِس الجديد؟
٣ أهي في الحديقة؟	٥ أأنتِ مَعي؟	٤ ألا يسكُن في بيروت؟
٦ أهذا بيتك؟	٨ أأنتُم مُحاسِبون؟	٧ أهذه الحقيبة ثقيلة؟
3.4	٢ كَيفَ وَجَدَت خاتمها؟	١ أينَ وَجَدَت خاتمها؟
٣ مَتَى وَجَدَت خاتمها؟	٥ لِماذا فَتَحوا الصَّندوق؟	٤ كَيفَ فَتَحوا الصَّندوق؟
٦ أينَ فَتَحوا الصَّندوق؟	٨ في أيَّة جامعة يَدرُس؟	٧ لِماذا يَدرُس التاريخ؟
٩ ماذا أَكَلَ؟	١١ أينَ أَكَلَ في مَطعَم؟	١٠ مَتَى أَكَلَ في مَطعَم؟
١٢ مَعَ مَن أَكَلَ؟		
3.5	٢ مَن	١ ما
٣ كَيفَ	٥ أيّ	٤ أينَ
٦ أيّة	٨ ماذا	٧ هَل
٩ مَتَى		١٠ لِماذا

II ◆ PAST TENSE

4 Regular basic verbs and sentence structure

4.1	٢ غَسَلْنا we washed	١ جَلَسْتُ I sat
٣ فَهِمَ he understood	٥ حَمَلْتُنَّ you (fem. pl.) carried	٤ كَتَبْتِ you (fem.) wrote
٦ خَرَجوا they (masc.) went out	٨ لَعِبْتَ you (masc.) played	٧ كَبُرَتْ she grew up
٩ طَبَخْتُمْ you (masc. pl.) cooked		١٠ فَهِمْنَ they (fem.) understood
4.2	٢ طَبَخَ	١ خَرَجْتُ
٣ غَسَلْتَ	٥ فَهِمْنا	٤ حَمَلْت
٦ شَرِبْتْ	٨ كَتَبْتُمْ	٧ جَلَسْنَ
٩ كَبُروا		١٠ لَعِبْتُنَّ
4.3	٢ شَرِبْتَ فنجان شاي.	١ شَرِبَ كوب حَليب.
٣ شَرِبَتْ عصير رُمان.	٥ شَرِبْتِ كوب ماء.	٤ شَرِبْنا عصير تُفّاح.
٦ شَرِبوا كولا.	٨ شَرِبْتُمْ عصير بُرتُقال.	٧ شَرِبْنَ عصير لَيمون.
4.4	٢ she wore	١ I hit
٣ we went down	٥ you (masc. pl.) jumped	٤ he searched
٦ they (fem.) left	٨ you (masc.) hated	٧ they (masc.) stole
٩ we escaped	١١ I did	١٠ you (fem.) laughed
١٢ he/it descended	١٤ you (fem. pl.) requested	١٣ she held
١٥ you (masc. pl.) reserved		

4.5	٣ رَسَمَتْ صورة.	٢ غَسَلَتْ المَلابِس.	١ شَرِبَتْ فِنجان قَهوة.
	٦ كَتَبَتْ رِسالة إلِكْترونيّة.	٥ لَعِبَتْ تِنِس.	٤ طَبَخَتْ الغَداء.
		٨ ذَهَبَتْ إلى الحديقة.	٧ رَكِبَتْ دَرّاجَتها.
4.6	٣ رَسَمْتُ صورة.	٢ غَسَلْتُ المَلابِس.	١ شَرِبْتُ فِنجان قَهوة.
	٦ كَتَبْتُ رِسالة إلِكْترونيّة.	٥ لَعِبْتُ تِنِس.	٤ طَبَخْتُ الغَداء.
		٨ ذَهَبْتُ إلى الحديقة.	٧ رَكِبْتُ دَرّاجَتي.
4.7	٣ طَلَبْتُ	٢ رَكِبَتْ	١ شَرِبوا
	٦ سَقَطَ	٥ دَخَلْنا	٤ جَلَسْتِ
	٩ رَجَعْتُمْ	٨ سَرَقَ	٧ حَمَلَتْ
	١٢ حَجَزْتُمْ	١١ رَقَصْنَ	١٠ سَكَنَ
4.8	٣ رَكِبَتْ	٢ رَجَعْتُمْ	١ دَخَلْنا
	٦ حَمَلَتْ	٥ شَرِبوا	٤ رَقَصْنَ
	٩ سَقَطَ	٨ حَجَزْتُمْ	٧ طَلَبْتُ
	١٢ جَلَسْتِ	١١ سَكَنَ	١٠ سَرَقَ
4.9	٣ سَرَقوها.	٢ بَحَثْنا عَنها.	١ دَخَلوهُ.
	٦ الأولاد شَرِبوهُ.	٥ رَقَصْتُ علَيهِ.	٤ ذَهَبْنا إلَيهِ.
	٩ خَرَجَت الحَشَرات مِنها.	٨ هل جَلَسْتِ علَيها؟	٧ مَتى رَجَعْتُمْ مِنهُ؟
	١٢ جَلَسوا علَيها.	١١ رَجَعْتُ إلَيهِمْ.	١٠ خَرَجوا مِنهُ.
	١٥ سَمِعْنا عَنهُ.	١٤ رَسَموها.	١٣ نَظَرْتُ إلَيهِنَّ.
			١٦ الرِجال حَمَلوها.
4.10	٣ إنّ الحِصان قَفَزَ مِن فَوقَ السِّياج.	٢ إنّ أُمّي دَفَعَت ثَمَن الفُستان.	١ إنّ شكري دَخَلَ الغُرفة.
	٦ إنّ الحَشَرات خَرَجَت من الشَّجَرة.	٥ إنّ الوَلَد شَرِبَ عصير البرتقال.	٤ إنّ ابنَتي دَرَسَت اللُّغة العربيّة.
	٩ إنّ اللِصّ سَرَقَ الحَقيبة.	٨ إنّ لَيلى طَبَخَت الغَداء.	٧ إنّ المُدير ذَهَبَ إلى مَكتَبِه.
			١٠ إنّ نادية تَرَكَت المَفاتيح على المائِدة.
4.11	٣ فَتَحَ اللُّصوص الشُّباك.	٢ خَرَجَت البَنات من البيت.	١ شَرِبَ الأولاد العصير.
	٦ رَسَمَ الأطفال صورة جميلة للمدرسة.	٥ حَضَرَت المُدَرِّسات الاِجتِماع.	٤ رَقَصَ كُلّ أَصدِقائي في الحَفلة.
		٨ عَمِلَ الرِجال حَتَّى الساعة التاسِعة مَساءً.	٧ دَخَلَت الطالِبات الجامِعة.
4.12	٣ سَمِعَ، ضَحِكوا	٢ خَرَجَت، لَعِبْـنَ	١ جَلَسَ، حَفِظوا
	٦ سَقَطَ، جَرَحوا	٥ رَكِبَتْ، ذَهَبْـنَ	٤ فَتَحَ، سَرَقوا
	٩ دَخَلَت، طَبَخْـنَ	٨ دَفَعَ، رَجَعوا	٧ ذَهَبَ، لَبِسوا
			١٠ تَرَكَ، رَقَصوا
4.13	٣ لِماذا ما حَضَرْتَ هذا الاِجتِماع؟	٢ ما سَمِعوا عن هذه المدينة.	١ ما رَكِبْتُ الطائِرة أَمس.
	٦ إنّ الطالِبات ما دَرَسْنَ الفَرَنسيّة السَّنة الماضية.	٥ ما خَرَجَتْ أُمّي من غُرفتها اليوم.	٤ ما حَفِظْنا المَسرَحيّة كلّها.
	٩ ما طَلَبْتُ فِنجان قَهوة.	٨ لِماذا ما تَرَكْتُم المَطعَم؟	٧ ما حَرَقَت الخِطابات والصُّوَر.
			١٠ الأولاد ما جَلَسوا على الأرض.

4.14

١ حَجَزَ شكري الفِرقة ولكِن ما بَحَثَ عن بَدلَتُه.

٢ ذَهَبَت أُمّ نادية إلى السوق ولكِن ما طَبَخَت الفَلافِل.

٣ غَسَلَ أبو نادية السيّارة ولكِن ما دَفَعَ ثَمَن الزُّهور.

٤ كَتَبَ عَمّ نادية القائِمة ولكِن ما طَلَبَ الخُبز.

٥ الأطفال رَسَموا (رَسَمَ الأطفال) الصُوَر ولكِن ما حَفِظوا مَسرَحيَّتَهُم.

4.15

١ هل حَجَزَ شكري الفِرقة؟ نعم، حَجَزَها. هل بَحَثَ عن بَدلَتِه؟ لا، ما بَحَثَ عنها.

٢ هل ذَهَبَت أُمّ نادية إلى السوق؟ نعم، ذَهَبَت إلَيه. هل طَبَخَت الفَلافِل؟ لا، ما طَبَخَتها.

٣ هل غَسَلَ أبو نادية السيّارة؟ نعم، غَسَلَها. هل دَفَعَ ثَمَن الزُّهور؟ لا، ما دَفَعَهُ.

٤ هل كَتَبَ عَمّ نادية القائِمة؟ نعم، كَتَبَها. هل طَلَبَ الخُبز؟ لا، ما طَلَبَهُ.

٥ هل الأطفال رَسَموا الصُوَر؟ نعم، رَسَموها. هل حَفِظوا مَسرَحيَّتَهُم؟ لا، ما حَفِظوها.

4.16

٣ سَرَقَ اللُّصوص حَقيبَتي... | ٢ شَرِبَ ابني حَليباً. | ١ هل حَجَزْتَ مِقعَداً على القِطار؟

٦ حَمَلْتُ الكُتُب الثَقيلة. | ٥ حَمَلَ سامِح حَقيبة كبيرة. | ٤ ...وسَرَقوا خاتِماً جَميلاً.

| ٨ ...ولكِن ما طَلَبنا السَّمَك . | ٧ طَلَبنا خُبزاً...

4.17

٣ تَخَل الطيّارون صالة الوُصول. | ٢ سَمِعْنا اللاعِبين في الحديقة. | ١ رَكِبَ المُسافِرون القِطار.

٦ خَرَجَ البَقّالون مِن سوق الخُضار. | ٥ هل تَرَكْتَ الطبّاخين بَعدَ الغَداء؟ | ٤ نَكَرْتُ المُمَثِّلين في خِطابي.

| ٨ لِماذا ما شَكَرَ اللاعِبون المُدَرِّبين؟ | ٧ جَلَسَ المُدَرِّسون بَعدَ الدَّرس.

5 Doubled verbs in the past tense

5.1

٣ رَدَدْنا على الرِسالة. | ٢ رَدَّ على أُمّه. | ١ هل رَدَدْتَ على الهاتِف؟

٦ مَتَى رَدَدْتِ على المُدير. | ٥ هل رَدَدْتُم على الدَّعوة؟ | ٤ لِماذا ما رَدَّت أمس؟

| ٨ ما رَدَدْنَ على المُدَرِّسة. | ٧ رَدَدْتُ أمس.

5.2

٣ شَكَكْتُ | ٢ قَصَّ | ١ عَدّوا

٦ بَثَّ | ٥ لَفَّتُ | ٤ تَمَّ

٩ ضَمَمْنَ | ٨ دَلَلْتَ | ٧ شَمِمْنا

١٢ مَرَرْتُنَّ | ١١ مَدَدْتُ | ١٠ ظَنَنْتِ

5.3

٣ قَصَّت | ٢ تَمَّ | ١ شَمَّ

٦ دَلَلْناها | ٥ مَدَّ | ٤ عَدَدْت

٩ لَفَفْتُم | ٨ ظَنّوا | ٧ شَكَكْنَ

١٢ مَرَّ شَمّوا | ١١ ضَمَّني | ١٠ رَدَدْتُ

5.4

٣ بَثَّت المَحَطّات هذا الخَبَر أمس. | ٢ لِماذا ما رَدَدْتُم؟ | ١ المُهندسون مَرّوا على البُرج.

٦ ما مَرَّت الطائِرات فوق أسبانيا. | ٥ قَصَّت البَنات الزُهور في الحديقة. | ٤ هل شَكَكْتُنَّ في الطبّاخ؟

٨ لَفَّ الأولاد حَولَ الحديقة وعَدّوا الشَجَر. | ٧ عَدَدْنا الضُّيوف عِندَ الباب.

5.5

بَثَّ التليفِزيون أمس حِواراً مع فوزي أبو شعرة حَلّاق المَلِك:

"قِصّتي هي أنَّني شَكَكْتُ وأنا طِفل أن عندي مَرَض خَطير لأنَّني في يَوم من الأيّام شَمِمْتُ رائحة غَريبة على وِسادَتي في الصَّباح، ثُمَّ وَجَدْتُ شعري كلَّه على الوِسادة وفي رأسي عَدَدْتُ ثلاث شعرات فَقَط. أنا عَدَدْتُها بِنَفسي!

مَرَرْتُ مع أبي على المُستَشفيات ولَفَفْتُ مع أمّي على كلّ الأطِبّاء ولكنَّهم رَدّوا "لا أمَل!" ظَنَنْتُ أنَّني سأعيش حياتي كلَّها بثلاث شعرات فقط.

وَجَدَني المَلِك وأنا تحت شَجَرة في الحَديقة فمَدَّ يَدُه نحوي وذَهَبْنا إلى القصر وضَمَّني الى العُمّال. ثم قَصَصْتُ شعر المَلِك مَرَّة وبعد ذلك أصبَحْتُ حلّاقُه الخاصّ. قصّتي هي دَليل على أن الحَياة غَريبة!"

5.6

بَثَّ التليفِزيون أمس حِواراً مع فوزي أبو شعرة حَلّاق المَلِك.

قصّتُه هي أنَّهُ شَكَّ وهو طِفل أن عندهُ مَرَض خَطير لأنَّهُ في يَوم من الأيّام شَمَّ رائحة غَريبة على وِسادته في الصَّباح، ثُمَّ وَجَدَ شعرهُ كلَّه على الوِسادة وفي رأسه عَدَّ ثلاث شعرات فَقَط. هو عَدَّها بِنَفسه!

مَرَّ مع أبيه على المُستَشفيات ولَفَّ مع أمّه على كلّ الأطِبّاء ولكنَّهم رَدّوا "لا أمَل!" ظَنَّ أنَّهُ سيَعيش حياته كلَّها بثلاث شعرات فقط.

وَجَدَهُ المَلِك وهو تحت شَجَرة في الحَديقة فمَدَّ يَدُه نحوه وذَهَبوا إلى القصر وضَمَّهُ الى العُمّال. ثم قَصَّ شعر المَلِك مَرَّة وبعد ذلك أصبَحَ حلّاقُه الخاصّ. قصّتُه هي دَليل على أن الحَياة غَريبة!

6   Weak verbs in the past tense

6.1

٣ وَلَدَتْ	٢ وَعَدْتَ	١ وَصَفوا
٦ وَقَعَ	٥ وَزَنّا	٤ وَصَلْتَ
٩ وَثَبْنَ	٨ وَضَعْت	٧ وَقَفَت
١٢ وَرِثْتُمْ	١١ وَصَلْنا	١٠ يَبِسَت

6.2

٣ وَجَدَ	٢ وَجَدْتْ	١ وَجَدَ
٦ وَجَدوا	٥ وَجَدَ	٤ وَجَدَتْ
	٨ وَجَدْتُ	٧ وَجَدْنَ

6.3

٣ وَعَدْتها	٢ وَجَدْتَ	١ وَزَنَ
٦ يَبِسَت	٥ وَقَعَ	٤ وَرِثْتُ
٩ وَضَعْت	٨ وَقَفْنا	٧ وَصَفوا
		١٠ وَلَدَتْ

6.4

١ زارَ he visited | زارَتْ she visited | زاروا they (masc.) visited | زُرْتُ I visited | زُرْتَ you (masc.) visited | زُرْتِ you (fem.) visited | زُرْنا we visited | زُرْتُمْ you (masc. pl.) visited | زُرْتُنَّ you (fem. pl.) visited | زُرْنَ they (fem.) visited

٢ صاحَ he shouted | صاحَتْ she shouted | صاحوا they (masc.) shouted | صِحْتُ I shouted | صِحْتَ you (masc.) shouted | صِحْتِ you (fem.) shouted | صِحْنا we shouted | صِحْتُمْ you (masc. pl.) shouted | صِحْتُنَّ you (fem. pl.) shouted | صِحْنَ they (fem.) shouted

6.5

١ قُلتُ ٢ ذابَ ٣ زُرتِ

٤ طارَت ٥ زارَ ٦ صاحَت

٧ صاموا ٨ بِعتُم ٩ زادَت

١٠ قُمنَ

6.6

زاروا صباح أمس المدينة القديمة. طافوا حول أسوارها وداروا حتّى وَصَلوا إلى باب السوق.

وَجَدوا بساطاً صغيراً في دُكّان. هي كان عندها بساط مِثله ولكنها باعَتْهُ لابنة عمّها.

فمالَت على البائع وقالَت لَهُ "ما ثَمَن البساط؟". قالَ البائع "مئة جُنيه" ولكن بعد ساعة باعَ البَساط لَهُم بخَمسين.

عادوا إلى الفُندُق في المساء وقالوا للمدير إنهُم زادوا شخصاً لأنَّ أخها وَصَلَ إلى الفندق وصاروا الآن ستّة بَدَلاً من خمسة.

6.7

١ كُنّا في مِصر. ٢ كانَ شُكري في المَكتَبة. ٣ كانَت سَميرة في بيتها.

٤ كُنتُ أمامَ البنك. ٥ هل كُنتَ مَشغولة؟ ٦ كانوا مع المُدرّس.

٧ كانَت الفِئران تَحت المائدة. ٨ كُنَّ في الحَديقة. ٩ كانَت البُحيرة هادئة.

١٠ كُنتُ المدير. ١١ كانَت الرسالة طويلة. ١٢ كانَت السيّارات في الشارع.

١٣ أينَ كُنتُـم؟ ١٤ كان البقّالون في سوق الخُضار/ البقّالون كانوا في سوق الخُضار. ١٥ هل كُنتُـنَّ في المدرسة؟

6.8

١ هل كانَت الشَّقّة جديدة؟ ٢ هل كانَت الرِّحلة قصيرة؟ ٣ هل كانَت السيّارة سريعة؟

٤ هل كان المَنظَر جميلاً؟ ٥ هل كانَت حَقيبَتك خفيفة؟ ٦ هل كُنتُـم أمامَ البحر؟

٧ هل كانَ ابنك صَبوراً؟ ٨ هل كانَ البَحر هادئاً؟ ٩ هل كان الطَّقس حارّاً؟

١٠ هل كُنتَ سَعيداً؟

6.9

١ لا، ما كانَت الشَّقّة جديدة إطلاقاً! ٢ لا، ما كانَت الرِّحلة قصيرة إطلاقاً! ٣ لا، ما كانَت السيّارة سريعة إطلاقاً!

٤ لا، ما كانَ المَنظَر جميلاً إطلاقاً! ٥ لا، ما كانَت حَقيبَتك خفيفة إطلاقاً! ٦ لا، ما كُنتُـم أمامَ البحر إطلاقاً!

٧ لا، ما كانَ ابنك صَبوراً إطلاقاً! ٨ لا، ما كانَ البَحر هادئاً إطلاقاً! ٩ لا، ما كانَ الطَّقس حارّاً إطلاقاً!

١٠ لا، ما كُنتَ سَعيداً إطلاقاً!

6.10

١ كان هناك سينما ولكن ما كان هناك مَسرَح. ٢ كان هناك بنك ولكن ما كان هناك مَكتَب البَريد.

٣ كانَت هناك مَحَلات كَثيرة ولكن ما كان هناك سوق. ٤ كان هناك جامع ولكن ما كانَت هناك كَنيسة.

٥ كانَت هناك مَدرَسة ولكن ما كانَت هناك جامعة. ٦ كانَت هناك مَحَطّة أُتوبيس ولكن ما كانَت هناك مَحَطّة قِطار.

6.11

١ لا، كان عندنا كِلاب السَّنة الماضية. ٢ لا، كان لَدَينا درّاجة مَكسورة الشَهر الماضي.

٣ لا، كان عندي ألم في رِجلي الأُسبوع الماضي. ٤ لا، كان عندَهُ تين طازج يَوم السَّبت الماضي.

٥ لا، كان لَنا سيّارة سريعة مُنذ سَنة. ٦ لا، كان لَهُ بَيت في البَحر الأحمَر مُنذُ سَنتَين.

٧ لا، كان لَدَيها شجرة طويلة في الحَديقة مُنذ ثلاث سِنين. ٨ لا، كان مَعي صُوَر أمس.

6.12

١ رَجا he requested | رَجَت she requested | رَجَوْا they (masc.) requested | رَجَوْتُ I requested |
رَجَوْتَ you (masc.) requested | رَجَوْتِ you (fem.) requested | رَجَوْنا we requested |
رَجَوْتُم you (masc. pl.) requested | رَجَوْتُـنَّ you (fem. pl.) requested | رَجَوْنَ they (fem.) requested

٢ دَعا he invited | دَعَت she invited | دَعَوْا they (masc.) invited | دَعَوْتُ I invited |
دَعَوْتَ you (masc.) invited | دَعَوْتِ you (fem.) invited | دَعَوْنا we invited |
دَعَوْتُم you (masc. pl.) invited | دَعَوْتُـنَّ you (fem. pl.) invited | دَعَوْنَ they (fem.) invited

6.13

١ دَعونا | ٢ شَكَوتُم | ٣ رَجَوتُ

٤ بدا | ٥ شَكَوْا | ٦ دَعَوتِ

٧ رَجَت | ٨ شَكَوْنَ | ٩ بَدَت

١٠ دَعا

6.14

١ رَمَى he threw | رَمَتْ she threw | رَمَوْا they (masc.) threw | رَمَيْتُ I threw | رَمَيْتَ you (masc.) threw | رَمَيْتِ you (fem.) threw | رَمَيْنا we threw | رَمَيْتُم you (masc. pl.) threw | رَمَيْتُنَّ you (fem. pl.) threw | رَمَيْنَ they (fem.) threw

٢ بَكَى he cried | بَكَتْ she cried | بَكَوْا they (masc.) cried | بَكَيْتُ I cried | بَكَيْتَ you (masc.) cried | بَكَيْتِ you (fem.) cried | بَكَيْنا we cried | بَكَيْتُم you (masc. pl.) cried | بَكَيْتُنَّ you (fem. pl.) cried | بَكَيْنَ they (fem.) cried

6.15

١ مَشَيتُ | ٢ جَرَيتُم | ٣ رَمَى

٤ بَكَيتِ | ٥ رَمَت، جَرَت | ٦ جَرَت

٧ بكَينا | ٨ مَشَوْا | ٩ بَكَيْنَ

١٠ جَرى، رَمَوْا

6.16

١ لَقِيَ he met | لَقِيَتْ she met | لَقوا they (masc.) met | لَقِيتُ I met | لَقِيتَ you (masc.) met | لَقِيتِ you (fem.) met | لَقِينا we met | لَقِيتُم you (masc. pl.) met | لَقِيتُنَّ you (fem. pl.) met | لَقِينَ they (fem.) met

٢ رَضِيَ he was pleased with | رَضِيَتْ she was pleased with | رَضوا they (masc.) were pleased with | رَضِيتُ I was pleased with | رَضِيت you (masc.) were pleased with | رَضِيت you (fem.) were pleased with | رَضِينا we were pleased with | رَضِيتُم you (masc. pl.) were pleased with | رَضِيتُنَّ you (fem. pl.) were pleased with | رَضِينَ they (fem.) were pleased with

6.17

١ نَسِيتُ اِسمهُ. | ٢ هل نَسيتِ اِسمي؟ | ٣ لَقِينا أمّي في السوق.

٤ هل رَضيتَ عن العُمّال؟ | ٥ نادية لَقِيَت شكري أمام السينما. | ٦ نَسِيَ شكري تَذكِرتَهُ.

٧ هل نَسِيَت نادية تَذكِرتها؟ | ٨ رَضِيَ المُهَندِسون (المُهَندِسون رضوا) عن المَشروع. | ٩ مَتى لَقيتُم الوَزير؟

١٠ لَقيناهُ أمس.

7 Hamzated verbs in the past tense

7.1

١ بَدَأت | ٢ سَأَلتُ | ٣ مَلَأَت

٤ سَئِمَ | ٥ أَذِنّا | ٦ أَخَذوا

٧ جَرُؤتِ | ٨ أَكَلتُم | ٩ أَمَروا

١٠ سَئِمْنا | ١١ أَسِفْتُ | ١٢ قَرَأتُنَّ

7.2

١ سَأَلتُ المُدير عن المَشروع. | ٢ أَخَذوا القطار إلى القاهرة. | ٣ مَتى قَرَأتُنَّ هذه الكُتُب؟

٤ مَلَأَت سميرة الزُجاجة بالعَصير. | ٥ لِماذا بَدَأت في هذا البَحث؟ | ٦ أَسِفْتُ على تَأخيري أمس.

٧ سَئِمَ أحمد من التِكرار في الفيلم. | ٨ هل أَكَلتُم الشوكولاتة؟

7.3

١ أَكَلتُهُ | ٢ ما أَكَلتُها | ٣ أَخَذتُهُم

٤ ما أَخَذتُها | ٥ قَرَأتُهُ | ٦ ما قَرَأتُها

٧ مَلَأتُها | ٨ أَخَذَهُ | ٩ ما أَخَذتُها

١٠ بَدَأوا فيهِ

7.4

١ مَلَأْنا   ٢ أَذَنَ   ٣ بَدَأُوا

٤ أَكَلْتُـم   ٥ سَأَلْنا   ٦ قَرَأْتِ

٧ أَخَذْتُ   ٨ سَئِمْنا   ٩ أَسِفَتْ

١٠ أَخَذْنَ   ١١ بَطُؤَ   ١٢ جَرُؤُوا

١٣ سَئِمْتُ   ١٤ أَمَرَتْني   ١٥ سَأَلْتُهُم

8 Dual verbs in the past tense

8.1

١ اللِّصّان أَخَذَا ساعتي.   ٢ أَينَ كُنتُما أَمس؟   ٣ الحارسان كانا عند الباب.

٤ هل نَسِيتُما مِفتاح السَّيّارة؟   ٥ المُوَظَّفان رَدًّا على رِسالة المُدير.   ٦ لِماذا ما بَحَثْتُما عن العَمَل؟

٧ هل البنتان قَصَّتا شعرهُما؟   ٨ المَرأتان ذَهَبَتا إلى السوق في الصباح.   ٩ أنتُما ما عَرِفْتُما الطَّريق.

١٠ الوَلَدان رَمَيا الكُرة.   ١١ المُلاكِمان بَطُؤَا بعد نِصف ساعة.   ١٢ الغريبان سَأَلاني عن فُندُق قَريب.

8.2

١ دَفَعَت، رَجَعَتا   ٢ دَخَلَت، بَدَأَتا   ٣ حَجَزَنَ، نَسِيا

٤ ذَهَبَت، شَكَتا   ٥ جرى، شَمّا   ٦ سَكَنَ، عَمِلا

٧ جَلَسَت، بَكَتا   ٨ أَخَذَ، حَمَلاها

8.3

١ حَمَلنا الصَندوقَين الثقيلَين.   ٢ سَأَلتُ الوَلَدَين عن الطَّريق.   ٣ هل قَرَأَ الكِتابَين؟

٤ كانا مُهَندِسَين في مِصر.   ٥ ضَمَّ الاجتِماع مُديرَين من الصين.   ٦ كانَتا طويلَتَين وجميلَتَين.

٧ هل رَكِبتُما الحِصانَين؟   ٨ هل كُنتُما مَشغولَين أمس؟   ٩ حَضَرتُ الاجتِماعَين.

١٠ وَجَدَت نادية حَشَرَتَين تحت الكتاب.   ١١ سَرَقَ اللِّصّ خاتِمَين جميلَين.   ١٢ رَمَيتُ القَميصَين القديمَين.

◆III PRESENT/FUTURE TENSE

9 Regular basic verbs

9.1

١ يَغْسِل he washes/is washing   ٢ يَذْهَب he goes/is going   ٣ يَكْتُب he writes/is writing

٤ يَحْمِل he carries/is carrying   ٥ يَطْبُخ he cooks/is cooking   ٦ يَفْهَم he understands/is understanding

٧ يَتْرُك he leaves/is leaving   ٨ يَرْجِع he returns/is returning   ٩ يَرْسُم he draws/is drawing

١٠ يَلْعَب he plays/is playing   ١١ يَحْرِق he burns/is burning   ١٢ يَضْحَك he laughs/is laughing

9.2

١ أَغْسِل I wash/am washing | تَغْسِل you (masc.) wash/are washing | تَغْسِلينَ you (fem.) wash/are washing | يَغْسِل he washes/is washing | تَغْسِل she washes/is washing | نَغْسِل we wash/are washing | تَغْسِلونَ you (masc. pl) wash/are washing | تَغْسِلْنَ you (fem. pl.) wash/are washing | يَغْسِلونَ they (masc.) wash/are washing | يَغْسِلْنَ they (fem.) wash/are washing

٢ أَخْرُج I go out/am going out | تَخْرُج you (masc.) go out/are going out | تَخْرُجينَ you (fem.) go out/are going out | يَخْرُج he goes out/is going out | تَخْرُج she goes out/is going out | نَخْرُج we go out/are going out | تَخْرُجونَ you (masc. pl.) go out/are going out | تَخْرُجْنَ you (fem. pl.) go out/are going out | يَخْرُجونَ they (masc.) go out/are going out | يَخْرُجْنَ they (fem.) go out/are going out

9.3

٢ نَضحَك we laugh/are laughing
٤ تَكتُبينَ you (fem.) write/are writing
٦ يَطلُبون they request/are requesting
٨ تَلعَب you (masc.) play/are playing
١٠ يَفهَمنَ they (fem. pl.) understand/are understanding

١ أَنظُر I look/am looking
٣ يَسمَع he hears/is hearing
٥ تَجمَعنَ they (fem. pl.) gather/are gathering
٧ تَترُك she leaves/is leaving
٩ تَحجِزون you (masc. pl.) reserve/are reserving

9.4

٣ تَغسِل
٦ تَسقُط
٩ يَرقُصونَ

٢ يَشرَب
٥ نَدرُس
٨ تَحرِقونَ

١ أَحمِل
٤ تَذكُرينَ
٧ يَبَحَثنَ
١٠ تَركَبنَ

9.5

٣ تَطبُخ زَينة الفَلافِل يوم الاثنَين.
٢ تَذهَب زَينة إلى السوق يوم الأَحَد.
١ تَلعَب زَينة التَنِس يوم السَّبت.

٦ تَدرُس زَينة الإنجليزيّة يوم الخَميس.
٥ تَغسِل زَينة المَلابِس يوم الأربِعاء.
٤ تَركَب زَينة حِصانها يوم الثُّلاثاء.

٧ تَذهَب زَينة إلى السينما يوم الجُمعة.

9.6

٣ أَطبُخ الفَلافِل يوم الاثنَين.
٢ أَذهَب إلى السوق يوم الأَحَد.
١ أَلعَب التَنِس يوم السَّبت.

٦ أَدرُس الإنجليزيّة يوم الخَميس.
٥ أَغسِل المَلابِس يوم الأربِعاء.
٤ أَركَب حِصاني يوم الثُّلاثاء.

٧ أَذهَب إلى السينما يوم الجُمعة.

9.7

٣ تَغسِلينَ
٦ يَدرُسونَ
٩ نَبحَث

٢ أَشرَب
٥ تَترُك
٨ يَذهَب

١ تَضحَكونَ
٤ تَسمَع
٧ يَجمَعنَ
١٠ يَحرِق

9.8

٣ طَبعاً، أَحضَرهُ كلّ أُسبوع.
٢ طَبعاً، أَقفِلهُ كلّ مَساء.
١ طَبعاً، أَغسِلها كلّ يوم.

٦ طَبعاً، أَدفَعهُ كلّ شَهر.
٥ طَبعاً، أَذهَب إلَيه كلّ يوم اثنَين.
٤ طَبعاً، أَحجِزها كلّ يوم سَبت.

٩ طَبعاً، يَلعَبنَهُ كلّ أُسبوع.
٨ طَبعاً، يَغسِلونَها كلّ يوم جُمعة.
٧ طَبعاً، تَكتُبها كلّ يوم أَحد.

١٢ طَبعاً، نَزرَعها كلّ رَبيع.
١١ طَبعاً، نَركَبها كلّ أُسبوع.
١٠ طَبعاً، نخرُج معهُ كلّ صَباح.

9.9

٢ لا نَطلُب منكم شيئاً.
١ لا أَذهَب إلى هذا المطعم.

٤ لا يركَب عَمّي الحِصان يوم الجُمعة.
٣ لا يحجِز لي أَحمَد مِقعَداً بجانب الشُّبّاك.

٦ لا ندرُس الرِّياضيّات كلّ يوم.
٥ إنّها لا ترقُص في الأَفراح.

٨ لا يسمَع التلاميذ الجَرَس فَلا يجلِسون على الأرض.
٧ لماذا لا تدفَعين الإيجار كلّ أُسبوع؟

١٠ لا يزرَع المُزارِع هذا الحَقل في الصَّيف.
٩ لا نشرَب القهوة بعد العشاء.

9.10

٢ لا تذهَب زَينة إلى السوق أَبداً!
١ لا يغسِل شكري السيّارة أَبداً!

٤ لا تلعَب سميرة مع أُختها أَبداً!
٣ صَديقتي فاطمة لا تكتُب لي أَبداً!

٦ زوجي أَنَس لا يحضُر اجتِماعات في المَدرَسة أَبداً!
٥ لا يقفِل أَحمد الباب أَبداً!

٨ لا تلبَس البنات (البنات لا تلبَسنَ) ملابِسهُنَّ الجديدة أَبداً!
٧ لا يركَب الأولاد (الأولاد لا يركَبون) دَرّاجاتهُم أَبداً!

9.11

٢ لماذا لا تذهَبين إلى السوق أَبداً، يا زَينة؟
١ لماذا لا تغسِل السيّارة أَبداً، يا شكري؟

٤ لماذا لا تلعَبين مع أُختك أَبداً، يا سميرة؟
٣ لماذا لا تكتُبين لها أَبداً، يا فاطمة؟

٦ لماذا لا تحضُر اجتِماعات في المَدرَسة أَبداً، يا أَنَس؟
٥ لماذا لا تقفِل الباب أَبداً، يا أَحمد؟

٨ لماذا لا تلبَسنَ ملابِسكُنَّ الجديدة أَبداً، يا بنات؟
٧ لماذا لا تركَبون دَرّاجاتكُم أَبداً، يا أولاد؟

10   Expressing the future

10.1

١ سَندخُل/سوف ندخُل   ٢ سَيركَب/سوف يركَب

٣ سَتدفَع/سوف تَدفَع   ٤ سَيجلِس/سوف يجلِس، سَيَنظُر/سوف يَنظُر

٥ سَيصنَعون/سوف يصنَعون   ٦ سَأبحَث/سوف أبحَث

٧ سَتسمَعون/سوف تسمَعون   ٨ سَأفتَح/سوف أفتَح

٩ سَيحضُر/سوف يحضُر، سَيرجَعون/سوف يرجَعون   ١٠ سَترسُم/سوف ترسُم، سيلعَبنَ/سوف يلعَبنَ

10.2

يا أصدِقائي، الغَد هو يوم زيارَتكُم!

سوف تذهبون إلى وسط المدينة بالباص، وستنزلون أمام البنك القَطَريّ. بيتنا قريب من هناك.

في البيت سنشرب قهوة وبعد ذلك سنخرُج. أوّلاً سنذهب إلى النادي، وأخي يوسُف سيذهب معنا أيضاً. سنلعب كرة القدم وكرة السَّلّة هناك وسوف نرجع في الساعة الواحدة للغَداء. قالَتْ أمّي إنّها ستطبخ لَنا الغَداء.

بعد الظُّهر سوف نَحضُر حفلة موسيقيّة، وسنسمع المُغَنّي اللُّبناني المَشهور، رَفيق خوري. حَجَزْتُ أربع تَذاكِر أمس، ولكنّنا سندفع غَداً. أخيراً سوف أذهب معكم إلى محطّة الباص في المساء.

أنا في اِنتِظاركم!

صديقكُم نور

10.3

١ بعد ذلك سنخرج   ٢ سندفع غَداً   ٣ ستنزلون أمام البنك القَطَريّ

٤ أخي يوسُف سيذهب معنا   ٥ ستطبخ لَنا الغَداء   ٦ سنلعب كرة القدم وكرة السَّلّة

٧ سنشرب قهوة   ٨ سنسمع المُغَنّي اللُّبناني المَشهور   ٩ سوف نرجع في الساعة الواحدة

١٠ سوف أذهب معكم إلى محطّة الباص   ١١ سنذهب إلى النادي

10.4

١ بعد ذلك سيخرج.   ٢ سيدفعون غَداً.   ٣ ستنزلين أمام البنك القَطَريّ.

٤ أُختي سميرة ستذهب معنا.   ٥ سيطبخنَ لَنا الغَداء.   ٦ سألعب كرة القدم وكرة السَّلّة.

٧ ستشرب قهوة.   ٨ ستسمعون المُغَنّي اللُّبناني المَشهور.   ٩ سوف ترجع في الساعة الواحدة.

١٠ سوف نذهب معكم إلى محطّة الباص.   ١١ ستذهبنَ إلى النادي.

10.5

١ هل ستطبخ سميرة السمك؟   ٢ أين ستلعبنَ كرة السلّة؟   ٣ كيف سأدفع؟

٤ هل سيحملون الحقيبة؟   ٥ متى سيرجع المدير؟   ٦ ماذا سنشرب؟

٧ أين ستتركون كُتُبي؟   ٨ هل المدرِّسات الجديدات سيعملنَ غَداً؟   ٩ ماذا سيحدث يوم السبت القادِم؟

١٠ متى ستحجز التذاكر؟

11   Doubled verbs in the present tense

11.1

١ أبي يَشُكّ في الاِبنة.   ٢ أُختي تَشُكّ في السائِق.   ٣ أخي يَشُكّ في الزَّوجة.

٤ جَدّي يَشُكّ في الاِبن.   ٥ جَدّتي تَشُكّ في المُمَرِّضة.   ٦ أولاد أُختي يَشُكّونَ في المُحاسِب.

٧ بنات أخي يَشْكُكْنَ في البُستانيّ.   ٨ أنا أَشُكّ في عامِل النَّظافة.

11.2

١ يَظُنّونَ   ٢ سَأَدُلّ   ٣ نَلُفّ

٤ تَمُرّينَ   ٥ لا تَرُدّ   ٦ نَبُثّ

٧ لا يَضُمّ   ٨ لا تَوَدّ   ٩ سَيَعُدْنَ

١٠ تَشُمّونَ   ١١ سَتتِمّ   ١٢ تَشْكُكْنَ

11.3

١ نَقُصّ الصُّوَر من المَجَلات.
٤ يَبثّ مُدَوَّنَتُهُ على الإنترنت.
٧ سوف يَدلّونَكَ على الطَّريق.

٢ هل تشكّون في الأسعار؟
٥ سوف يشُمُمْنَ رائحة السمك.
٨ ألا تدلّين الضُّيوف إلى مقاعِدهم؟

٣ أمرّ على هذه اللافِتة كلّ يوم.
٦ إنّها لا تظنّ أن هناك أمَل.

11.4

١ سَأَعُدّ/سوف أَعُدّ
٤ تَظُنّ
٧ لا يشُكّ
١٠ لا تَلقُّينَ

٢ لا يَرُدّونَ
٥ سأَرُدّ
٨ لا تَبُثّ

٣ نَوَدّ
٦ لا تَشُمّ
٩ نَمُرّ

12 Weak verbs in the present tense

12.1

١ أرِن
٤ تَضَع
٧ لا يَثِبونَ
١٠ لا تَعِدونَ

٢ سوف يَجِد/سَيَجِد
٥ تَقِف
٨ سوف يَيْبَس/سَيَيْبَس
١١ تَلِد

٣ لا نَصِف
٦ سوف نَرِث/سَنَرِث
٩ تَدَعِين
١٢ سوف تَقَعْنَ

12.2

١ يَزِن البَقّال الجُبن والزَّيتون.
٤ يَقِف القطار في قَريَتِنا.
٧ نَقِف أَمَام شُبّاك التَذاكِر.
١٠ لماذا لا تَثِبونَ من فوق السور؟

٢ أجِد صُوَراً كثيرة على الإنترنت.
٥ نَصِف السِّباق في الراديو.
٨ تَيْبَس الزُّهور بِسَبَب حَرارة الشَّمس.

٣ تَعِد جَدَّتها بِهَدِية غالية.
٦ إنّ الأولاد يَصِفون مَلامِح اللصّ.
٩ هل تَضَعِين البيتزا في الفُرن صباحاً؟

12.3

١ لا، سأجِدهُ بعد الظُّهر.
٤ لا، سأعِدها بعد الظُّهر.
٧ لا، سيَصِلون بعد الظُّهر.

٢ لا، سأزِنهُ بعد الظُّهر.
٥ لا، ستَضَعها في غُرفتها بعد الظُّهر.
٨ لا، سيَصِفها بعد الظُّهر.

٣ لا، سأضَعها في الدرج بعد الظُّهر.
٦ لا، سيَصِل بعد الظُّهر.

12.4

١ أعود I return/am returning | تَعود you (masc.) return/are returning | تَعودينَ you (fem.) return/are returning | يَعود he returns/is returning | تَعود she returns/is returning | نَعود we return/are returning | تَعودونَ you (masc. pl.) return/are returning | تَعُدْنَ you (fem. pl.) return/are returning | يَعودونَ they (masc.) return/are returning | يَعُدْنَ they (fem.) return/are returning

٢ أَبيع I sell/am selling | تَبيع you (masc.) sell/are selling | تَبيعينَ you (fem.) sell/are selling | يَبيع he sells/is selling | تَبيع she sells/is selling | نَبيع we sell/are selling | تَبيعونَ you (masc. pl.) sell/are selling | تَبِعْنَ you (fem. pl.) sell/are selling | يَبيعونَ they (masc.) sell/are selling | يَبِعْنَ they (fem.) sell/are selling

12.5

١ يقول
٤ يَذوب
٧ يَزورونَ
١٠ يميل
١٣ يبِعْنَ

٢ تَصوم
٥ يَطوفونَ
٨ يَزيد
١١ نَعود

٣ أقوم
٦ تَدور
٩ تَصيح
١٢ تَطير

12.6

١ يميل هذا البيت إلى اليَسار.
٤ يبيعونَ أَفضَل أَنواع المِلح.
٧ يَزيد عَدَد السُّوّاح كلّ سَنة.
١٠ متى تقول لي الحَقيقة؟

٢ لماذا تصيحين؟
٥ لا تطير الدُّيوك.
٨ هل يذوب الصابون في الماء؟
١١ كيف يتعودونَ إلى المَصنَع؟

٣ يدور المُحَرِّك بصُعوبة.
٦ سميرة دائماً تزور أمّها يوم السبت.
٩ لا أصوم بِسَبَب مَرَضي.
١٢ يَطُفْنَ حول البُرج.

12.7

١ أمس نامَت الخالة فاطِمة في غُرفة سارة ولكنّها سَتنام الليلة في غرفة ماري.

٢ أمس نامَ أبو سميرة في فُندُق ولكنّه سَينام الليلة في غُرفة أَحمد.

٣ أمس نامَت سميرة في غُرفتها ولكنّه سَتنام الليلة في غُرفة سارة.

٤ أمس نامَ أطفال سميرة في غرفة الجُلوس ولكنّهُم سَينامون الليلة في غرفة الطَّعام.

٥ أمس نامَت بَنات سامي في غرفة ماري ولكنّهُنَّ سَينَمْنَ الليلة في المَكتَب.

٦ أمس نامَ أولاد فاطِمة في المَكتَب ولكنّهُم سَينامون الليلة في خَيمة في الحَديقة.

٧ أمس نامَ البَبغاء في الحَمّام ولكنّه سَينام الليلة في المَطبَخ.

٨ أمس نامَت الكِلاب في المَطبَخ ولكنّها سَتنام الليلة في الجَراج.

12.8

٢ سوف نكون/سنكون شُكري في المَكتَبة.

٤ سوف أكون/سأكون أمامَ البنك.

٦ سوف يكونون/سيكونون مع المُدرّس.

٨ سوف يكُنَّ/سيكُنَّ في العِراق.

١٠ سوف تكون/ستكون المدير.

١٢ سوف تكون/ستكون السيّارات أمام المَدخَل.

١٤ هل ستكونون في المدرسة؟

١ سوف نكون/سنكون في مِصر.

٣ سوف تكون/ستكون سَميرة في بيتها.

٥ هل ستكونين مَشغولة؟

٧ سوف تكون/ستكون الكِلاب في الحديقة.

٩ سوف يكون/سيكون الكتاب ثقيلاً.

١١ سوف تكون/ستكون الرِّحلة طويلة.

١٣ سوف يكون/سيكون البقّالون في سوق الخُضار.

12.9

٣ سَـتكونين

٦ سَـيكُنَّ

٩ سَـتكونونَ

٢ أكون

٥ يكون

٨ يكونون

١ سَنكون

٤ تكون

٧ سَـتكون

١٠ سَـتَكُنَّ

12.10

١ سوف تكون/سَتكون هناك فِرقة كبيرة في حَفل الزِّفاف.

٢ سوف يكون/سَيكون هناك مُطرب شَهير في حَفل الزِّفاف.

٣ سوف يكون/سَيكون هناك ألعاب ناريّة في حَفل الزِّفاف.

٤ سوف تكون/سَتكون هناك نافورة شوكولاتة في حَفل الزِّفاف.

٥ سوف يكون/سَيكون هناك حَمام في حَفل الزِّفاف.

٦ سوف يكون/سَيكون هناك ضُيوف من كُلّ العالَم في حَفل الزِّفاف.

٧ سوف تكون/سَتكون هناك زُهور على كل مائِدة في حَفل الزِّفاف.

٨ سوف تكون/سَتكون هَديّة لِكلّ ضَيف في حَفل الزِّفاف.

12.11

٢ سَيَكون عِندَنا سيّارة السنة القادِمة.

٤ سَيَكون عِندَها صُداع في الصباح.

٦ سَيَكون لِأختي ثلاجة جديدة.

٨ سَيَكون لَنا مَطبَخ صغير في الشقّة الجديدة.

١٠ هل سَيَكون لَكُنَّ صُوَر كثيرة في المَجلّة؟

١٢ هل سَيَكون مَعَكَ قَلَم؟

١٤ أمّهُم ستّكون مَعَهُم.

١٦ سَيَكون لَدَينا اِجتِماع يوم السبت.

١٨ سَيَكون لَدَيه حَقائِب كثيرة.

٢٠ هل سَيَكون لَدَيكُنَّ وقت؟

١ سَيَكون عِندي مَكتَب في الطابِق الخامِس.

٣ سَيَكون عِندَ البقّال تين طازِج الأسبوع القادِم.

٥ سَيَكون عِندَهُم ستّة مَقاعِد في سيّارتهم الجديدة.

٧ سَيَكون للمُهَندِسين مطعم خاصّ.

٩ سَيَكون لي دور كبير في الفيلم.

١١ سَيَكون مَعي المِفتاح.

١٣ هل سَيَكون مَعَكِ كِتابي؟

١٥ هل سَيَكون مَعَكُم الكلب؟

١٧ سَيَكون لَدى المدينة مَسرَح جديد السَنة القادِمة.

١٩ سوف يكون لَدَيهم جِناح كبير في المَعرَض.

12.12

١ هذه المَرأة تَشكو من حَجم الحَمّام.

٣ هذه الشابّة تَشكو من حَجم السَرير.

٥ هؤُلاء النِّساء يَشكونَ من الموسيقى الصاخِبة.

٧ هؤُلاء الأطفال يَشكونَ من حمّام السِّباحة المَقفول.

٢ هذا الوَلَد يَشكو من التليفزيون المَكسور.

٤ هؤُلاء الرِّجال يَشكونَ من عَدَم وُجود الماء الساخِن.

٦ هذا الشابّ يَشكو من تكييف الهَواء.

٨ أنا أشكو من كل هذه المَشاكِل!

12.13

١ نَدعو   ٢ تَشكو   ٣ يَدعونَ

٤ يَرجو   ٥ يَبدو   ٦ تَشكينَ

٧ نَرجوكُم   ٨ تَبدو   ٩ سَأدعو

١٠ تَشكو

12.14

١ يَمشي   ٢ أمشي   ٣ تَمشونَ

٤ تَمشينَ   ٥ يَمْشينَ   ٦ تَمشي

٧ تَمشي   ٨ يَمشونَ   ٩ تَمشينَ

12.15

١ أمشي   ٢ يَمشون   ٣ سَنَمشي

٤ يَبكي   ٥ سَتَرمين   ٦ تَمشي

٧ يَبكي   ٨ أمشي   ٩ يَرمي

١٠ يَرمينَ

12.16

١ أَلْقَى I meet | تَلْقَى you (masc.) meet | تَلْقَيْنَ you (fem.) meet | يَلْقَى he meets | تَلْقَى she meets | نَلْقَى we meet | تَلْقَوْنَ you (masc. pl.) meet | تَلْقَيْنَ you (fem. pl.) meet | يَلْقَوْنَ they (masc.) meet | يَلْقَيْنَ they (fem.) meet

٢ أرْضَى I am pleased with | تَرْضَى you (masc.) are pleased with | تَرْضَيْنَ you (fem.) are pleased with | يَرْضَى he is pleased with | تَرْضَى she is pleased with | نَرْضَى we are pleased with | تَرْضَوْنَ you (masc. pl.) are pleased with | تَرْضَيْنَ you (fem. pl.) are pleased with | يَرْضَوْنَ they (masc.) are pleased with | يَرْضَيْنَ they (fem.) are pleased with

12.17

١ أنسى اسمها دائماً.

٢ نَلقى أُمّنا في السوق دائماً.

٣ يَرضونَ عَن العُمّال دائماً.

٤ يَلقى شُكري نادية أمام السينما دائماً.

٥ يَنسى شُكري تَذكرته دائماً.

٦ هل تَلقَينَ سميرة في النادي دائماً؟

٧ تَنسَينَ كِتابكِ دائماً.

٨ تَنسى نادية مِفتاح الصُّندوق دائماً.

٩ هل تَلقى الوزير في مَكتبه دائماً؟

١٠ إنّ المُهنْدِسات يَرضَينَ عن المَشروع دائماً.

12.18

١ لا أنْساها أبداً.

٢ لا أنْساهُ أبداً.

٣ لا ألْقاهُم أبداً بعد المدرسة.

٤ لا ألْقاهُنَّ أبداً في مركَز التَّسَوُّق يوم الجمعة.

٥ لا يَنْساهُ أبداً.

٦ لا تَلْقاهُنَّ أبداً في الحَديقة.

13 Hamzated verbs in the present tense

13.1

١ read, sleeps   ٢ apologize, lateness   ٣ You (masc. pl.), newspaper

٤ eating, cake   ٥ reading, subject   ٦ will, drinks

٧ never, fed up   ٨ me, now   ٩ fill, hope

١٠ starting, our   ١١ viewers, these   ١٢ dare, in

١٣ takes, hand   ١٤ children, feel

		13.2
١ لا يَقرَأ سمير قبل أن يَنام.	٢ نَأسِف عَن تَأخيرنا.	٣ سَنَقرَأ عَنهُ في الجَريدة غَداً.
٤ لِماذا يَأكُل كَعكة أُخته؟	٥ يَبدو أنَّك تَقرَأ عن المَوضوع.	٦ سوف يَأخُذنَ المشرويات إلى الشاطِئ.
٧ لا تَسأَم سوزي من سَماعها أَبداً.	٨ هل سَيَأذَن لَكُم بالخُروج الآن؟	٩ إنَّ الأطفال يَمْلأُونَ قُلوبنا بالأَمَل.
١٠ أبدَأ الآن في تَرتيب أُموري.	١١ هل تَسأَمينَ من هذه البَرامِج.	١٢ لا تَجرُؤ أمّي على النَّظَر في المِرآة.
١٣ تَأخُذ الحمامة اللَّوزة من يَدها.	١٤ نَأكُل الحلوَى ونشعُر بالنَّشاط.	

14 Dual verbs in the present tense

14.1

١ تَعرِفان	٢ يَجريان	٣ يَنسَيان
٤ تَقولان	٥ يَسكُنان	٦ تَشرَيان
٧ تَسمَعان	٨ يَحضُران	٩ تَرِثان
١٠ تَبحثان		

14.2

	14.2
١ كُلّ يوم يقرَآن الجريدة بعد الإفطار.	٢ كُلّ يوم يذهَبان إلى السوق في الساعة العاشرة.
٣ كُلّ يوم يشرَبان قهوة في السوق.	٤ كُلّ يوم يلقَيان أصدِقائهُما في الحديقة.
٥ كُلّ يوم يَأكُلان الغَداء في مطعم إيطاليّ.	٦ كُلّ يوم ينامان لمُدّة ساعة بعد الغداء.
٧ كُلّ يوم يزوران المكتبة في الساعة الثالثة.	٨ كُلّ يوم يحملان الكُتُب للبَيت.
٩ كُلّ يوم يلعَبان الشَّطرَنج قبل العَشاء.	١٠ كُلّ يوم يَأكُلان العَشاء في الساعة السابعة.
١١ كُلّ يوم يكتُبان الخِطابات بعد العشاء.	١٢ كُلّ يوم ينامان في الساعة العاشرة والنِّصف.

14.3

	14.3
١ كلّ يوم يَأكُل أبي وأمّي الغداء ويَنامان لمُدّة ساعة.	٢ دائماً تَصِل الأختان معاً وتشرَبان القهوة.
٣ يَقِف أنور وحسن هناك وسيحملان الحقيبة إلى غُرفتك.	٤ تلعَب البنتان الشَّطرَنج ولا ترُدّان على الهاتف.
٥ كلّ يوم يذهب الطالِبان إلى المَكتَبة و يقرَآن كُتُباً.	٦ يدرُس أنور وسميرة الفَرَنسيّة ولكنّهُما لا يفهمان هذه القصّة.

 FORMS OF THE VERB

15 Forms II, III, and IV

15.1

	PAST TENSE	PRESENT TENSE
SINGULAR		
أنا I	حَسَّنْتُ	أُحَسِّن
أنتَ you (masc.)	حَسَّنْتَ	تُحَسِّن
أنتِ you (fem.)	حَسَّنْتِ	تُحَسِّنين
هُوَ he/it (masc.)	حَسَّنَ	يُحَسِّن
هِيَ she/it (fem.)	حَسَّنَتْ	تُحَسِّن

(continued)

		PAST TENSE	PRESENT TENSE
PLURAL			
we	نَحنُ	حَسَّنّا	نُحَسِّن
you (masc. pl.)	أنتُم	حَسَّنْتُم	تُحَسِّنون
you (fem. pl.)	أنتنَّ	حَسَّنْتُنَّ	تُحَسِّنَّ
they (masc.)	هُم	حَسَّنوا	يُحَسِّنون
they (fem.)	هُنَّ	حَسَّنَّ	يُحَسِّنَّ

		PAST TENSE	PRESENT TENSE
SINGULAR			
I	أنا	كَسَّرْتُ	أُكَسِّر
you (masc.)	أنتَ	كَسَّرْتَ	تُكَسِّر
you (fem.)	أنتِ	كَسَّرْتِ	تُكَسِّرين
he/it (masc.)	هُوَ	كَسَّرَ	يُكَسِّر
she/it (fem.)	هِيَ	كَسَّرَتْ	تُكَسِّر
PLURAL			
we	نَحنُ	كَسَّرْنا	نُكَسِّر
you (masc. pl.)	أنتُم	كَسَّرْتُم	تُكَسِّرون
you (fem. pl.)	أنتنَّ	كَسَّرْتُنَّ	تُكَسِّرْنَ
they (masc.)	هُم	كَسَّروا	يُكَسِّرون
they (fem.)	هُنَّ	كَسَّرْنْ	يُكَسِّرْنَ

15.2

Did Nadia break the glass? ١

No, the children broke the glass. ٢

Is the government improving the road to the city? ٣

No, they are not improving it at all. ٤

What are you studying, Amira? ٥

I am studying English in Bahrain. ٦

Did the guests break their plates in the Greek wedding? ٧

Did you study Arabic at university? ٨

Did you improve the team's skills this year? ٩

No, but we will improve them next year. ١٠

15.3

١ رَحَّبنا

٢ أُعَدِّل

٣ تُنَظِّف

٤ نَكَّرِت

٥ يُدَرِّسون

٦ تُـجَهِّز

٧ قَطَّعنَ

٨ سَنُفَتِّشون

٩ حَمَّلتُ

١٠ يُفَضِّلون

١١ نُدَرِّب

١٢ يُدَخِّن

15.4

٣ قَطَّعنَ	٢ سَتُفَتِّشونَ	١ حَمَلْتُ
٦ يُدَخِّن	٥ يُدَرِّسون	٤ رَحَّبنا
٩ تُنَظِّف	٨ نُدَرِّب	٧ يُفَضِّلون
١٢ تُعِدّ	١١ ذَكَّرتِ	١٠ سَأُعَدِّل

15.5

1. The young prince is coming to the restaurant tomorrow.

2. It is his birthday.

3. An important person from the palace will inspect the restaurant before the visit.

4. To check cleanliness, train the staff how to greet the prince, and teach them what to do while he is there.

5. He will adjust the tables, set up a large table beside the window, and may move some flower pots around.

6. To fix the torn curtain and buy the most beautiful flowers in town.

7. He will present the birthday cake to the prince when he welcomes him at the door.

8. He wants Ahmed to heat the tea for the bodyguards.

15.6

we will prepare	سوف نُجَهِّز
I organize	أُنَظِّم
you clean	تُنَظِّف
so that he inspects	لِيُفَتِّش
and so that he trains you (pl.)	ولِيُدَرِّبِكُم
and so that he instructs you (pl.)	ولِيُعَلِّمكُم
I will adjust	سَأُعَدِّل
I will set up/arrange	وسَأُرَتِّب
we improve	نُحَسِّن
I move	أُحَرِّك
you fix	تُصَلِّح
I will remind you	سَأُذَكِّرك
they cost me	تُكَلِّفني
I will welcome/greet	سَأُرَحِّب
I will present	وسَأُقَدِّم
he will cut it up	سَيُقَطِّعها
you heat up	تُسَخِّن
we thought	فَكَّرنا
I believe	أُصَدِّق
he prefers	يُفَضِّل

15.7

٣ ساعَدتُ ابنَتي في دُروسها.	٢ سافَرَ المَلِك بطائِرة خاصّة.	١ شاهَدنا التليفزيون.
٦ ذاكَرَت سميرة للامتِحان.	٥ أبي وأمّي حادَثا المدرِّس.	٤ هل سابَقتُم البَنات؟
٩ هل راجَعتِ الدُّروس يا نادية؟	٨ شارَكَت الوَزيرة في هذا الاجتِماع.	٧ لِماذا جادَلتَني؟
١٢ مَتَى غادَرَ القِطار؟	١١ إنّ النِساء هاجَرنَ إلى أمريكا.	١٠ قاتَلنا من أجل الحُرّية.

١ جادَلْتُ أبي في مَوضوع الإمتحانات.   ٢ إنه يُعامِلني وكأنّني طِفل.   15.8

٣ ناقَشنا هذا مَعَهُ أمس.   ٤ قاتَلَ أجدادنا من أجل الحرّية.

٥ أُحادِثهُما عن ابنهما كُلّ يَوم.   ٦ أنتُم دائماً تُجادِلون المُدير.

٧ متى سَتَحادِثْنَ المديرة عن الخِدمة؟   ٨ جالَسناها أمس.

أُسابِق، نُسافِر، لِنُشاهِد، أُراجِع، يُحادِثني، أُجادِلهُ، وأُناقِشهُ، أُقاتِل، تُشارِك، تُساعِدني، يُعامِلني، أُغادِر، سَأُهاجِر   15.9

١ أسْرَع/يُسْرِع   ٢ أحْسَن/يُحْسِن   ٣ أرسَل/يُرسِل   15.10

٤ أخْبَر/يُخْبِر   ٥ أخْرَج/يُخْرِج   ٦ أقْلَع/يُقْلِع

٧ أنْعَش/يُنْعِش   ٨ أصْبَح/يُصْبِح   ٩ أنْقَذ/يُنْقِذ

١ أحسَنت في الامتحانات. أحسَنْتُ في الامتحانات.   ٢ سَتُرسِل النتائِج غداً. سَيُرسِلونَ النتائِج غداً.   15.11

٣ أنقَذْنا الطفل من النهر. أنقَذَ الطفل من النهر.   ٤ سَيُصبِح قائد الفريق. سَأُصبِح قائد الفريق.

٥ أخبَروا الناظر عن الحفلة. أخبَرتِ الناظر عن الحفلة.   ٦ سَتُصلِح الكمبيوتر. سَيُصلِحنَ الكمبيوتر.

١ لِماذا تُخرج الكمبيوتر من الغُرفة؟   ٢ أسْرَعتُ إلى المُستَشفى.   ٣ هل سَتُنْقِذينَ زَميلهُ أيضاً؟   15.12

٤ سوف نُنْعِش الاقتِصاد.   ٥ أقْلَع دون أن يُخبِر القائد.   ٦ هل سَتُحْسِنون في الامتِحان؟

٧ أنْقَذوا أخي من السِّجن.   ٨ أصْبَحْنَ فَقيرات بعد الحَرب.

١ أخو الكاتِب   ٢ في بِلاد العَدو   ٣ من رِسالة   15.13

٤ من المَطار الحربيّ   ٥ في اللَيل   ٦ لأنّهُ أخَذَ الطائرة بدون إذن

٧ في السِّجن   ٨ على الشاطِئ

16　Forms V and VI

١ هي لا تَتَذَكَّر اسمي.   ٢ سَأتَذَكَّر هذا اليَوم.   ٣ هل تَذَكَّرتِ حَقيبتك؟   16.1

٤ نعم، تَذَكَّرتُها.   ٥ أنتم لا تَتَذَكَّرون عيد ميلادي أبداً.   ٦ تَذَكَّرناهُ في العام الماضي.

٧ هل تَتَذَكَّرينَ الحَرب؟   ٨ أتَتَذَكَّرها قَليلاً.

١ يتحدَّث/يتكلَّم جرجس العربيّة واليونانيّة بطلاقة.   16.2

٢ يتحدَّث/يتكلَّم جاك الفرنسيّة بطلاقة والعربيّة قليلاً.

٣ تتحدَّث/تتكلَّم فاطمة الفارسيّة بطلاقة والفرنسيّة قليلاً.

٤ يتحدَّث/يتكلَّم أحمد الفارسيّة والعربيّة بطلاقة والانجليزيّة قليلاً.

٥ تتحدَّث/تتكلَّم لوسي الصينيّة بطلاقة واليابانيّة قليلاً.

٦ يتحدَّث/يتكلَّم سامي الانجليزيّة بطلاقة والألمانيّة قليلاً.

٧ تتحدَّث/تتكلَّم ماري الفرنسيّة والألمانيّة بطلاقة واليونانيّة قليلاً.

٨ (أنا) أتحدَّث/أتكلَّم العربيّة والانجليزيّة بطلاقة والفرنسيّة قليلاً.

١ نَتَعَلَّم   ٢ تَعلَم   ٣ تَعَلَّم   16.3

٤ عَلمنا   ٥ يَتَعَلَّمون   ٦ عَلِمْنَ

٧ تَتَعَلَّمون   ٨ عَلِمتُ

16.4

٣ أَتَصَرَّف	٢ تَحَسَّنَت	١ تَتَحَرَّك
٦ يَتَعَلَّمون	٥ تَتَحَرَّك	٤ تَتَسَلَّق
٩ تَتَذَكَّرِين	٨ تَعَلَّمنا	٧ تَسَلَّقَ اللِّصّ
١٢ تَعَلَّمتُم	١١ نَتَصَرَّف	١٠ تَفَرَّقَت

16.5

٢ إنّ الرِّجال تَقاتَلوا في هذا الوادي.

٤ هؤُلاء الأطفال يَتَقاتَلون على قِطعة الخُبز.

٦ المَجلِس يَتَناقش الآن في هذه المشكلة.

٨ إنّني أَتَكاسَل في الحرارة.

١ إنَّنا نَتَحادَث بِلُغة ويلز.

٣ كَلبي يَتَكاسَل ويَنام بعد أن يَأْكُل.

٥ الأُختان تَتَقاتَلان من أَجل المال.

٧ يا شابّات، هل تَـحادَثْتُـنَّ في هذا المَشروع؟

17 Forms VII, VIII, and X

17.1

٣ انْسَحَبَ	٢ يَنْقَسِمون	١ انْقَلَبَ
٦ انْقَلَبَت	٥ سَوفَ تَنْسَحِب	٤ انْعَكَسَ
	٨ تَنْكَسِر	٧ تَنقَسِم

17.2

٢ خالي مَمدوح انصَرَفَ الساعة العاشرة والنصف مساءً.

٤ أبي وأمّي انصَرَفا الساعة الحادية عشرة والنصف مساءً.

٦ بَنات مَمدوح انصَرَفْنَ الساعة الواحدة والنصف صباحاً.

٨ صَديقتي مها انصَرَفت الساعة الثانية والنصف صباحاً.

١٠ أنا انصَرَفتُ الساعة الرابعة صباحاً!

١ جدّتي انصَرَفت الساعة التاسعة مساءً.

٣ عَمَّتي سارة انصَرَفت الساعة الحادية عشرة مساءً.

٥ أبناء سارة انصَرَفوا الساعة الواحدة صباحاً.

٧ صَديقي يونِس انصَرَفَ الساعة الثانية صباحاً.

٩ وَليد وماري انصَرَفا الساعة الثالثة صباحاً.

17.3

٣ ج/ه/د اجْتَهَد/يَجْتَهِد	٢ ج/م/ع اجْتَمَع/يَجْتَمِع	١ ب/س/م ابْتَسَم/يَبْتَسِم
٦ س/م/ع اسْتَمَع/يَستَمِع	٥ ق/د/ب اقْتَرَب/يَقْتَرِب	٤ ح/د/م احْتَرَم/يَحْتَرِم
	٨ ن/ظ/ر انْتَظَر/يَنْتَظِر	٧ ع/ق/د اعْتَقَد/يَعْتَقِد

17.4

٣ سَتَحْتَفِل	٢ ارتَفَعَت	١ يَسْتَمِع
٦ يَحتَرِم	٥ اجتَمَعنا	٤ انتَظَروا
٩ ابتَسَم، اقتَرَبتُ	٨ تَستَمِعنَ	٧ نَجتَهِد
		١٠ أعتَقِد، تَنتَظِر

17.5

٣ نحن نَـجتَمِع اليوم يا زُمَلائي لِنَحتَفِل

٦ أنا أودّ أن يَزيد هذا النَّجاح

٩ أعتَقِد أنّكم تَتَساءَلون

٢ أودّ أن أَستَمِع إلى اقتراحاتكُم

٥ التُّجار في السوق يَنتَظِرون بِضائِعنا

٨ وهذا يا زملائي لأنّكم تَـجتَهِدون

١ يَحتَرِم كلّ الوُكَلاء شَرِكَتنا

٤ ارتَفَعَت المُبيعات في العام الماضي

٧ لِتَحسين الإنتاج

١٠ وتَرتَفِع هذا العام أيضاً

17.6

٣ اسْتَعْلَمَ	٢ اسْتَخْدَمَت	١ اسْتَـمْتَعْنا
٦ اسْتَكْبَرَت	٥ يَستَخْرِجون	٤ تَسْتَحْسِنين
٩ استَحْسَنتُ	٨ تَسْتَعْلِمون	٧ يَسْتَقْبِل
١٢ يَسْتَكْبِرون	١١ اسْتَقْبَلْنا	١٠ اسْتَـمْتَعْنَ

17.7

١ الطَّبّاخون في مَطْعَمنا يَستخدِمون زيت الزَّيتون.

٢ سوف تَستَقبِل الضُّيوف عند الباب.

٣ اِسْتَقبَلَت هذه المَحَطّة ثلاثة مَلايين راكِب في العام الماضي.

٤ هل اِستَخدَمتُم هذا البَرنامَج في عَمَلكم؟

٥ اِستَمتَعتُ بزيارة البُرج والمَتحَف.

٦ إنّك تَستَكبِر عَلَينا مُنذُ أن رَبَحْت جائِزة المِليون دولار.

٧ إنّنا نَستخرج البَترول والغاز الطَّبيعيّ من هذه الآبار.

٨ اِستَعلَمَ الرَّجُل عن مَواعيد القطارات.

٩ إنّ النِساء اِستَحسَنَّ فُستان العَروس.

١٠ هل تَستَخدمينَ الإنترنت في المَدرَسة؟

18 Irregular verbs in the derived forms

18.1

١ أعتَقِد أن فاطمة تُحِبّ الأرانِب ولكنّها لا تُحِبّ البَطّ.

٢ أعتَقِد أن زوج فاطمة يُحِبّ الدَّجاج والبطّ ولكنّه لا يُحبّ السَّمَك.

٣ أعتَقِد أن منير يُحِبّ الأرُزّ ولكنّه لا يُحبّ الكُسكُس.

٤ أعتَقِد أن زوجة منير تُحِبّ البَطاطِس ولكنّها لا تُحِبّ الجَزَر.

٥ أعتَقِد أن أطفال فاطمة يُحِبّون البيتزا ولكنّهم لا يُحبّون الفَلافِل.

٦ أعتَقِد أن بنات منير يُحْبِبْنَ عَصير التُّفاح ولكنّهن لا يُحْبِبْنَ عَصير البُرتُقال.

18.2

١ فاطمة أَحَبَّت الأرانِب بالجَزَر

٢ زوج فاطمة أَحَبَّ البَطّ بالكُسكُس

٣ مُنير أَحَبَّ السمك بالأرُزّ

٤ زَوجة منير أَحَبَّت الدجاج بالبطاطس

٥ أطفال فاطمة أَحَبّوا البيتزا وعَصير البرتقال

٦ بنات منير أَحْبَبْنَ الفلافل وعَصير التُّفاح

٧ أنا أَحْبَبْتُ كُلّ المَأكولات!

18.3

١ Form II رَدَّدْتُ (I repeated) | أُرَدِّد (I repeat)

٢ Form VIII اِحْتَلَلْتُ (I occupied) | أَحْتَلّ (I occupy)

٣ Form X اِسْتَحْقَقْتُ (I deserved) | أَسْتَحِقّ (I deserve)

٤ Form II سَبَّبْتُ (I caused) | أُسَبِّب (I cause)

٥ Form VIII اِمْتَدَدْتُ (I extended) | أَمْتَدّ (I extend)

٦ Form IV أَعْدَدْتُ (I prepared) | أُعِدّ (I prepare)

٧ Form X اِسْتَمْرَرْتُ (I continued) | أَسْتَمِرّ (I continue)

٨ Form V تَرَدَّدْتُ (I hesitated) | أَتَرَدَّد (I hesitate)

٩ Form II قَرَّرْتُ (I decided) | أُقَرِّر (I decide)

18.4

1. Nadia prefers chicken.

2. Ahmed prefers fish.

3. He threatens to occupy/take over the kitchen and eat fish every day.

4. Nadia thinks the wife should be responsible for what happens in the kitchen.

5. She was going to call her mother.

6. He says that it is delicious and beneficial.

7. She hangs up and gives him a beautiful smile.

8. Nadia wins the argument.

18.5

١ نَسْتَيْقِظ

٢ وَقَّعَ

٣ يَسْتَوْرِدون

٤ تَتَوَقَّف

٥ تُوَزِّع

٦ سَيُوَظِّف

٧ أُوَفِّر

٨ يَسَّرَ

٩ نَتَوَقَّع

١٠ تَتَوافَق

18.6

١ سَنَتَّفِق على الاجتِماع في البنك.

٢ سَيوصِل المُهَندِسون أنابيب الماء إلى البُيوت.

٣ سَتُودِع نادية الشيكات في حسابها.

٤ سَتُوقِظ أُسرَتي كلّها بِتِليفونك!

٥ سأتَّصِل بِمدير البنك في مَكتَبه.

٦ إنّ الأطفال سَيوصِلون الكلِمات والصُّوَر.

٧ هل سَتَتَّفِقون على الحَفلة؟

٨ إنّ النِساء سيَتَّصِلْنَ بالمدرِّسة يوم الخميس.

18.7

٢ غَيَّرنا قائمة الطَّعام لِفَصل الشِّتاء.

٤ لماذا غَيَّرتِ قائمة الطعام؟

٦ تَسَوَّقنَ معاً يوم الخميس الماضي.

٨ حاوَلنا أن نَرُدَّ على هذه الأسئلة أمس.

١ تَضايَقَ أحمد من أُخته قليلاً.

٣ متى تَتَسَوَّقون معاً؟

٥ أنتَ لا تُحاوِل أن تَرُدَّ على الأسئلة.

٧ تَضايَقتُ من هذه الموسيقى.

18.8

٢ مُنير يُريد جِزاماً من الجِلد.

٤ أطفال فاطمة يُريدون كُتُباً فَرَنْسيّة.

٦ نادية وزَوجها يُريدان مَفْرَشاً من القُطن.

١ أُمّ أميرة تُريد زُجاجة عِطر.

٣ زَوجة مُنير تُريد قَلادة فَضّيّة.

٥ بنات مُنير يُرِدنَ شكولاتة.

18.9

٢ مُنير لا يَحتاج إلى جِزام من الجِلد.

٤ أطفال فاطمة لا يَحتاجون إلى كُتُب فَرَنْسيّة.

٦ نادية وزَوجها لا يَحتاجان إلى مَفْرَش من القُطن.

١ أُمّ أميرة لا تَحتاج إلى زُجاجة عِطر.

٣ زَوجة مُنير لا تَحتاج إلى قَلادة فَضّيّة.

٥ بنات مُنير لا يَحتَجنَ إلى شكولاتة.

18.10

٣ خَوَّف/يُخَوِّف

٦ ناوَل/يُناوِل

٩ صَوَّت/يُصَوِّت

١٢ لَوَّث/يُلَوِّث

٢ تَطَوَّر/يَتَطَوَّر

٥ تَصَوَّر/يَتَصَوَّر

٨ اِستَراح/يَستَريح

١١ أَدار/يُدير

١٤ تَعاوَن/يَتَعاوَن

١ أجاب/يُجيب

٤ اِختار/يَختار

٧ أضاف/يُضيف

١٠ تَزَوَّج/يَتَزَوَّج

١٣ عاوَن/يُعاوِن

18.11

٣ تَطَوَّرت

٦ تَعاوَنّا

٩ أُريد، يُعاوِنني

١٢ ناوَلتُهُ

١٥ نَستَطيع، نُضيف

٢ سيَتَزَوَّج

٥ تَتَصَوَّر

٨ سيُخيف

١١ سَتَتَلَوَّث

١٤ اِختَرتُ

١ يُدير

٤ اِستَرَحْنا

٧ صَوَّتوا

١٠ لَوَّثت

١٣ أَجَبتِ

18.12

٣ Form II

٦ Form III

٩ Form VIII

٢ Form VIII

٥ Form X

٨ Form II

١ Form III

٤ Form IV

٧ Form VII

١٠ Form IV

18.13

٣ اِشتَرَيتُم

٦ اِسْتَثْنَت

٩ سأُعْطي

١٢ يُنادينَ

٢ سَمَّينا

٥ يُصَلّونَ

٨ سَتَنْتَهي

١١ أَنْهى

١ أُلاقي

٤ تَرتَدينَ

٧ غَنَّيتَ

١٠ يَنْحَني

18.14

١ My husband returned from work, had lunch, then went to sleep.

٢ Hey, Khalil, your father is calling you!

٣ We will name our daughter Dalia because it's my grandmother's name.

٤ He gave me a small box for my mother.

٥ We finished our exams (tests) and went to the club.

٦ Anwar prays in the new mosque.

She sings and plays the *oud* and piano. ٧

We will meet our friends in front of the cinema. ٨

We amused ourselves by eating popcorn and watching movies. ٩

The friends had dinner together in the fish restaurant. ١٠

I hope to visit you (all) next year. ١١

The workers meet in this cafeteria (coffee shop) every morning. ١٢

Will you be wearing the new yellow dress? ١٣

I will buy a black hat from this store. ١٤

Sarah finished writing the novel in December. ١٥

18.15

influenced, writings ٣	late ٢	confirmed, morning ١
blamed, forgot ٦	stood, congratulated ٥	started, arrived ٤
rewarded, gave ٩	rented, sea ٨	believe, happiness ٧
founded, inherited ١٢	influence, this ١١	hurt, sit ١٠
wondered, arrived ١٤		built, thousands ١٣

18.16

٢ هَنَّأَت أُختي العروس والعريس.

٤ لماذا حاوَلَت أَن تُؤَثِّر على القاضي؟

٦ أَسَّسَت جَدَّتي الشَّركة وأنا وَرِثتُها عَنها.

٨ تَساءَلنَ عن سرِّ الأهرامات.

١٠ سَيُنشِئ الملك قَصرهُ الجديد هنا.

١٢ تَأَخَّرَ أحمد فما ذهبنا إلى السينما.

١٤ هل تَأَثَّرتُم بماله؟

١ رَقَبَتي تُؤلِمُني.

٣ سَيَبتَدِئ الحفل حين تَصِل أمّي.

٥ كافأنا ابننا وأَعطيناهُ دَرّاجة.

٧ سَأَستأجِر شَقّة كبيرة تُطِلّ على الحديقة.

٩ آمَنَ الفراعنة بِقُدرة النُّجوم.

١١ أَخَذتُها لأنَّها نَسِيَت الكتاب.

١٣ هل أَكَّدتِ الحَجز؟

V MOODS OF THE VERB AND VERBAL NOUNS

19 The subjunctive

19.1

١ أَسكُنَ أنا | تَسكُنَ أنتَ | تَسكُني أنتِ | you (masc.) تَسكُنَ أنتَ | يَسكُنَ هو he | تَسكُنَ هي she

٢ تَسكُنا أنتُما you (dual) | يَسكُنا هما they (masc. dual) | تَسكُنا هما they (fem. dual)

٣ نَسكُنَ نحن we | تَسكُنوا أنتم you (masc. pl.) | تَسكُنَّ أنتن you (fem. pl.) | يَسكُنوا هم they (masc.) | يَسكُنَّ هن they (fem.)

19.2

٣ نَزور أمَّنا قبل السَّفَر.

٦ يرجَع إلى البيت للغداء.

٩ يَجلِسنَ على الأرض.

١٢ تَتَزَوَّجا؟

٢ تَترُكوا الحَقائب عند الباب.

٥ أزورَهُم قريباً.

٨ يناموا الساعة التاسعة.

١١ نَتَّصِل بِمدير البنك.

١ أَلعَب التنس كلّ يوم.

٤ تَركَبي دَرّاجَتكِ في الحَديقة؟

٧ يَحضُرا اجتِماعاً يوم الخَميس.

١٠ يُنَظِّموا لَها حفلة.

19.3

٣ يأمَلونَ ألّا يناموا بَعد الظُّهر.

٦ نرجو منكُما ألّا تَستَمِعا إلى الراديو.

٢ أَمَرَتني أمّي ألّا أُساعِد أَخي.

٥ هل من المُمكِن ألّا أَشتَري السيّارة؟

٨ أتمَنّى ألّا تجدوا الكَنز المَدفون.

١ يَجب ألّا تُغادِري الآن، يا نادية.

٤ حاوَلوا ألّا يَتَضايَقوا من أُختِهم.

٧ طَلَبتُ منه ألّا يَجلِس على الأرض.

١ لِيَلعَب   ٢ لِتُساعِدي   ٣ أَتَسَلَّق
٤ يَشتَروا   ٥ تَتَعَلَّم   ٦ نُراقِب
٧ لِتَعرِفنَ   ٨ لا تَحتَرِق   ٩ لِيَشكُروا
١٠ لا تَسمَعنا   ١١ تَأْخُذوني   ١٢ لِيَستَقبِلا

19.5

١ لن أَدرُس الهَندَسة في الجامِعة.   ٢ لن يَزوروا المَزرَعة.
٣ لن أَقُصَّ شَعري.   ٤ لن تَدفَعي أكثر من خمسة، يا سميرة.
٥ لن تَسمَع أُختي نَصيحَتي.   ٦ لن تَذهَبوا إلى الشاطئ غداً.
٧ لن نَبدَأَ قبل الساعة الخامِسة.   ٨ لن يَملأوا حمّام السِباحة بالماء.
٩ لن يُخَوِّف كَلبك الأطفال.   ١٠ لن يُوَقِّع المَلِك هذه الرِّسالة.
١١ لن تُعِدّي العَقد قَبلَ يَوم الخَميس.   ١٢ لن تَكونوا أصدِقاء بَعدَ اليوم.
١٣ لن تَحتَفِل بعيد ميلادك غداً.   ١٤ أَبي وأُمّي لن يَستَقبِلا الضُّيوف عند الباب.
١٥ لن تَعود ماري إلى زَوجها.   ١٦ لن يَبيعوا السَّمَك هنا.
١٧ لن تُعِدّي الدجاج.   ١٨ لن يُسَبِّب لَك مَشاكِل.
١٩ لن يُفَتِّشوا المَطعَم المَوجود بِجانِب النَّهر.   ٢٠ أنتُما لن تَكونا مُهِمَّين في حَياتنا.

20 The jussive

20.1

١ أَستَمِعْ أنا I | تَستَمِعْ أنتَ you (masc.) | تَستَمِعي أنتِ you (fem.) | يَستَمِعْ هو he | تَستَمِعْ هي she

٢ تَستَمِعا أنتُما you (dual) | يَستَمِعا هما they (masc. dual) | تَستَمِعا هما they (fem. dual)

٣ نَستَمِعْ نحن we | تَستَمِعوا أنتم you (masc. pl.) | تَستَمِعنَ أنتن you (fem. pl.) | يَستَمِعوا هم they (masc.) | يَستَمِعنَ هن they (fem.)

20.2

١ الطَّقس حارٌّ فلنَأكُلْ آيس كريم.   ٢ الحديقة واسِعة فلنَلعَبْ كُرة القَدَم.
٣ المَنظَر جَميل فلنَأخُذْ صورة.   ٤ النَّهر هادِئ فلنركَبْ قارِباً.
٥ هذه السَّندَويتشات لَذيذة فلنَرجَعْ هُنا للغَداء.   ٦ هذه الحَقائِب رَخيصة فلنَدخُل المَحَلّ.
٧ السينما قريبة فلنُشاهِدْ الفيلم الجَديد.   ٨ لا أعرِف الطَّريق إلى السينما فلنَسأَلْ الشُّرطيّ.

20.3

١ لم نذهَبْ إلى البَحر الأحمَر، ذَهَبْنا إلى البَحر المُتَوَسِّط.   ٢ لم تذهَبْ جِدَّتنا معنا، ذَهَبَتْ خالَتنا معنا.
٣ لم يَتَسَلَّقْ أبونا جَبَلاً تَسَلَّقَ بُرجاً.   ٤ لم تَنكَسِرْ آلة التَّصوير، انْكَسَرَتْ مَظَلَّة الشَّمس.
٥ لم نُغادِرْ بعد الغَداء، غادَرْنا بعد العَشاء.   ٦ لم تَركَبي جَمَلاً رَكِبْتِ حِماراً.
٧ لم ألعَبْ كُرة القَدَم، لَعِبْتُ الكُرة الطائِرة.   ٨ أبونا وأُمّنا لم يَطبُخا سَمَكاً على الشاطئ، طَبَخا دَجاجاً.

20.4

١ لم يَخرُجْ المُدير من المَكتَب.   ٢ لم تَسكُنْ سَميرة في هذا الشارِع.
٣ لم يَعرِفوا سَبَب هذا الاجتِماع.   ٤ لم تُنَظِّفوا الأرض جَيِّداً.
٥ لم تَتَعَلَّمي من أخطائك.   ٦ لم أركَبْ سيّارة بهذه السُّرعة في حَياتي.
٧ لم نَتَحَدَّثْ في هذا المَوضوع أمام الأولاد.   ٨ لم تَتَذَكَّري عيد ميلادي!
٩ لم يَضحَك المُشاهِدون كَثيراً.   ١٠ لم تُصلِحْ هذه المائِدة المَكسورة.
١١ لماذا لم تَطبُخْنَ السمكة؟   ١٢ البَنات لم يَستَمتَعْنَ بِزيارة القَصر القَديم.
١٣ أكَل الرِّجال ولم يَدفَعوا الحِساب.   ١٤ لم أشكُرْ صَديقي على الهَدية.
١٥ لم يَنصَرِفوا لكنَّني لم أطلُبْ الشُّرطة.   ١٦ وَردة وأحمد لم يَتَحادَثا معي في مَوضوع زَواجِهما.

١ أَرُدُّ أنا | تَرُدُّ أنتَ | تَرُدِّي أنتِ | you (masc.) | يَرُدُّ هو he | تَرُدُّ هي she

٢ تَرُدّا أنتُما | you (dual) | يَرُدّا هما they (masc. dual) | تَرُدّا هما they (fem. dual)

٣ نَرُدُّ نحن we | تَرُدّوا أنتَم you (masc. pl.) | تَرُدُدْنَ أنتن you (fem. pl.) | يَرُدّوا هم they (masc.) | يَرُدُدْنَ هن they (fem.)

١ لماذا لم تَرُدَّ على الهاتِف؟

٢ لم يَرُدِّ الولد على أمّه.

٣ فَلْنَرُدَّ على الرِّسالة.

٤ لماذا لم تَرُدِّي أمس؟

٥ فَلْنَرُدَّ على الدَّعوة.

٦ سَأَلْتُ البنات ولكنَّهُنَّ لم يَرُدُدْنَ.

٧ فَلْنَرُدَّ على الهاتِف.

٨ لم يَرُدّوا لأنَّهُم كانوا في الحديقة.

١ لم تَمُرَّ الطائرة فوق أسبانيا.

٢ لم تَبُثَّ المَحَطّة هذا الخَبَر أمس.

٣ لم تُحِبّ سميرة الفَلافِل.

٤ لَمْ نَعُدِّ الضُّيوف عند الباب.

٥ لماذا لم تَقُصّي شعرك؟

٦ لم نُغَيِّر قائمة الطَّعام.

٧ لم يَضُمَّني المُدَرِّب للفَريق.

٨ لم يَستَحِقّوا كلَّ تلكَ المَشاكِل.

٩ أبي وأَمّي لم يُعِدّا الحَقيبة للسَّفَر.

١٠ لِماذا لم تَرُدّ؟

١ أطِرْ أحتَجّ I | تَطِرْ تَحتَجّ you (masc.) | تَطيري تَحتاجي you (fem.) | يَطِرْ يَحتَجّ he | تَطِرْ تَحتَجّ she

٢ تَطيرا تَحتاجا you (dual) | يَطيرا يَحتاجا they (masc. dual) | تَطيرا تَحتاجا they (fem. dual)

٣ نَطِرْ نَحتَجّ we | تَطيروا تَحتاجوا you (masc. pl.) | تَطِرْنَ تَحتَجْنَ you (fem. pl.) | يَطيروا يَحتاجوا they (masc.) | يَطِرْنَ يَحتَجْنَ they (fem.)

١ تَطِرْ

٢ فَلنَنَمْ

٣ أحتَجّ

٤ فَلنَزُرْهُ

٥ تَزِدْ

٦ يَستَطِعْ

٧ فَلنُضِفْ

٨ أصُمْ

٩ يَقُمْنَ

١٠ يَعُودا

١١ تَختَرْ

١٢ فَلنَبِعْ

١٣ تَقولي

١٤ تَستَريحوا

١ لم أرِم الكتاب على الأرض.

٢ لماذا لم تَمشِ إلى بيتي؟

٣ لم يَجروا إلى المدرسة.

٤ نحن مُتَأَخِّرون، فلنَجرِ.

٥ لم تَرمِ سميرة الكرة.

٦ لماذا لم ترمي الكرة؟

٧ مَشَت البنات ولكِنَّهُنَّ لم يَجرينَ.

٨ فلنَرمِ العصا للكلب.

٩ ألم تَمشيا إلى الحديقة؟

١٠ لَدَينا وقت كَثير، فلنَمشِ إلى المتحف.

١ لِماذا لم تُعطي التَّذكِرة لِزُمَك؟

٢ لم نَلقَ سارة في الحَديقة.

٣ لم تَجرِ نادية في سِباق الأُمَّهات.

٤ لم أشْتَرِ قُبَّعة في السوق.

٥ لم نَدعُ صَديقنا على العَشاء.

٦ لم يُعْطِني أحمد الكتاب.

٧ لم يَمشوا في الصَّحراء لمُدّة طويلة.

٨ لم تَنتَهِ سارة من كِتابة الرِّواية.

٩ لم يَشكُ المُوَظَّفون من حَرارة المَكتَب.

١٠ إنَّ الصَّديقين لم يَتَلاقَيا في النادي.

١١ لم يَجرِ الأولاد وَراء السيّارة ولم يَرموا الزُّهور.

١٢ لم تَرتَدي الفُستان الجديد في الحفل.

١٣ لم نَرضَ عن الخِدمة في المَطعَم.

١٤ لم يُعْطِنا المُدير مِفتاح الباب.

١٥ لم أرجُ منكُم الاِمتِناع من التَّدخين.

21 The imperative

21.1

١ اُنْظُرْ!   ٢ اُتْرُكِي!   ٣ اِقْرَأوا!

٤ اِجْمَعْ!   ٥ خُذِي!   ٦ أَعْطِ!

٧ أَخْرِجوا!   ٨ اِبْتَسِمي!   ٩ اِجْلِسْنَ!

١٠ طِرْ!   ١١ رَتِّبا!   ١٢ تَقَدَّموا!

١٣ ضَعي!   ١٤ اِنْسَ!   ١٥ قَرِّرْنَ!

١٦ جِدّوا!   ١٧ غَيِّرْ!   ١٨ اِسْتَمَعا!

١٩ اِسْتَيقِظي!   ٢٠ رَكِّزوا!

21.2

1. Collect all the empty cola bottles.
2. Put them in this box.
3. Change the sheets.
4. Tidy the bed.
5. Look under the bed.
6. Give me these empty pizza boxes.
7. Remove this sock from the pizza box.
8. Put it in the laundry basket.
9. Open the window.
10. Take these plates and glasses to the kitchen.
11. Leave them next to the sink.
12. Throw the remains of this old sandwich in the trash.
13. Wake up!

21.3

يا نادية غُرفَتك قَذِرة! اِجْمَعي زُجاجات الكولا الفارغة كلّها، وضَعيها في هذا الصَّندوق. غَيِّري المِلايات ورَتِّبي السَّرير. اِنظُري تحت السَّرير! أَعْطيني عُلَب البيتزا الفارغةَ هذه! أَخْرِجي هذا الجَورب من عُلبة البيتزا يا نادية وضَعيه في سَلّة الغَسيل! اِفتَحي الشُّباك. خُذي هذه الأطباق والأكواب إلى المَطبَخ واتُركيها بِجوار الحَوض. اِرمي بَقايا هذا السندَويتش القَديم في الزِّبالة. متى سَتتَعلَّمين يا نادية! اِستَيقِظي!

21.4

١ لا تَنْظُرْ!   ٢ لا تَتْرُكِي!   ٣ لا تَقْرَأوا!

٤ لا تَجْمَعْ!   ٥ لا تَأْخُذي!   ٦ لا تُعْطِ!

٧ لا تُخْرِجوا!   ٨ لا تَبْتَسِمي!   ٩ لا تجْلِسْنَ!

١٠ لا تَطِرْ!   ١١ لا تُرَتِّبا!   ١٢ لا تَتَقَدَّموا!

١٣ لا تَضَعي!   ١٤ لا تَنْسَ!   ١٥ لا تُقَرِّرْنَ!

١٦ لا تجِدوا!   ١٧ لا تُغَيِّرْ!   ١٨ لا تَسْتَمَعا!

١٩ لا تَسْتَيقِظي!   ٢٠ لا تُرَكِّزوا!

21.5

لا تَيْأَسوا يا شَباب! ولا تَشُكّوا أَبداً في أنّكم الفَريق الأَفضَل.

لا تَنْظُروا إلى النَّتيجة الآن، ولا تَدعوا الأهداف الستّة تُؤَثِّر على عَزيمتكم.

في الشوط الثاني لا تَتْرُكوا "كاكي" و"مِشمِش" يَلمِسان الكُرة.

يا إبراهيم، لا تَدَع "ميمو" يَهرب مِنك في وَسَط المَلْعَب.

يا أحمد، رَكِّز على "فرفور" حَتّي لا يَغيب عن عَينك لِثانية واحدة.

لا تَتَقَدَّموا كلّكم معاً. لا تَمنَحوهُم مَساحات خالية في المَلْعَب. لا تُعطوهم الوقت لِلتَّفكير.

لا تَنسوا تَعليماتي، وأَكيد لَن يَستطيعوا أن يُسَجِّلوا ستّة أهداف أُخرى في الشوط الثاني.

21.6

١ لا تَنسوا تَعليماتي   ٢ رَكِّز على "فرفور"   ٣ لا تَتَقَدَّموا كلّكم معاً

٤ لا تَيْأَسوا يا شَباب!   ٥ لا تَنْظُروا إلى النَّتيجة الآن   ٦ لا تَدَع "ميمو" يَهرب مِنك

٧ لا تَشُكّوا أَبداً في أنّكم الفَريق الأَفضَل   ٨ لا تُعطوهم الوقت لِلتَّفكير   ٩ لا تَتْرُكوا "كاكي" و"مِشمِش" يَلمِسان الكُرة

١٠ لا تَدعوا الأهداف السِتّة تُؤَثِّر على عَزيمتكم

22 The verbal noun

22.1

١ "dancing" from the verb رَقَصَ/يَرْقُص

٢ "sitting" from the verb جَلَسَ/يَجْلِس

٣ "writing" from the verb كَتَبَ/يَكْتُب

٤ "return(ing)" from the verb رَجَعَ/يَرْجِع

٥ "looking" from the verb نَظَرَ/يَنْظُر

٦ "riding" from the verb رَكِبَ/يَرْكَب

٧ "understanding" from the verb فَهِمَ/يَفْهَم

٨ "planting/agriculture" from the verb زَرَعَ/يَزْرَع

٩ "exiting" from the verb خَرَجَ/يَخْرُج

١٠ "saying" from the verb قالَ/يَقول

١١ "opening" from the verb فَتَحَ/يَفْتَح

١٢ "passing" from the verb مَرَّ/يَمُرّ

١٣ "eating" from the verb أَكَلَ/يَأْكُل

١٤ "reply(ing)" from the verb رَدَّ/يَرُدّ

١٥ "description" from the verb وَصَفَ/يَصِف

١٦ "reading" from the verb قَرَأَ/يَقْرأ

١٧ "shouting" from the verb صاحَ/يَصيح

١٨ "being/existence" from the verb كانَ/يَكون

١٩ "forgetting" from the verb نَسِيَ/يَنْسى

٢٠ "sleep(ing)" from the verb نامَ/يَنام

22.2

١ استِقْبال reception

٢ تَنْظيف cleaning

٣ تَحَدُّث speaking

٤ مُساعَدة help(ing)

٥ تَسَلُّق climbing

٦ انْسِحاب withdrawal

٧ إصْلاح reform(ing)

٨ احْتِفال celebration

٩ استِعْلام inquiring

١٠ تَدْخين smoking

١١ ابْتِسام smiling

١٢ إرْسال sending

١٣ مُشاهَدة viewing

١٤ تَكاسُل being lazy

١٥ احْتِرام respect

١٦ تَصَرُّف behaving/behavior

١٧ مُراجَعة review(ing)

١٨ تَرْتيب organization/tidying

١٩ تَعْديل adjustment

٢٠ استِخْراج extraction

22.3

١ ممنوع التَّدخين في الحديقة

٢ ممنوع الكِتابة على المكاتب

٣ ممنوع التَّحَدُّث مع سائِق الباص

٤ ممنوع الخُروج من المدرسة

٥ ممنوع تَسَلُّق السور

٦ ممنوع السِّباحة في النهر

٧ ممنوع مُشاهَدة التليفزيون بعد الساعة التاسعة

٨ ممنوع استِخدام الكمبيوتر قبل الغداء

٩ ممنوع الصِّياح في المَمَرّ

١٠ ممنوع التَصَرُّف دون احْتِرام

22.4

١ يُحِبّ أبي مُشاهَدة كُرة السَّلّة.

٢ أُريد كِتابة رواية.

٣ يَوَدّ الولد تَسَلُّق الشَّجَرة.

٤ يأمَلونَ زيارة أوروبا.

٥ هل تُحِبّ القِراءة؟

٦ رَجَوْنا منهُنَّ الجُلوس على الأرض.

٧ طَلَبْتُ منكُم تَرْك الحَقائِب عَند الباب.

٨ طَلَبَت مِنّي أمّي احْتِرام المُدَرِّسين.

٩ هل تَستَطيعينَ استِقبال خالَتِك في المَطار؟

١٠ يأمَلونَ تَغْيير قائِمة الطعام قبل بِداية الصَّيف.

١١ أرادَت نادية زيارة صديقتها يَوم الجُمعة.

١٢ يَوَدّ حُضور الاجتِماع يوم الخَميس.

١٣ نرجو منكُما الاستِماع إلى الراديو.

١٤ يَتمَنّى أحمد استِخدام الكمبيوتر.

١٥ حاوَلوا حَلّ مَشاكِلهُم.

22.5

١ d

٢ b

٣ f

٤ g

٥ a

٦ h

٧ e

٨ c

23 Unusual verbs

23.1

١ أَقِي I guard | يَقِي he guards | وَقَيْتُ I guarded | وَقَى he guarded
لَمْ أَقِ I didn't guard | لَمْ يَقِ he didn't guard

٢ أَفِي I fulfill | يَفِي he fulfills | وَفَيْتُ I fulfilled | وَفَى he fulfilled
لَمْ أَفِ I didn't fulfill | لَمْ يَفِ he didn't fulfill

23.2

١ رَوَيْتُ القِصّة للأطفال.

٢ نَنوي أن نَذهَب إلى السوق غداً.

٣ رَوَتْ لنا المُدرِّسة قِصّة علي بابا.

٤ هل تَنوي أن تَطبُخ هذا السمك؟

٥ لم نَروِ لها تَفاصيل قِصّتنا.

٦ سَنَروي لكُم القِصّة كلّها.

٧ لا تَنوي نادية أن تَحتَفِل بعيد ميلادها.

٨ لم أنوِ السَّفَر هذا الصباح.

٩ هل سَتَروينَ كلّ شيء لأمّك؟

١٠ لا نَنوي أن نَروي التَّفاصيل هنا.

23.3

٣ جِئتَ	٢ يَجيء	١ جاءَ
٦ يجِئ	٥ جِئنا	٤ جِئتُ
٩ تَجيء	٨ جِئنَ	٧ سَيَجيئون
١٢ جاءَتْ	١١ سَتَجيئون	١٠ أجيءَ

23.4

٣ يَأتي	٢ أتى	١ آتي
٦ يَـأتونَ	٥ أتَتْ	٤ سنَأتي
٩ ستَأتي	٨ تأتِ، ساتي	٧ أتَيْتُـنَّ
	١١ أتَيْتُما	١٠ نأتِ

23.5

٢ نَرى حصاناً في الصورة.	١ رَأَيْتُ المَلِك.
٤ أينَ رَأَيْتُـنَّ المَلِكة؟	٣ أوَدّ أن أرى أمّي.
٦ تَرى أمّ أحمد أنّهُ عنيد.	٥ رَأَيْناها في الشُّرفة مع الملك.
٨ رَأَوْا مَركَباً على النَّهر.	٧ أنا لا أرى أنّهُ عنيد.
١٠ يَرى بَعض الناس أن المِشمِش مُفيد للصحّة.	٩ أخي وأُختي هناك وهما يَرَيان المركب أيضاً.

23.6

1. She saw the prime minister and his wife.
2. She saw the famous actress "Carmella Kareem."
3. She saw the famous football player "Farfour."
4. She saw the prince in the golden carriage.
5. She saw the bride and her beautiful dress.
6. She saw the king and queen in the royal carriage.
7. She saw the white horses.
8. She saw the royal family on the balcony of the palace.

23.7

١ أرى رئيس الوُزَراء وزوجته.

٢ أرى المُمثِّلة المَشهورة "كرامِلّة كريم."

٣ أرى لاعِب الكُرة المَشهور "فَرفور."

٤ أرى الأمير في المَركَبة الذَهبيّة.

٥ أرى العَروس وفُستانها الجَميل.

٦ أرى المَلِك والمَلِكة في المَركَبة المَلَكيّة.

٧ أرى الخُيول البَيضاء.

٨ أرى العائلة المَلَكيّة في شُرفة القَصر.

23.8

١ رَأى شكري رئيس الوُزَراء ولكنّهُ لَمْ يَرَ زَوجَته.

٢ رَأَتْ سارة الأمير ولكنّها لَمْ تَرَ العَروس.

٣ رَأَتْ زوجة شكري المَركبة الذَهبيّة ولكنّها لَمْ تَرَ الخُيول البَيضاء.

٤ رَأى أطفال سارة (أطفال سارة رَأوا) المُمثِّلة المَشهورة ولكنّهُم لَمْ يَرَوْا لاعِب الكُرة المَشهور.

٥ رَأى خالِد وسميرة (خالد وسميرة رَأيا) وُصول الضُّيوف ولكنّهُما لَمْ يَرَيا العائلة المَلَكيّة في الشُّرفة.

23.9

٢ لَيسَ شُكري في المَكتَبة.

٤ لَستُ أمامَ البنك.

٦ لَيسوا مع المُدرِّس.

٨ لَيسَت البُحيرة هادئة.

١٠ لَيسَ الباب مَفتوحاً.

١٢ لَستُم مُتَأَخِّرين.

١ لَسنا في مِصر.

٣ لَيسَت سَميرة في بيتها.

٥ لَستِ مَشغولة الآن.

٧ لَيسوا مهندسين في العراق.

٩ لَستَ المدير.

١١ لَيسَت السيّارات في الشارع.

١٣ أَلَستُـنَّ في المدرسة؟

23.10

٢ لَيسَت نادية في أمريكا.

٤ لَيسَت أُختي طويلة.

٦ ألَيسَ ابنك طَبّاخاً؟

٨ ألَستَ في المدرسة؟

١٠ ألَيسَت الكُتُب في الحقيبة؟

١ لَستُ في الحديقة.

٣ لَيسَ شكري عنيداً.

٥ لَيسَت السيّارة أمام البيت.

٧ لَسنا مدرّسين.

٩ لَيسَ هذا القَميص نَظيفاً.

23.11

٢ هناك جمنازيوم ولكن لَيسَ هناك حمّام سِباحة.

٤ هناك حديقة ولكن لَيسَ هناك مَقاعد.

٦ هناك اِسطبلات رُكوب الخَيل ولكن لَيسَ هناك مِضمار.

١ هناك ملعب كرة القَدَم ولكن لَيسَ هناك ملعب جولف.

٣ هناك كافتيريا ولكن لَيسَ هناك مَطعَم.

٥ هناك ملعب أطفال ولكن لَيسَ هناك مُنزَلِق.

23.12

٢ لا، لَيسَ لَدَينا درّاجات الآن.

٤ لا، لَيسَ عِندَ البقّال تين طازج الآن.

٦ لا، لَيسَ لِابنَتنا بيت في البَحر الأَحمَر الآن.

٨ لا، لَيسَ مَعي صُوَر العائلة اليَوم.

١ لا، لَيسَ عندنا كِلاب الآن.

٣ لا، لَيسَ عندي أَلم في رِجلي الآن.

٥ لا، لَيسَ لِابننا سيّارة سريعة الآن.

٧ لا، لَيسَ لَدَينا شجرة طويلة في الحديقة الآن.

23.13

٣ دَحْرَجْتَ you (masc.) rolled

٦ غَرْغَروا they (masc.) gargled

٢ زَلْزَلَتْ it/she shook

٥ دَنْدَنّا we hummed

٨ طَقْطَقَتْ it (fem.) crackled

١ تَـمْتَـمْتُ I muttered

٤ ثَرْثَرْتُـم you (masc. pl.) chattered

٧ زَخْرَفَ it/he adorned

23.14

٢ نُثَرْثِر we chatter, are chattering

٤ تُزَخْرِفينَ you (fem.) decorate, are decorating

٦ يُدَنْدِنونَ we hum, are humming

٨ تُتَـمْتِم you mutter, are muttering

١ تُتَرْجِمونَ you (masc. pl.) translate, are translating

٣ تُطَقْطِق it (fem.) crackles, is crackling

٥ يُغَرْغِرْنَ they (fem.) gargle, are gargling

٧ يُزَلْزِل it/he shakes, is shaking

23.15

٣ دَحْرَجَتْ

٦ يُطَقْطِق

٢ نُغَرْغِر

٥ تَـمْتَـمْتُ

٨ تُزَخْرِفْن

١ تُثَرْثِرينَ

٤ يُزَلْزِل

٧ تَرْجَموا

23.16

٣ تَـمْتَـمْتُ

٦ يُطَقْطِق

٢ سَتُزَخْرِفْنَ

٥ تُثَرْثِرينَ

٨ دَحْرَجَتْ

١ تَرْجَموا

٤ نُغَرْغِر

٧ يُزَلْزِل

23.17

٢ تُحِبّ سامية أن تَتَفَلْسَف في التاريخ.

٤ تُحِبّ صديقات سامية أن تَتَفَلْسَفْنَ في الأَدَب.

٦ تُحِبّ أميرة وسميرة أن تَتَفَلْسَفا في الأخلاقيات.

١ يُحِبّ خالد أن يَتَفَلْسَف في الطَّبيعة البَشَرِيّة.

٣ يُحِبّ أصدقاء خالد أن يَتَفَلْسَفوا في نَظَرِيّة التَّطَوُّر.

٥ يُحِبّ محمود ونادر أن يَتَفَلْسَفا في عِلم الوَراثة.

24 Compound tenses and conditional sentences

24.1

١ كُنْتَ (قَدْ) وَجَدْتَ القَلَم. You (masc.) had (already) found the pen.

٢ كانَتْ (قَدْ) فَعَلَتْهُ. She had (already) done it.

٣ كُنّا (قَدْ) اشتَرَينا ملابِس. We had (already) bought clothes.

٤ كانوا (قَدْ) غادَروا البيت. They (masc.) had (already) left the house.

٥ كانَ (قَدْ) مَشَى إلى المَحَطّة. He had (already) walked to the station.

٦ كانَتْ (قَدْ) صَلَّحَتْ الكُرسيّ المَكسور. She had (already) repaired the broken chair.

٧ كُنَّ (قَدْ) ذَهَبْنَ إلى النادي. They (fem.) had (already) gone to the club.

٨ كُنّا (قَدْ) شَرِبنا العَصير. We had (already) drunk the juice.

٩ كانَتْ (قَدْ) اسْتَيْقَظَتْ. She had (already) woken up.

١٠ كانوا (قَدْ) أَكَلوا الكَعك. They had (already) eaten the cookies.

١١ كُنْتُمْ (قَدْ) بِعتُم السيّارة. You (masc. pl.) had (already) sold the car.

١٢ كُنْتُ (قَدْ) اسْتَخدَمْتُ الكُمبيوتر. I had (already) used the computer.

١٣ كُنْتِ (قَدْ) رَدَدْتِ على الهاتِف. You (fem.) had (already) answered the telephone.

١٤ كُنّا (قَدْ) رَأَينا المَلِك. We had (already) seen the king.

١٥ كانا (قَدْ) رَتَّبا غُرفَتهُما. They (masc. dual) had (already) tidied their room.

24.2

١ كُنْتُ (قد) خَرجتُ   ٢ كانَت (قد) نَفَذَتْ   ٣ كانَ (قد) غادَرَها

٤ كانوا (قد) دَفَعوا   ٥ كُنتِ (قد) طَبَخْتِه   ٦ كُنتَ (قد) فَتَحْتُهُ

٧ كانا (قد) عادا   ٨ كانَتْ (قد) تَعَشَّتْ

24.3

١ لا، كُنتُ أَعمَل كَنَجّار ولكن الآن أَعمَل كَمُهَندِس.

٢ لا، كانَت تَعمَل كَمُدرِّسة ولكن الآن تَعمَل كَمُفَتِّشة.

٣ لا، كانَ يَدرُس في بَيروت ولكن الآن يَدرُس في باريس.

٤ لا، كانَتْ تُقيم في الكُوَيت ولكن الآن تُقيم في عُمان.

٥ لا، كُنّا نُسافِر إلى أمريكا كلَّ صَيف ولكن الآن نُسافِر إلى فَرَنسا.

٦ لا، كان يَكتُب مَقالات لجَريدة "الأهرام" ولكن الآن يَكتُب مَقالات لجَريدة "الدُّستور".

24.4

١ كانَتْ زَينة تَلْعب كُرة القَدَم يوم السَّبت.   ٢ كُنتُ أُقيم في دِمَشق.

٣ كانَ عَمّي يَركَب الخَيل.   ٤ كُنّا نَسْمَع قِصَصاً غَريباً عَن هذا البيت.

٥ كانَ الأولاد يَصِلونَ إلى المَدرَسة الساعة الثامِنة.   ٦ كُنتَ تَنْسَى عيد ميلادي.

٧ كانوا يَظُنّون أن هُناك أَمَل.   ٨ هل كُنتُم تَسْتَمِعون إلى الموسيقى قَبلَ النَّوم؟

٩ هل كُنتِ تُنَظِّفينَ الأرض؟   ١٠ كانَ الأصدقاء يَتَلاقَوْنَ في النادي.

١١ كانَ الصَّيّاد يَذهَب إلى النَّهر في الفَجر.   ١٢ كُنّا نَتَحَدَّث عن تَحسين الإنتاج.

١٣ كانَتْ البنات يَبْتَسِمْنَ كَثيراً.   ١٤ كانَ أبي وأَخي يَطبُخانِ الغَداء كلّ يوم.

24.5

١ إذا/إن ذَهَبتُ إلى الحفلة فَسَألْبس فُستاني الجَديد.   ٢ إذا/إن أَخَذتَ هذا الطَّريق فَسَتَصِل إلى المَطار.

٣ إذا/إن أَعطَيتُكُم الدولارات كلَّها فَسَتُنفِقونَها في أسبوع.   ٤ إذا/إن اشتَرَينا سَمَكة فَسَنَشويها على الفَحم.

٥ إذا/إن جاءَني العَقد فَسَأُوَقِّعهُ اليوم.   ٦ إذا/إن قَرَأَ أبي مُدوَّنتي فَسَيَأْخُذ الكمبيوتر منّي.

24.6	١ إن أُختك استَيقَظَت...
٢ إذا شَعَرتَ بالجوع...	
	٣ إذا أرَدتَ أن تَجلِس في الحديقة...
٤ إن اتَّصَلَت جَدّتك بالهاتِف...	
	٥ إذا رَأَيتَ البُستانيَّ...
٦ إذا وَجَدتَ مفاتيحي...	
	٧ إذا رَنَّ الجَرَس...
٨ إن أرَدتَ أن تَستَمِع إلى الموسيقى...	

24.7	١ لَو كانَ أبي جاءَ لَنَلعَب التنس.
٢ لَو كانَ إبراهيم وَجَدَ المَفاتيح لَوَضَعَها على المائدة.	
	٣ لَو كانَت سميرة وَصَلَت قَبلي لَحَجَزَت لي مقعداً.
٤ لَو كُنتُ غنيّاً لَاشتَرَيتُ يَختاً كبيراً.	
	٥ لَو كُنتِ سَمِعتِ الجَرَس لَفَتَحتِ الباب.
٦ لَو كانوا عَرفوا لَشاهَدوا الأخبار.	

25   The passive

25.1	١ وُلِدَت أمّي في باريس عام ١٩٥٤.
٢ وُلِدَ جَدّي في حيفا عام ١٩٢٨.	
	٣ وُلِدَت جَدّتي في القُدس عام ١٩٣١.
٤ وُلِدَ أخي في بيروت عام ١٩٧٦.	
	٥ وُلِدَت أختي في الكُويت عام ١٩٧٨.
٦ وُلِدتُ في عَمّان عام ١٩٨٠.	
	٧ وُلِدَت زَوجتي في إربد عام ١٩٨٢.
٨ وُلِدَ ابني في عَمّان عام ٢٠٠٧.	
	٩ وُلِدَت ابنتي في جَرَش عام ٢٠٠٩.
١٠ وُلِدَ التَّوأَم (التوأم وُلِدا) في أمريكا عام ٢٠١٢.	

25.2	١ وُجِدَ الكِتاب.
٢ بيعَت السيّارة.	
	٣ كُتِبَ اسمي.
٤ سُرِقَت ساعتي.	
	٥ فُتِحَ الشُّبّاك.
٦ أُضيفَ البَصَل للَّحم.	
	٧ شُرِبَ عصير البرتقال.
٨ حُجِزَت الصالة للحَفل.	
	٩ قيلَ إنَّهُم لُصوص.
١٠ تُرِكَت المَفاتيح على المائدة.	
	١١ حُمِّلَ الفيلم من الإنترنت.
١٢ وُرِثَت المَزرَعة عن الجَدّ.	
	١٣ رُسِمَت صورة جميلة للمُدرِّسة.
١٤ أُستُخدِمَ زيت الزيتون في هذا الطَبَق.	
	١٥ أُستُخرِجَت النواة من المِشمِش.

25.3	١ يُقطَف التُّفاح في أُكتوبِر.
٢ تُنَظَّف الأرض كلَّ يوم.	
	٣ يُضاف السُّكِّر إلى العَصير.
٤ تُباع الملابس في أمريكا.	
	٥ تُنقَل الصناديق إلى المَصنَع.
٦ كلَّ يوم يُترَكون في الحديقة لِمُدّة ساعة.	
	٧ يُقال إن الأميرة جميلة.
٨ تُعَبَّأ الكُتُب في صَناديق.	
	٩ يُستَخدَم زيت زيتون دائِماً في هذا المَطعَم.
١٠ تُسرَق لُعَب من السوق كلَّ يوم.	

25.4	١ يوجَد كُرسيّ في الحَديقة.
٢ توجَد كُتُب على الكرسيّ.	
	٣ توجَد مَحَطّة أُتوبيس في وَسَط المدينة.
٤ يوجِد جامِع بجانب النَّهر.	
	٥ توجَد مَحَلّات كثيرة قَريبة من بيتنا.
٦ توجَد سيّارة للبيع.	
	٧ توجَد مَلابِس في الدُّرج.
٨ توجَد مَشاكِل كثيرة بهذا المَشروع.	
	٩ يوجَد لُصوص وراء السور.
١٠ توجَد الزُّهور على كلّ مائدة.	

25.5	١ تُقطَف، تُعَبَّأ، تُنقَل
٢ تُنَظَّف، تُفصَل، تُقطَع	
	٣ يُضاف، يوضَع، يوضَع، يُترك
٤ يُعَبَّأ، يُرَصّ	
	٥ تُغلَق، تُحَمَّل، تُنقَل، لِتُوَزَّع

26 Review

26.1

SINGULAR

I	جَرَيْتُ/أَجْري	رُزْتُ/أزور	عَدَدْتُ/أَعُدّ	خَرَجْتُ/أَخْرُج
you (masc.)	جَرَيْتَ/تَجْري	رُزْتَ/تَزور	عَدَدْتَ/تَعُدّ	خَرَجْتَ/تَخْرُج
you (fem.)	جَرَيْتِ/تَجْرينَ	رُزْتِ/تَزورينَ	عَدَدْتِ/تَعُدّينَ	خَرَجْتِ/تَخْرُجينَ
he/it (masc.)	جَرى/يَجْري	زار/يَزور	عَدَّ/يَعُدّ	خَرَجَ/يَخْرُج
she/it (fem.)	جَرَتْ/تَجْري	زارَتْ/تَزور	عَدَّتْ/تَعُدّ	خَرَجَتْ/تَخْرُج

PLURAL

we	جَرَيْنا/نَجْري	رُزْنا/نَزور	عَدَدْنا/نَعُدّ	خَرَجْنا/نَخْرُج
you (masc. pl.)	جَرَيْتُمْ/تَجْرونَ	رُزْتُمْ/تَزورونَ	عَدَدْتُمْ/تَعُدّونَ	خَرَجْتُمْ/تَخْرُجونَ
you (fem. pl.)	جَرَيْتُنَّ/تَجْرينَ	رُزْتُنَّ/تَزُرْنَ	عَدَدْتُنَّ/تَعْدُدْنَ	خَرَجْتُنَّ/تَخْرُجْنَ
they (masc. pl.)	جَرَوْا/يَجْرونَ	زاروا/يَزورونَ	عَدّوا/يَعُدّونَ	خَرَجوا/يَخْرُجونَ
they (fem.)	جَرَيْنَ/يَجْرينَ	زُرْنَ/يَزُرْنَ	عَدَدْنَ/يَعْدُدْنَ	خَرَجْنَ/يَخْرُجْنَ

DUAL

you (dual)	جَرَيْتُما/تَجْريانِ	رُزْتُما/تَزورانِ	عَدَدْتُما/تَعُدّانِ	خَرَجْتُما/تَخْرُجانِ
they (masc. dual)	جَرَيا/يَجْريانِ	زارا/يَزورانِ	عَدّا/يَعُدّانِ	خَرَجا/يَخْرُجانِ
they (fem. dual)	جَرَتا/تَجْريانِ	زارَتا/تَزورانِ	عَدَّتا/تَعُدّانِ	خَرَجَتا/تَخْرُجانِ

26.2

١ يوم السَّبت مساءً سَتذهَب إلى السينما مع نادية.
٢ يوم الأحد صباحاً سَتأخُذ الساعة المكسورة إلى المحَلّ.
٣ يوم الأحد مساءً سَتكتُب خطاباً لِجدّتها.
٤ يوم الاثنين صباحاً سَتغسِل الملابس.
٥ يوم الاثنين مساءً سَتحضُر اِجتماعاً في المدرسة.
٦ يوم الثُلاثاء صباحاً سَتردّ على الرسالة الإلكترونية من البنك.
٧ يوم الثُلاثاء مساءً سَتلعَب التنس في النادي.
٨ يوم الأربِعاء صباحاً سَتذهَب إلى السوق.
٩ يوم الأربِعاء مساءً سَتطبُخ العَشاء لأمّها.
١٠ يوم الخميس صباحاً سَتغسِل السيّارة.
١١ يوم الخميس مساءً سَتقرَأ كتاباً.
١٢ يوم الجُمعة صباحاً سَتجري ثلاثة أميال.
١٣ يوم الخميس مساءً سَتأكُل في المطعم الجديد.

26.3

١ نَعم، طَبَخْتُهُ.
٢ نَعم، فَتَحْتُهُ.
٣ نَعم، حَجَزْتُها.
٤ نَعم، وَضَعْتُها في الجَراج.
٥ نَعم، أخَذْتُهُمْ إلى الحديقة.
٦ نَعم، قَرَأْتُها.
٧ نَعم، زُرْتُهُ.
٨ نَعم، وَجَدْتُها.

26.4

١ تتحسّن
٢ سابقتُ
٣ تتذكّرين
٤ استمتعتُ
٥ سنستقبل
٦ يتقاتلون
٧ سيُعلن
٨ كسّر
٩ ابتسموا
١٠ يستخدمون
١١ درّسوا
١٢ يسافران
١٣ تنظّفنَ
١٤ تنقسم

٢ لن يُسافِروا بطائِرة خاصّة.

١ لن أَكتُب خِطاباً للوَزير.

٤ لم أَركَب جَمَلاً في مِصر.

٣ لم نَحتَفِل بِعيد ميلاد زوجي.

٦ لم يَجِدوا الخاتِـم في السيّارة.

٥ لن يَبيعوا السيّارة في العام القادِم.

٨ لم تَرتَدِ الفُستان الجديد.

٧ لن نَتَـحَدَّث في هذا المَوضوع أمام الأولاد.

١٠ لم تزِدْ الأسعار هذا العام.

٩ لِماذا لم تَطبُخْنَ السمكة؟

١٢ لِماذا لم تَقُصِّ شَعرك؟

١١ لن يُسَبِّب لَك مَشاكِل.

١٤ لم تَستَطِعْ نادية أن تَستَقبِل خالَتها في المَطار.

١٣ لن تَـجري سميرة في سِباق الأُمَّهات.

١٥ لِماذا لم تَرُدّوا على الهاتِف؟

١٦ لن يُعِدّ المُدير العَقد قَبلَ الساعة الخامِسة.

٢ بكر، افتَح الشبّاك.

١ جميلة، ضَعي حَقيبتك هناك.

٤ أنور، أرسُم صورة بيت.

٣ وردة، اغسِلي هذا الطَبَق.

٦ سارة، ساعِدي أنور من فضلك.

٥ منى وفريدة ونبيلة، أَخرِجنَ هذه المِلابس من الغرفة.

٨ لوسي وتوم وكريم، رتِّبوا الكُتُب.

٧ حسين وجيهان ومها، أَعطوا الناظِر هذه الدَّعوة.

١٠ بدر، عَدِّل هذه الصُّوَر.

٩ فاطمة وزينة ونورا، انتَظِرنَ هنا.

١٢ نادر وزينب، اطلُبا كُرة من المُدَرِّب.

١١ أميرة، احمَلي هذا المكتب إلى هناك.

١٤ محمد، قِف بِجانب الباب.

١٣ زهرة وجمال وحسن، عُدّوا الأَقلام.

١٦ ابراهيم، قُل لي، ماذا فعلتَ؟

١٥ أشرف وشريفة، اقفِلا صندوق اللُعَب.

١٧ بسرعة يا أَولاد! تَـحَرَّكوا! أَسرِعوا!

٣ يُستَخرَج

٢ تُنقَل

١ يوضَع

٦ تُعَبَّأ

٥ يُصَبّ

٤ يُضاف

٨ توضَع

٧ تُـحَمَّل